Plain Yarns From the Fleet

BY THE SAME AUTHOR

Independent Traveller
Britons Abroad
The Opaque Society
The Maltese Islands
No More Heroes
The Grand Days of Travel
Just Across the Channel

Plain Yarns From the Fleet

The Spirit of the Royal Navy during its Twentieth-Century Heyday

Charles Owen

Foreword by Admiral Sir Charles Madden Bt, GCB

SUTTON PUBLISHING

First published in 1997 by
Sutton Publishing Limited · Phoenix Mill
Thrupp · Stroud · Gloucestershire · GL5 2BU

Paperback edition first published in 1998

British Library Cataloguing in Publication Data
A catalogue record for this book is available from the British Library

ISBN 0 7509 1985 X

Cover illustration, main picture: A squadron of British battleships in line ahead, c. *1935. (IWM HU55811)*

Typeset in 10/13pt Sabon.
Typesetting and origination by
Sutton Publishing Limited.
Printed in Great Britain by
WBC Limited, Bridgend, Mid-Glamorgan.

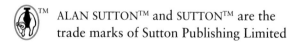

Contents

Foreword

I came from a Naval family. In the First World War my father was Chief of Staff to Admiral Jellicoe in his flagship *Iron Duke*, and later Second in Command to Admiral Beatty at the surrender of the German Fleet which I witnessed as a boy from an Admiralty tug. My own first sea appointment as a Midshipman was to the same HMS *Iron Duke*.

In the Second World War I had the good fortune to serve under Admiral A.B. Cunningham in his flagship HMS *Warspite*. He was our most famous fighting Admiral of this war and *Warspite* was a very special ship, and I still attend the annual meetings of those who served in her and loved her.

I welcome this book with its vivid reminders of the great days of the Navy from 1900 to 1945 not only for recalling old memories but for appraising the character and achievements of the people, officers and ratings, who made the Navy what it was, though the author does not hide from the reader some of the Navy's disasters and failures during this period.

The author's own sea service during the Second World War was in destroyers, the hardest worked class of ship of all, but it is not only the author's view that prevails. A feature of the book is the weaving into his narrative of the recollections and opinions of a wide range of contemporary officers and ratings and the picture that emerges is both entertaining as well as enlightening.

This book is a tribute to the high morale of the Navy in triumph and disaster, a spirit nurtured by that achieved in the individual ships, above all perhaps by the good-humoured respect and support among and between officers and men, a feeling of 'all in the same boat', a determination to make their own ship the best.

To all who admire or may be interested in the exploits of the Navy during the first half of the present century I commend this book.

Charles Madden

Acknowledgements

I am very much indebted to Admiral Sir Charles Madden for his appraisal of this work during its two-year evolution; while not sharing all the author's opinions, for his consistent encouragement; for his foreword to the book and the excerpts from his memoirs.

For guidance or assistance with particular episodes, including in most cases the provision of unpublished material, I am more than grateful to a number of retired naval personalities, ratings as well as officers,[1] notably Geoffrey Brooke, Bob Burns, Ian Fleming-Williams, Donald Goodbrand, John Gower, Rear Admiral Edward Gueritz, Richard Hodges, Sidney Hutchison, Victor Loosemore, Admiral Sir William O'Brien, my brother Major General John Owen Royal Marines, Ann Rodney and Margaret Seeley; to R.W.A. Suddaby for facilitating access to Imperial War Museum archives, and to Barbara Sanderson for her admirable story about wartime travel.

For invaluable suggestions and for introductions, I offer warm thanks to John and Clare Arrigo, Lady Elizabeth Baxendale, Michael Berger, Lady Carnwath, Elizabeth Collins, Jack Goering, Professor Victor Griffiths, Patricia Countess Jellicoe, Sir Bryce Knox, Patience Pain, Rex Smith, Patrick Tailyour, John Wells and Gill Young.

For practical help, advice and encouragement I salute Admiral Sir Peter Ashmore, Alistair Donald, Colin Greaves, William King, my daughter Caroline Knox, Peter Linklater, Matthew Little of the Royal Marines Museum, Campbell McMurray with John Buckeridge and other members of the staff at the Royal Naval Museum, John Marriott for his contribution to some of the 'yarns' about life in Malta, Charles Omell, my son Rupert Owen, Brian Patterson of the Portsmouth Dockyard Trust, Gareth Shannon of the Society of Authors, Douglas Smith, Patsy Spicer, Viktor Wickman and his Maritime Collection in Malta, Richard Woodman, Sophia Wright and John Wyllie.

1 Ranks are given here only to admirals and to those at comparable levels in other walks of life.

I have much appreciated the willing and efficient services of several libraries – the London Library, the libraries of the Imperial War, the Royal Naval and the Royal Marines museums, and of the Royal United Services Institute; the central libraries of Valletta (Malta) and Portsmouth; and the Marylebone branch of the City of Westminster libraries, not least for their ability to search nationwide for books not readily available through other channels.

My sincere thanks are due to the following for permitting reproduction of the book's illustrations:

Viktor Wickman's Maritime Collection, Malta: 2, 3, 20.
Imperial War Museum: 5, 6, 7, 13, 14, 28, 32, 35, 37, 41, 42, 44.
Portsmouth Royal Dockyard Historical Trust: 8, 21, 22, 24, 25, 27, 38.
Royal Marines Museum: 9, 46.
Royal Naval Museum: 10, 49.
By kind permission of Clive Debenham, grandson of Arthur Debenham, portrait photographer of Ryde: 11, 12.
Richard Hodges: 15.
Geoffrey Brooke archives: 17, 26, 29, 39, 40.
John Arrigo's private collection: 18, 19.
Sir Charles Madden's private collection: 31, 45.
National Maritime Museum: 36.
Sidney Hutchison's private collection: 43, 48.
Victor Loosemore: 47.
N.R. Omell Galleries, London: 50.
The author's own collection: 1, 4, 16, 23, 30, 33, 34.

Finally, I acknowledge with affection my publisher's vote of confidence in commissioning the book; the word processing skills and good-humoured diligence of Pat Holliday; the timely editorial advice of Linden Lawson; Patrick Tailyour for his kind offer to compile the index.

Far from least, I acknowledge with love and gratitude the indispensable role of Felicity, my wife and mentor, to whom this book is dedicated, as my chief researcher and, generally, in keeping me up to the mark.

Charles Owen
London, 1996

Prologue: Rulers of the Waves

From Trafalgar to recent times the Royal Navy has played a dominant role in world affairs. In those heady days of the far-flung British raj – the only large-scale empire in history based essentially on sea power – the Navy was the chief instrument of the *pax britannica*. It acquired a mystique, a glamour, a reputation of infallibility. While this owed much to legend and romance, it was also the expression of a confident, hard-headed, but colourful professionalism, the more impressive for dispensing pomp without pomposity, for being serious without solemnity.

With the help of numerous anecdotes, some contributed specially, others culled from archives or published works, some critical, others eulogistic, this book seeks to probe and evaluate the phrase contained in its subtitle – the spirit of the Royal Navy during its twentieth-century heyday. The service's style and endeavours were at their most visible and influential during the first half of the century, the period covered by the book. This was largely due to the evolving impact of modern communications enabling not only everyday eccentricities of the so-called 'Silent Service' to be recorded, but its reactions and, indeed, contributions to the dramas and tensions preceding two world wars as well as the wartime battles and campaigns themselves.

To have been part of the Navy at this time or, otherwise, a close witness of some of its activities was, to say the least, a stirring experience. Thus the crowds, a few decades ago, keyed up for the great event, watched from the Valletta ramparts as the British Mediterranean Fleet returned to Malta. They never failed to be moved by the precision and elegance of the manoeuvres as, squadron by squadron, flotilla by flotilla, the stately mass of white-ensigned men-of-war crowded their way into harbour. No other navy could match this spectacle or create the same sense of occasion. To the Maltese onlookers the fleet's arrival, the martial music, the eloquent ceremonial and the burst of life as the ships' picket boats and pinnaces fanned out towards the landing stages brought new purpose, a sense of renewal and, of course, the welcome clatter of money in the island's tills.

What was the Navy doing in those days, how did its people function, and what led to the high esteem and affection in which they were held? And when, at last, the great test, the great opportunity came in 1939, was the Navy up to it?

Our story begins in 1900.

FISHER'S NAVY, 1900–31

CHAPTER ONE

Stormy Days

At the start of this century, after the relative obscurity of the Victorian period, the Royal Navy rose to a new zenith of public esteem. The sailor, the bearded 'Jack Tar', was a celebrity. Children of both sexes wore suits or dresses bearing the naval sailor's collar. The smoker bought his tobacco in packets or tins displaying the reassuring face of the familiar icon. Cigarette cards were issued in series of types of warship or ranks of naval personnel – to collect a full set was a cause of celebration. Characteristic songs and anthems, such as 'Rule Britannia', 'A Life on the Ocean Wave', and 'All the Nice Girls Love a Sailor', provided an emotional or joyful edge to the burgeoning cult. The newspapers carried regular and prominent reports on naval affairs – even the fleets' gunnery practices, the hit scores of individual ships presented in a competitive format with photographs of the winning gunners, provided meat for the public apppetite on a par with the exploits of football stars and jockeys.

Then, as the years went by, in peace and war, the spotlight fell increasingly on the top brass, on widely acclaimed, sometimes controversial household names such as Jack Fisher, Charles Beresford, John Jellicoe, David Beatty, Roger Keyes, Joe Kelly, W.W. Fisher. These names still have a heroic resonance.

Throughout this period, respectful noises-off continued unabated – plays and films, from the happy-go-lucky *The Middle Watch* to the more tight-lipped *The Flashing Stream*; songs from Gilbert and Sullivan to all-join-in music hall; adventure novels from the likes of Bartimeus, Taffrail, Westerman; autobiographies by retired senior officers, in the dry style of reports of proceedings; and the growing cacophony of news and comment via radio, on cinema screens and in the ever-expanding press. The 'Silent Service' was becoming less reticent – by the 1930s, journalists were being made increasingly welcome at special events and, in the summer months, following a cheerful round of visits to seaside resorts by warships of the Home Fleet, there were the widely popular Navy Weeks at Portsmouth, Plymouth and Chatham.

In 1939, at the outbreak of the Second World War, Britons at home and abroad felt confident the Navy would see them through.

* * *

'All the Nice Girls Love a Sailor . . .' – these jaunty lines from the song 'Ship Ahoy', published in 1909, were an instant hit. Arch, provocative and by the standards of those days sexy, the song stirred women of all ages. To some, the concluding line of this verse, '. . . And You Know What Sailors Are', hinted at risk, with luck a rather delicious kind of danger, to others a romantic idyll on some foreign, palm-fringed shore. While the song encouraged yearning, it seemed prudently also to offer warning – yearn away, it seemed to say, but for mum's sake, and heaven's, take care.[1]

Translated into a marching tempo, the rhythm turned every head. During the Second World War the officer leading the naval guard of honour at the head of a long Warship Week procession recorded:

> The accompanying Royal Marine band broke with gusto into the 'Ship Ahoy' tune just as my 100-strong contingent of sailors rounded the corner of the main square and advanced upon the dais. The crowd, surging forward to the barrier, burst spontaneously into a prolonged cheer. As handkerchiefs fluttered or hands were clapped the smiling faces, particularly those of the women, were alight with joy. My sailors with their slightly rolling gait loved it. Of course, they earned extra plaudits for *appearing* not to be affected, their professionalism, as they well knew, being part of the show; chins up, eyes ahead, ready to be turned on order towards the VIP on the dais, rifles with fixed bayonets at the slope, their drill had to remain impeccable.
>
> There was a specially stirring moment when, at the end of a similar occasion in Northampton, we entrained for London. My contingent having disdained the offer of motor coaches to carry us to the rail station, we assumed our full ceremonial gear and, band playing, marched unexpectedly through the streets. People, taken by surprise, poured on to the pavements from shops and offices, while policemen appeared from nowhere to clear our path through the traffic. By the time we reached the station, several hundred enthusiastic citizens were following in our wake, many of them pursuing us to the departure platform through willingly opened gates.
>
> Our two reserved carriages were at the rear of the waiting train and as this got under way our band began to play. Through the open windows of our carriages, the strains of 'All the Nice Girls Love a Sailor' could suddenly be heard. The crowd, until this moment boisterous, fell silent. Some of the women continued to wave but most just stood there; and as the train gathered speed and the sailors at the windows, now off duty, smiled and waved goodbye, I was

amazed to see on many faces, tears streaming uncontrollably down the cheeks. When the train cleared the station the band stopped playing and, for a while, all of us, too moved for words, sat quietly in our seats.[2]

No less rousing, albeit in a heartier way, was the vigorous shanty, notably its verse:

A Life on the Ocean Wave,
A Home on the Rolling Deep,
Where the Scattered Waters Rave
And the Winds Their Revels Keep.

Anyone who has served his time at sea or travelled widely across the oceans will recognize in the lilt of these words the motion of a ship as it dips into the swell at the start of a voyage, and some of the mystery, wildness, grandeur and unpredictability, the anger and benignity, of the oceans.[3]

The unfathomable power of those fickle, watery wastes brings home to man his fragility as a unit in nature's universe in a way no other element can match. His mixed feelings of achievement and humility after battling through a hurricane, of relief and then of discovery on gaining the shelter of a new harbour, contribute to his sense of belonging, with other ocean-going seamen, to a race apart. No song could be more eloquent about the effect of deep waters upon the soul, or explain better how an experienced, weather-hardened navy assumed a lead in resilience, humanity and self-assurance over its sister services as well as its rivals.

Too jingoistic for today's unheroic tastes, but in its imperialistic era an anthem to induce pride, pugnacity and high morale, was the splendid:

Rule Britannia,
Britannia Rule the Waves:
Britons Never, Never
Shall be Slaves![4]

To the officer class of the early twentieth century these words expressed more than sentiment – they sounded an emotional call to patriotism, to the honour of bearing arms in the service of their country. The awe-struck youth on the threshold of a career in the mighty Royal Navy, awaiting admittance to the cadet training ship, was already gripped, as was his mother:

It was the hour preceding dinner, and a small boy in the uniform of a Naval Cadet stood on the balcony of our hotel at Dartmouth. . . . His thoughts went back along the path of the last few years that had followed his father's death. . . . Years of thrift and contrivance, new clothes foresworn, a thousand

> renunciations – this had been his mother's part, that her son might in time bear his share of the Empire's burden.
>
> She came out on the balcony as the sun dipped behind the hills. . . . It is rarely given to men to live worthy of the mothers that bore them; a few – a very few – are permitted to die worthy of them. . . . She accompanied him on board the following day. . . . 'Number 32, you are, sir,' said the Petty Officer; and as he spoke she knew the time had come when her boy was no longer hers alone.[5]

Thus was popular fiction enlisted, willingly, in the service of Empire. Here is our young cadet, now a full-blown naval lieutenant bloodied by war, looking back:

> Memories, ah, memories! Haphazard, half revealed through the mists of years. Grim old cradle of the Eternal Navy, there lies on my desk a blotting-pad hewed from your salt timbers; it may be that some whimsical ghost strayed out of its abode to provoke these recollections. Does it, I wonder, unite with other ghosts from chiselled garden seat or carved candle-stick, and there on the moonlit waters of the Dart refashion, rib by rib, keel and strake and stempost, a Shadow Ship? And what of the Longshoremen Billies that plied for hire between the shore and the after-gangway. . . . that shell-backed fraternity? Gone to the haven of all good ships and sailormen: and only the night wind, abroad beneath the stars, whispers to the quiet hills the tales of sharks and pirates and the Chiny seas that once were yours and ours.
>
> But what familiar faces throng once more the old docks and cluster round the empty ports! . . . You crowd too quickly now, you whose fair names are legion, so that the splendour of your sacrifices blur and intermingle. The North Sea knows you and the hidden Belgian minefields; the Aurora Borealis was the candle that lit some to bed, and the surf on the beaches of Gallipoli murmurs to others a never-ending lullaby. Ostend and Zeebrugge will not forget you, and the countless tales of your passing shall be the sword hilt on which our children's children shall cut their teeth.
>
> From out of that Shadow Ship lying at her moorings off the old Mill Creek comes the faint echoes of your boyish voices floating out across the placid tide. Could we but listen hard enough we might catch some message of good hope and encouragement from you who have had your Day:
>
> *'We are the Dead. . . .*
> *To you from failing hands we throw*
> *The torch: be yours to hold it high:*
> *If ye break faith with us who die,*
> *We shall not sleep. . . .'*
>
> There shall be no faith broken. God rest you, merry Gentlemen.[6]

* * *

Among the heartbreaking realities of life at the outset of the First World War, no beacon of patriotism shone brighter than that illuminated by a letter in London's *Morning Post.* A mother whose sixteen-year-old was among a posse of cadets, newly-joined from Dartmouth, their training incomplete, posted in the rush of mobilization to three elderly cruisers and killed when their ships succumbed to enemy torpedoes, wrote:

> God knows how we all mourn for and with those of our sisters whose sons' names already figure on the Roll of Honour, and should the Admiralty see fit to remove our sons from the danger zone our relief would be immeasurable. Nevertheless, for my own part, if my son can best serve England at this juncture by giving his life for her, I would not lift one finger to bring him home. If any act or word of mine should interfere with or take from him his greatest privilege, I could never look him in the face again . . .[7]

And what of the mass of stalwart hearts of oak at the lower, less romantic levels of naval life? As Admiral Chatfield rather loftily recorded a few decades later, having remarked on the rating's 'hard and trying' life of fifty years previously, always at the mercy of weather and emergencies peculiar to service at sea, 'no sailor can go to his hammock with a complete certainty that he will not be roused in the night. He sits at meals on a hard wooden form at a hard wooden mess table with fifteen or more shipmates, one of perhaps twenty messes in a compartment. Privacy is at a discount. . . . The sailor knows his life is strange and peculiar, but that thousands of his race have led it before him, that if he has discomfort he will never have monotony, that if he leave his wife and children not too well provided for, he can save money and look forward to a new honeymoon; and anyhow he is doing what must be done if England is to live. Sailors are a special brand, rather unlike anyone else, and it is an absorbing interest to command them.'[8]

The admiral's cheerful reference to the lot of the sailor's wife on the eve of the First World War raises many questions. In brief, the answer to most of these is that, thanks to an explosion of welfare activity led by the great reformer Agnes Weston, and supported by a host of volunteers, including the wives of service officers, the sailor's wife might well be poor but she need not be lonely. Agnes Weston:

> The number of sailors' wives that have passed through our meetings would number millions if totalled up. We value the friendship of our sailors' wives very exceedingly, and the sight on any Monday at Devonport or Portsmouth of our large hall filled with the wives, once seen, is not to be forgotten. They represent men serving all over the world, as can be seen when the names of foreign stations are announced, and those connected with them put up their hands.

> We have a sick committee of sailors' wives, and they organise bazaars and various other means of getting up money. A portion of this money is voted to the 'Victoria Jubilee Nurses'. These admirable nurses are available at all times for maternity and district nursing. We have our clubs of various kinds, our library, our stalls for materials, ready-made clothing, &c., and, above all, our crêche for the little ones. Babies in arms can be brought into the hall, and sometimes one hundred babes are present, blowing their little steam whistles pretty loudly. . . . We make our Monday afternoons as bright as possible – plenty of singing, always a short Bible-reading, and then something fresh every week. They do enjoy these meetings. . . . Of course such large gatherings have to be so controlled that talking should be at a minimum. They may talk as much as they like before the meeting opens, but once the gong is sounded there must be silence.[9]

Silence! Discipline! Hardship! Merciless exploitation! Let one of the few authentic lower deck voices of that period speak for the overriding spirit and self-assurance of the ratings. Sidney Knock, a naval stoker:

> If the strength of the British Navy lies in its fashion of policing the seas, its success is due to the incomparable courtesy of the men of the lower deck. . . . Naval men have shown what is meant by the term 'Navy fashion' whenever tact and human understanding were called for . . . and this human factor is the most powerful instrument in creating a Service that is unique in the history of the nation. . . . The lower deck is a wonderful institution. Certainly polish, culture and formality in the conventional sense are lacking, but its code of honour, its ethics, are as rigid as those of an English Public School.[10]

* * *

The two stars of the Navy's Edwardian high-wire act were, of course, the admirals Charles Beresford and Jack Fisher. These two powerful and colourful men, united in their determination to win ever more hitting power for the British battle fleet, were too often divided over means. Beresford, a wealthy and swashbuckling Irish peer, prominent in political and Debrett-level circles in London, was, comparatively, an admiral of the old school. Like Fisher, a product of the sail-driven navy, he had become a popular, high profile, hands-on leader, well loved and respected among the lower ranks of his seagoing commands. During the first decade of the century he was a vigorous force in public opinion from his positions as Commander-in-Chief of the Mediterranean and, from 1907 to 1909, Channel Fleets.

Among his less endearing and, perhaps, more revealing traits was his attachment to his bulldog, Cora. This truculent, overfed animal took her exercise on the flagship's normally spotless quarterdeck – a member of the admiral staff always on hand to clean up promptly after the bitch's indiscriminate bowel and bladder movements. Beresford's assumption that a uniformed member of a warship's company should be so employed was typical of the vanity and insensitivity of an admiral whose flashes of vision, at least in the short term, could be clear-sighted and of value as both a goad and a corrective to Fisher's ambitions.

Fisher, of humbler, middle-class origin, with a mercurial temperament, had by choice risen up a more technology-conscious stream to occupy the posts of Second, and from 1904 to 1910, First Sea Lord during the same decade. In the vanguard of thought about warships' function and design and, in particular, the potential of the latest gunnery techniques, he soon gained prominence in a world centred on the rapidly evolving, steampowered battleship. In essence, for all its grandeur and sophistication, it was little more than a mobile gun platform, yet seen by most strategists as the decisive weight in the scales of international power.

Fisher was a charismatic leader and public figure with a vitality and a programme of reforms that was to find a ready echo and response at every forward-looking level from the new-age admirals and captains to the most junior officers and ratings. He was widely admired for his verve and determination.

> A religious man, he would often start his day at 06.00 with prayers in Westminster Abbey, to be followed after an early breakfast by twelve hours at the Admiralty, sometimes with one short break for lemonade and biscuits. For relaxation at the end of this stint, he loved best to gird himself in epaulettes, white gloves and gold-lined trousers, hurry to a ball and, having marshalled a bevy of young partners with the right blend of gaiety, beauty, stamina and good breeding, dance the whole night through. Girls, responding to his zest and ebullient self-assurance, liked being put on their mettle, not least by his skill and grace as a ballroom dancer; while, in return, their high spirits and evident pleasure in his company served to replenish his own stocks of vitality . . . Not bad for a man who was already, by modern definition, at retiring age.[11]

Fisher's *pièce de résistance* was the battleship *Dreadnought* which, brought into service in 1906, made all existing battleships obsolete. Over the next ten years it was the worldwide forerunner of 140 modern capital ships, in service or building – 45 of these being British, 26 German, 17 American, 16 French and the remainder shared among a further 8 of the would-be naval powers. During this period design of these ships continued to evolve – in Britain's fleet the calibre of the centre-line guns grew from 12 in to 15 in, the battery being ranged and fired from a single control position. Propulsion became oil instead of coal based, with speeds, of the battle cruiser version, rising to 26 knots. The wireless became increasingly important as a means of communication.

Revolutionary changes in manpower, organization and training were initiated by Fisher to serve the growing and more complex British Fleet. The Navy's engineering and technical arms were given new roles and status, with a building programme of barracks, training schools and extended dockyard facilities to match, the townscapes and dynamism of naval bases like Portsmouth being transformed. The officers' cradle was rehoused ashore at Osborne and Dartmouth to accommodate the expanding 13½-year-old cadet entry, soon to be augmented by an ex-public school entry at 17½ as well as by a more accessible ladder of promotion to officer rank from the lower deck.

This radical upheaval throughout a traditionally slow-to-change service placed many senior officers out of their intellectual depth. This was a source of the animosity directed towards Fisher, fuelled by Beresford's vociferous resentment at being threatened with extinction himself. In one respect, however, the Beresford castigations had merit. As a means, as he saw it, of clipping Fisher's wings and achieving a more acceptable use of naval resources, Beresford campaigned vigorously for the introduction of an Admiralty war staff charged with the foundation of long-term policies based on systematic research and planning. While Fisher paid lip service to the concept, he had not the least intention of succumbing – as he saw it he had much to achieve, time was short, and to be side-tracked into extra chat and paperwork beyond those generated by his existing hand-picked team of acolytes was sheer obstruction.

Fisher, like his predecessors as First Sea Lord, considered it his prerogative to make all the major decisions single-handed. While this attitude enabled him to create a navy ready for his view of Armageddon, his plans, such as they were, precluded effective liaison with the army or with potential allies on the Continent. Preparations for campaigns other than those primarily based in the North Sea, for which he was so busily refashioning the Navy, had no place on his agenda. Would his successor continue Fisher's good work or would the new incumbent, in turn, start reshaping the Navy to his own liking? As we shall see, the absence of a viable staff at the Admiralty was almost to cost Britain the forthcoming U-boat war.

Meanwhile, despite the squabbling in high places and some occasional in-house complaints, usually over pay differentials, as the expanding personnel adjusted to rapidly changing circumstances, morale in the Navy could not have been higher. As a seagoing panjandrum, Beresford had attracted an enthusiastic following, but with power at the Navy's Whitehall headquarters so firmly in Fisher's hands, Beresford's influence was already on the wane. It was further diminished following his removal from the Channel Fleet a year before time, and by Winston Churchill's slur that Beresford was one of those who 'before they get up, they do not know what they are going to say; when they are speaking, they do not know what they are saying; and when they have sat down, they do not know what they have said.'

By 1910, however, there were enough owners of out-of-joint noses in high places to deflect Fisher from his path and, under a quieter successor at the Admiralty, set the scene for a two-year period of consolidation. 'Grimly certain

1.) In the British public's view, everyone serving in the Royal Navy in the early years of the century, whatever his rank or rating, famous or anonymous, was hero material. The famous bearded sailor, icon of manliness, was used proudly by Player's as a model to advertise their tobacco.

4.) A popular magazine featured John Fisher who, as Second and then as First Sea Lord, revolutionized the Navy in the years preceding the First World War.

2. & 3.) Studio photographs of a petty officer, with helmet, and a leading seaman were enough, no doubt, to bring tears to the eyes of the folks back home.

that war with Germany would come in the summer of 1914,' Fisher had the Navy's main fighting strength concentrated in the North Sea, to which end a number of overseas dockyards had been reduced or closed and 150 old ships condemned. After nearly a century of easy-going peace, the Navy had been shaken to its foundations by a revolution achieved 'ruthlessly, relentlessly, remorselessly'. 'Our Navy at this moment could take on all the Navies of the world. Let 'em all come,' Fisher had boasted at a critical stage in his fight for resources. The cry 'We want eight and we can't wait,' referring to the number of new battleships sought by Fisher from hesitant politicians for the 1909–10 building programme, had been taken up country-wide in the press, at meetings and by placard-bearing processions.

According to his friends at this time Sir John Fisher was 'the greatest sailor since Nelson, . . . a genius, a demi-god, transcendental embodiment of continuing energy'. According to his enemies he was 'unscrupulous and vindictive, an intriguer and self-seeker, a tyrant'. In the Admiralty's campaign to secure government approval for the additional battleships, it had been said that 'McKenna (First Lord) would resign if he did not get his way. . . . If Fisher (First Sea Lord) too resigned, it would be a somewhat more serious matter . . . but a good deal more serious if Lloyd George (Chancellor of the Exchequer) resigned . . . and it was whispered that, if McKenna resigned, Grey (Foreign Secretary) would resign with him.' In the end, as Winston Churchill has recorded, 'a curious and characteristic solution was reached. The Admiralty had demanded eight ships, the economists offered four and we finally compromised on six.'[12]

The Fisher momentum was resumed in 1912 with the appointment of Churchill as First Lord, upon whose drive, prompted by Fisher from the sidelines, the Navy now depended. The fleet that would take up its war stations in August 1914 would include most of the sixty-one battleships and battlecruisers reviewed ceremonially, with grim foresight, at Spithead the previous month. It was a truly formidable armada, and a visible outcome of Fisher's genius, in Churchill's words 'incomparably the greatest assemblage of naval power ever witnessed in the history of the World'; and the instrument which, everyone expected, would on its own decide the coming war.

Historians have tended to play up the discordant noises and animosities of this period as though these had eroded the nation's will to win and the Navy's readiness for war. While the quarrels and disagreements at the highest political and military levels undoubtedly confused some issues and retarded some decisions, the thrust was evident. The main effect of this was to induce in the public mind a growing sense of excitement, a prelude to the surge of patriotism that would soon herald the outbreak of the war.

As for the Navy, the continuing debates about its development merely added an extra glow to the spotlight of esteem and expectation in which the officers and men were basking. As they saw it, their service, ever-expanding, newly-equipped and geared increasingly to war, was on a high. Its personnel were and saw themselves as more than a match for anything the Germans might try to throw at them – and when the two fleets met eventually in battle, in the first decisive, set-piece encounter since Trafalgar, Britain's enemy would undoubtedly be trounced. England, the Empire, freedom, democracy – all depended on it, and the Navy would again win a famous victory.

* * *

When the great day came, on 31 May 1916, it started well enough. Admiral Beatty's battle cruiser squadron lured the enemy fleet towards the advancing British battleships. His commander-in-chief, Admiral Jellicoe, manoeuvred his great armada into a single line with deft precision, and with it crossed the German 'T'. By this classic device, the object of much thought, training and practice over the years, all the British heavy guns could concentrate on, and, in turn, annihilate the leading German warships before the latter's supporters could be organized into a retaliatory order of battle.

So far so good. The time was 1800 in the calm hazy North Sea summer evening, off the coast of Jutland. The severe losses incurred by Beatty's squadron as it laid its bait would surely soon be avenged. In the ensuing set-piece battle, the natural successor to Trafalgar, superior British tactics and weight of gunfire must prevail. The Germans were brave and efficient but, as newcomers to warfare afloat, they lacked the tradition of victory at sea. Anything short of a British triumph was unthinkable.

By two bold moves the Germans won a breathing space. By means of an emergency all-together turn-away at high speed, a manoeuvre which the British had considered impracticable, and of a massed destroyer torpedo attack against Jellicoe's ships, the German battle fleet extricated itself from the British trap.

In response, Jellicoe made his first serious misjudgement. Instead of facing up to the threat from torpedoes and giving instant chase to the retreating enemy, Jellicoe turned his battleships away from the torpedo-firing destroyers. The correct defence against this form of attack was for the target ships to turn end-on towards the enemy and thus 'comb' the approaching torpedo tracks. Where these tracks were running more or less at right angles to their prey's line of advance, a choice was offered – the target ships could swing towards the enemy to steam forward between the tracks, or they could veer away, with similar effect, while putting more distance between them and their attackers. According to the doctrine of the time, largely of his own making, Jellicoe chose the latter course and in doing so lost touch with his main enemy in the gathering darkness.

The next step for Jellicoe was to concentrate his own ships and, because of the risk of confusion in the darkness, try to avoid further battlefleet actions until daylight. He felt sure, and here was his second misjudgement, that there would be

5.) While glamorous portraits of David Beatty abounded, here was no mere pin-up star. Destined to be lauded as one of Britain's three greatest fighting admirals in the twentieth century, Beatty, having led the battle-cruisers at Jutland, succeeded John Jellicoe in command of the Grand Fleet, to end his career in the 1920s as a First Sea Lord of outstanding distinction.

6. & 7.) The other two battle-hardened stars were Jellicoe (left), stalwart Commander-in-Chief of the British Fleet at Jutland, and A.B. Cunningham (right), whose Mediterranean Fleet was engaged from 1940 in some of the toughest combat in the history of naval warfare.

enough time to smash the Germans the next morning when, with his own fleet reorganized, conditions would once again be in his favour. The main question was how to ensure that the enemy could not slip away through the minefields to his home ports.

Jellicoe considered that he had this battle in the bag. Unfortunately, the intelligence available to him during that night was incomplete because of a failure by the Admiralty to pass on some crucial information from enemy sources. This was compounded by the omission by outlying units of his own fleet to keep him informed about German ships' movements which they could see, but, as they must have known, Jellicoe could not. So, alas, when dawn stole over the silent sea, the enemy was nowhere to be seen – far from being to the westward of Jellicoe, as he supposed, the Germans were to the south-east, and already more or less under the protection of minefields guarding the approaches to their bases. The opposing forces were by now so far apart that, even in good visibility, re-engagement would have been out of the question.

Thus the greatest missed opportunity of the war ended in anticlimax. The outcome of the battle involving over 200 warships, lasting more than twelve hours, covering an area larger than the Irish Sea, dealt a shattering blow to British self-assurance. Who won, or was it just a draw?

The German battle fleet, having regained the shelter of its harbours, did not venture out again. In strategic terms this was a British victory but at a high cost for, so long as the enemy battleships remained in being, the vastly expensive Grand Fleet, based on Scapa and Rosyth, and ever ready for battle, was obliged to maintain its active presence in the North Sea. Meanwhile, the Germans were able quickly to switch resources into their one potential war-winner, the U-boat which, by the summer of 1917, besides despatching much of Britain's wealth to the bottom of the Atlantic, was bringing the country to the brink of crisis and, consequently, within sight of a total German victory. At the same time, Britain's ultimately decisive weapon, the blockade of Germany, was being thwarted by the diversion of British naval forces to meet the prevailing battle fleet and U-boat threats.

In tactical terms, with the losses of heavy ships at Jutland more or less equal (British fleet: 3 lost, 8 damaged; German fleet: 2 lost, 10 damaged) and the greater part of the Grand Fleet (including 26 undamaged heavy ships) able to resume its seagoing deployment within hours of regaining its bases, the British might well, if only by a short head, claim victory. The head would have been longer and more decisive given British shells that, in their ability to pierce German armour, were a match for the enemy's projectiles, and British decks that offered stronger protection against plunging German shells which, fired at extreme ranges, were descending almost vertically on to their relatively vulnerable targets.

But there was another factor, the psychological factor, and here, due to the Admiralty's incompetence and Jellicoe's lack of imagination in the immediate aftermath of battle, the British were undoubtedly the losers. While Jellicoe was steaming back towards Scapa, where he arrived on the afternoon of 2 June, he chose to delay his dispatches, the reports from his own fleet being incomplete. Meanwhile, the Germans, with their far more sophisticated awareness of public psychology, put their propaganda machine into top gear without awaiting all the detail. Their early announcements claimed a German victory and, failing contradiction from the other side, only one conclusion could be drawn. So, while the British press, primed by a halting Admiralty communiqué, hesitated, foreign newspapers, including those in neutral countries, were running banner headlines: 'British Losses Great! . . . British Fleet Almost Annihilated!' As Lord Beaverbrook records, 'Consternation and alarm . . . spread throughout the nation and to the allied countries.' Thus, in the absence of clear-cut news, aghast at the possibility that the Royal Navy had failed, the country seethed with a mixture of fear and fury.

Whatever the faults and fumbles in Whitehall, the blame lies heavily on Jellicoe. As Grand Fleet supremo, he owed it to his officers and men, to the traditions of his service, to public goodwill and, for that matter, to himself, to blow loud and clear the trumpet of success. But Jellicoe had schooled himself in tight-lipped reticence and, in his view, no admiral need utter until he had something definite to say and then no doubt the less said the better.

Perhaps Jellicoe had for too long carried the lonely burden of the Grand Fleet commander. His vast responsibilities had been endlessly impressed upon him. While outwardly calm, cheerful, ever ready with words of encouragement for others, inwardly the doubts gnawed at him – doubts about his equipment's efficiency, his ships' fire power, the security of their base, the efficacy of their escorts. Unlike ministers in cosy Whitehall offices and generals dressing for dinner in châteaux far behind the firing line, Jellicoe, in the British fighting admirals' tradition, lived and worked in the confined space of a warship. Throughout their waking hours he was under the close scrutiny of the officers and men with whom he might at any moment enter battle.

While this contact had advantages in order-giving and morale-building, isolation from the centres of power and direction in Whitehall was a constant cause of frustration and anxiety. The to and fro of laboriously-drafted correspondence on an ever-widening range of topics, long waits for replies to urgent questions and the doubts and difficulties of interpretation added constantly to the strains of responsibility. Because of the hierarchical ways of the Navy and the deliberate aloofness of a senior officer's below-decks life, these concerns could be little shared and never admitted.

For leaders like Jellicoe respite lay mainly in vigorous exercise. In harbour by day they paced the decks of their flagships, eating up the miles; and in the afternoons they went ashore, not into the arms of their womenfolk, but to stride manfully up the hills and over the moors, hardening their bodies. Thus by self-discipline, besides quenching sexual urges, the admirals freed and cleansed their minds ready for tomorrow's problems. In particular, as they saw it, physical fitness was the key to mental alertness and it was their absolute duty to ensure that their minds would be in tiptop running order when the great test came.

Despite his health-inducing regime, Jellicoe was showing signs of staleness, with a tendency to minor ailments in the months before Jutland. There is no doubt, even so, that in the opening phases of the great battle, the admiral's alert mind was working at peak efficiency. Up to the moment when the battlefleets began their engagement, his thought processes could not be faulted. But had he the stamina to keep his brain at full pitch throughout the long, confusing and distracting hours of battle and conjecture?

Another factor was little noticed by the historians: the conditions under which a fleet commander was obliged to make clear-cut decisions, with his own flagship in action, were truly appalling. In the North Sea mistakes were liable to be made by officers standing on bridges, often exposed to the icy wind and spray and subjected to the devastating effect not only of the enemy's fire but of the blast and flash of the forward gun-turrets. There is no more shattering experience than to be near the muzzles of great naval guns – the interval between the sounding of the warning 'fire' bell and the explosion prohibits constructive thought. The exhaustion resulting from prolonged experiences of this kind helps to explain Jellicoe's failure to make enough, promptly, of his fleet's achievements in his post-Jutland dispatches. If he had been less numbed or fatigued in the battle's aftermath he might have used the hours steaming towards Scapa more imaginatively. As the one leader who could have 'won the war in an afternoon', might it not be said of Jellicoe that this admiral's burden was greater than any man should have been called upon to bear?

Whatever may be the answer to that question or the verdict on his performance at Jutland, Jellicoe carried himself with dignity through his disappointments into old age, his quiet air of authority and twinkling good humour intact. He was the epitome of leadership and, indeed, the very stuff of the dreams and ambitions of all those starry-eyed young officers in the Bartimeus mould.

CHAPTER TWO

Doldrums

Soon after Jutland, John Jellicoe was called to the Admiralty to become First Sea Lord, being replaced by David Beatty as Commander-in-Chief of the Grand Fleet. With this fleet, still hungry for a Trafalgar-style victory, safely in Beatty's hands the Admiralty now had every chance and, from Lloyd George the new prime minister, every encouragement to get to grips with the growing U-boat menace.

To this end Jellicoe, with the additional title of Chief of Naval Staff, could call on a new galaxy of staff officers, all in eager pursuit of a solution. But old habits die hard. Jellicoe seemed unable to let go of the reins and to grasp new concepts. Every conceivable measure against the marauding U-boats was tested, except the one which, in the end, did the trick – the convoy system.

Convoys, the name given to organized groups of merchant ships accompanied by their own guard of warships, remained out of favour. This was partly due to the mistaken belief that escorts of sufficient strength could be provided only if the Grand Fleet were put at risk by robbing it of some of its protecting warships. But it was mainly, and absurdly, because a convoys-based strategy was seen by the diehards as so overtly defensive, so overtly contrary to the long-cultivated offensive spirit, as to pose a threat to naval and national morale.

Meanwhile, although the losses were mainly in the Atlantic, the waters nearer home were not immune. During one week in September 1916, when that area was being patrolled 'offensively' by 49 destroyers, 48 torpedo boats, 7 'Q' ships and over 400 armed auxilaries, 3 U-boats operating between Beachy Head and Eddystone sank 30 ships and escaped. During the first three months of 1917 in the war zone at large 800 merchant ships fell victim to the U-boats.[1] Then, even in the critical month of April 1917, by which time losses of merchant ships from U-boat attack were clearly fast outstripping replacements, and production of U-boats was fast outstripping losses, Jellicoe admitted to the cabinet that 'our policy is heading straight for disaster', but could offer no positive suggestions.

At last, the American, Admiral Sims, having learned from Jellicoe that the amount of shipping being sunk by U-boats was three or four times larger than that being published in the press, and the American ambassador having reported to his president that Britain was facing defeat by the German submarines, something had to be done. By Christmas it was, indeed, done. Jellicoe was removed from office, and thanks to the new, flourishing convoy system the graph of merchant ship losses was plunging downward as that of U-boat losses soared upward.

* * *

The charismatic David Beatty was the man of action par excellence, a leader who, whatever his feelings, exuded optimism, dash and that rare quality among admirals of his era, a decisiveness tempered by a proper concern for the views of his advisers. He thrived on danger – the noisier and bloodier the battle, the calmer his mind and the more implacable his will to win. During the last two uncertain years of the war, when the military reverses and casualties on the western front vied with the losses at sea to U-boat attack to bring Britain to its knees, Beatty was the one man capable of keeping the Grand Fleet in fighting trim in pursuit of that ultimate triumph – the smashing of the German fleet.

In 1910, having been bloodied in colonial skirmishes at the turn of the century and having shown exceptional promise on his way up the ladder, Beatty, on promotion at the age of thirty-eight to Rear Admiral, became the Navy's youngest flag officer for over 100 years. Within two years his chance to shine in Whitehall came when Churchill, as First Lord of the Admiralty, made him his naval secretary. From this post Beatty rose on the eve of the First World War to command the battle cruiser squadron, the powerful advance guard of Jellicoe's Grand Fleet.

> At this time, Beatty was a handsome, active, youthful-looking man who carried responsibility without visible effort. Evertything about him was highly individual; his uniform with its slightly horsy cut, six buttons on his monkey jacket instead of the usual eight, a very broad peak to the cap he wore at the well-known Beatty tilt. At first glance the keen strong face was a little grim and haughty, an impression soon removed by his frank speech, lively eyes and a personal magnetism almost as tangible as a visible aura. Powerful, broad-shouldered, lithe, he looked a fighter; poised and ready, wary, thoughtful; calculating rather than impetuous. Clearly a man who could be relentless and did not suffer fools gladly, but you would know where you stood with him.[2]

During the last peacetime summer of 1914, leading a ceremonial visit to the Russian port of Kronstadt, Beatty 'made a tremendous impression. His youthful, clean-shaven face caused many Russians, accustomed to seeing admirals with beards to their waist, to mistake Beatty for his own Flag Lieutenant. But Beatty's manner was unmistakably one of command. His square jaw and the jaunty angle at which he wore his cap suggested the sea dog. He spoke in a voice which would have carried over the howl of a gale.' Before long, he would be widely known for his bulldog air, . . . his postcard photo being in every newsagent's window.[3]

Beatty's readiness to go his own way is recalled by Ernle Chatfield, his Flag Captain in the battle cruiser HMS *Lion*: 'Most people who have been signally honoured with a great Command over the heads of others would have made the occasion one for showing great zeal and attention to duty. Not so Beatty. He would have his holiday (in Monte Carlo) and arrive just when he, and no one else, considered it right and opportune. Audacity was in his nature. . . . ' The idea of Beatty as a thoughtful strategist and tactician may have appeared strange to those who saw him 'as a Prince Rupert, dashing and happy-go-lucky in the spirit of the hunting field. True he had all the fascinating qualities of a brave leader ready to do all and dare all.' But, as Chatfield emphasizes, when Beatty made his decisions they were based not only on the habit of guidance from his staff officers and the response of his captains to previous evolutions, but 'on his capacity, by careful mental preparation, to form a judgement rapidly, without hesitation or visible anxiety. . . . No one could live in continual contact with him without being affected by his force of character and fearlessness.'[4]

In November 1918, a few days after the armistice, Beatty's Grand Fleet, now comprising over 40 modern battleships and battlecruisers, 30 light cruisers and 100 destroyers, received in formal surrender the demoralized and unkempt German fleet, its crews, too long at bay in their harbours, now sullen with bolshevism and discontent. This was a much-publicized event but, alas, the thoughts of the officers and men of the British Fleet now focused on demobilization, a somewhat hollow victory.

Beatty had long believed that no man can shoulder great responsibilities unless he is physically fit. 'In harbour he landed every morning before breakfast, pulling himself ashore in a skiff if the tide allowed, for a brisk walk. Dealing with paperwork during the forenoon he usually remained on his feet, standing at a high desk, rapidly picking out the essential; letters and papers quickly finding their way into two trays marked OUT and BALDERDASH.' Visitors and office business were dealt with until the early afternoon when, if his ship was at Rosyth, his preferred base, Beatty would join his wife and two small sons at their temporary home. 'After some hard sets of tennis, a round of golf or a long walk he would be back on board at 7 p.m. He always changed for dinner, a leisurely meal eaten with his staff or with guests. If there was a cinema show on board he would attend it. From August 1914 to November 1918 he slept on board his ship every night.' Also, 'he made a point of being known in other ships of his fleet, attending such functions as boxing matches and concert parties. Often he would conclude the proceedings with a brief, sailor-like talk, giving his men his views and firing them with his own conviction that the constant practices, weary waiting and arduous sweeps over an empty sea would one day be rewarded in victorious battle.'[5]

'I told you they'd have to come out,' Beatty said ruefully to his men as the surrendered German ships came to anchor at Scapa. Now, at last, back in Rosyth he could resume a more normal married life, and from April 1919, when his fleet was disbanded, Beatty was to be free of the cares of office for a while.

* * *

Of all the honours showered upon Beatty at this time by an admiring nation none moved him more than an invitation from the men of the Grand Fleet to be their guest at a banquet in Portsmouth where, his car having been hauled through the crowded streets by naval gun teams, he was received with bursts of rousing, heartfelt cheers. But enthusiasm was far from the norm among British sailors recently home from sea. To many of them demobilization had been a case of too many fits and not enough starts – now, in the postwar industrial turnaround, there were too many applicants for too few vacancies in too many trades and districts. The nation, exhausted by war, was tightening its belt and in the public services economy cuts, including reductions in salaries and wages, were soon to be the order of the day.

In the Navy, despite a long overdue increase in pay in 1919, there was much dissatisfaction. Chatfield has recorded his concern about the lot of his yeoman of signals whose wife 'lives in a small house in Portsmouth. I send her all I can but she can hardly exist and pay her rent. Next door there are munition workers who are wealthy, their wives and daughters wearing fur coats and playing their new pianos. It is hard to bear.'

As Chatfield explained, by the early 1920s the disarmament-mongers were becoming vocal. With a new League of Nations, all seemed set fair for permanent peace. 'Do away with armaments and war will vanish . . .' and, in particular, there were outcries in press and parliament against naval expenditure. Each chancellor of the exchequer would soon be 'vying with his predecessor in reducing the defence budget to a new minimum figure'.[6]

Also hard at work was the insidious new creed of communism. Faced with the growing power and influence of socialism and trade unions, the establishment was shuddering quietly at the thought that a workers' revolution could take hold even in Britain. Industrial unrest, culminating in the coal strike of 1926, hinted at the ugly prospect of civil war. Would the police and the armed forces stand firm, come what may?

Naval personnel were disinclined to militancy. Grievances about pay and local pockets of unrest about leave or working conditions had erupted occasionally in recent years and left no trace. Anger, if felt, was directed at the system, meaning the Admiralty, and animosity by disaffected groups towards their own officers was virtually non-existent. During the 1920s,

> in a modern navy of craftsmen, recruited from the sons of craftsmen, trade unionism was something of respected worth and socialism a valid doctrine but the lower deck was not strongly politically conscious. The men were there because they had chosen to be there. A majority . . . were proud of king and country . . . and believers of empire and the superiority of the Anglo-Saxon race. That their officers were extremely class-conscious was not the way they saw it. To them, officers were still merely a privileged part of the life to which they subscribed. There was the comfortable wardroom and the spartan mess-deck but both were inside the British warship and God help those who trod upon the lion.[7]

W.B. Harvey, who spent seventeen years on the lower deck, records the prevailing attitude of ships' companies in the between-wars period as being 'a reluctant and therefore completely genuine pride in belonging to a great navy. . . . ' His messmates sometimes 'beefed' but expressed in many ways their sense of achievement in 'holding their rate' in a 'hard' ship, 'winning the Fleet Regatta or Marathon Race, or wearing the cap tally ashore of the smartest ship. . . . They were by no stretch of the imagination servile,' and anyone who suggested 'that they were serfs would very quickly have had his features if not his opinions altered. . . . There was very little self-pity or envy, though conditions were sometimes harsh and justice unashamedly rough.'[8]

* * *

Every British warship, particularly while on foreign service, was regarded by its complement with masochistic fervour as their home from home. Despite the cheek-by-jowl conditions, each rating, even on the crowded mess decks, had a corner or a 'billet' which others recognized as his space. Off duty, within the prevailing hubbub, a man's wish to be alone with his thoughts or with the task of writing to wife or family was respected. There was rivalry rather than collaboration with the crews of other ships, in each man's opinion his own being the best. Whenever they were on view, afloat or ashore, officers and men alike, behind their flip manner, were quietly conscious of their role as representatives not just of their country, not just of their navy but of their own rather special man-of-war.

Indeed the 'square-rigged' sailor sported a cap ribbon announcing his ship's name in gold letters. He was happy also to display on his blue-collared, bell-bottomed, sexy, figure-hugging uniform other signs of identity and, incidentally, of higher pay: a badge to denote rank if above the able rate; another to define a technical qualification in, say, gunnery, torpedoes, stoking or signalling; and, according to his length of service, up to three 'good-conduct' badges. Petty officers in their peaked caps and more urbane suits wore the equivalent badges but, denoting their grander, more worldly status, no longer their ship's name.

The working day began early. Even in harbour in peacetime, reveille was at 0530. Having lashed up their hammocks, donned working rig and swallowed a cup of cocoa, the men fell in at 0615 to be detailed for cleaning duties above and below decks. All being shipshape and the later-rising officers now in evidence, the colours-hoisting ceremony took place at 0800 by which time everyone on the lower deck, having breakfasted, was in the correct dress for the day. At 0845 more housekeeping and at 0915 formal 'divisions', including commander's or first lieutenant's inspections, prayers and allocation of the forenoon drills and maintenance tasks. And so on until 1600 when, following the end-of-day assembly, all those not required to keep watch were allowed off duty and, if leave were given, free to go ashore, all-night leave being granted if ships were in their home ports or in ports which could offer appropriate facilities.

Discipline was upheld by custom and usage, prompted by peremptory order-giving by officers and senior ratings when the occasion demanded, a process guided and underpinned by accepted, clear-cut codes of punishment. As Sidney Knock, a former naval stoker, recalls, there were stipulated penalties for most breaches of discipline and every sailor knew where he would stand in the wake of misdemeanours. Besides a stint of extra duties, up to three hours absence over leave would cost the culprit one day's pay. For twenty-four hours absence, given no previous convictions for the same offence, punishment was fifteen days' pay plus seven days in cells, but up to fourteen days in cells if the ship had been under sailing orders.

A period in cells was no sinecure. A typical cell, usually below decks in the fore part of the ship, measured 6 ft by 4 ft, its furniture comprising a thick plank, to serve as a bed, and a small wooden table. Diet, traditionally, for the first three days might comprise only ship's biscuits and water, after which 'white bread, unsweetened tea and cocoa twice daily and a pint of potato soup for dinner.' The prisoner might be required to pick 2 pounds of oakum every day and take regular exercise under an armed sentry, while on Sundays, conspicuously garbed, he would attend divine service on the quarterdeck, 'this being considered the *worst part of the punishment*'.

Another punishment involved deprivation of good conduct badges, with a consequent loss of pay and possibly a black mark against the offender's promotion prospects. Generally after hearings on the open deck punishments were doled out with minimum ceremony by the captain or second-in-command but the more serious ones became the subject of a warrant read aloud to the whole ship's company, while those of exceptional severity would emerge, in time, from the deliberations of a court-martial with all the attendant gun salutes, full-dress parades and pageantry. By such rituals was the mystique of authority enhanced.[9]

Tom Cable, who served twenty-six years on the lower deck, from boy seaman in the late 1920s, to chief petty officer, sums up life at sea:

The world in which the lower deck rating lived was one of hardship and discomfort, eating and sleeping in a confined space, seeing the same faces 24 hours a day, week in, week out, often for years at a time. It is little wonder that on occasion he turned to drink and women during the few hours he escaped. Bad language was part and parcel of life on ship but never on shore and never in the presence of women. His demeanour and character were bywords in foreign countries. He played his sport in the spirit in which it was intended, not only for the honour of his ship but for love and devotion to his country and all this on a mere pittance. . . .

The hardship experienced in bad weather at sea produces very special qualities enabling men to exist in peace and harmony. It matters little how many creature comforts are provided on board a ship, the power of the sea is unrelenting. In my time to achieve these ends the years of training were hard and tough. In the days of sail when ships spent months at sea, homosexuality was the rule, the old timers taking under their wing a young seaman, guarding him, giving him delicacies and in general treating him as a beautiful female. Such boys were called 'Wingers' and in my early days a blind eye was turned to this practice. For most men, however, women, prostitutes included, were put on a pedestal for in them sailors found two things missing in their life of celibacy – love and sympathy – even when it was only during an all night session with a lady of easy virtue. In times of peace the sailor was often reckoned to be a drunkard and a womanizer but in war, a hero. In truth he was underpaid and overworked, in spite of which, he was one of the country's greatest ambassadors.[10]

* * *

In November 1919 Beatty was appointed First Sea Lord, a post he was to hold for the unusually long period of nearly eight years. The Americans, having in their view saved the Allies' bacon by joining them against the Germans in 1917, the penultimate year of the war, were now prominent among the star turns at the peace conferences. The more they saw of the fragility of the world around them the more committed they became to developing their navy as 'second to none'. At the same time, in the interests of economy and to encourage the peace process, the swollen navies of the leading powers were to be reduced in size. The vital questions were how to agree ratios and how to measure strengths – and to answer these the United States, Britain, France, Italy and Japan were, from 1921, to confer together in Washington.

Beatty, in all his glory, that is Admiral of the Fleet, David, Earl Beatty of the North Sea and of Brooksby GCB, OM, GCVO, DSO, DCL, LLD, Grand Officer of the Military Order of Savoy and holder of the American Distinguished Service Medal, the Japanese Order of the Rising Sun, the Grand Cordon of the Order of Leopold,

8. & 9.) During the Edwardian period, behind the bright image, life on the lower deck was far from glamorous. While the daily rum distribution was a highlight (right) among the lowest lights was coaling ship day (below).

the French Croix de Guerre (Bronze Palm), the Grand Cross of the Star of Rumania, the Grand Cross of the Legion of Honour, the Greek Order of the Redeemer Grand Cross, the Chinese Order of the Excellent Crop First Class and the Gold Medal of La Solidarad of Panama, was to lead the uniformed element of the British delegation. His reception in America was rapturous, the more so because, to add to his other accomplishments, he could boast Irish ancestry and an American wife, a Field, a member of the wealthiest commercial elite.

In those days a nation's importance in the league of world powers was measured by its strength in battleships. At the outset, therefore, Beatty's aim must have been to maintain Britain's lead in that ponderous and expensive commodity. Little could Beatty have guessed that the Navy over which he presided was soon to suffer at the hands of the Americans, and in peacetime at that, a defeat greater, in loss of major warships, than any in its long and glorious history. For the capital ship ratio on the agenda, on a much reduced scale, was: United States 5, Britain 5, Japan 3, France 2, Italy 2. This was a marked comedown for a power that hitherto had boasted a navy equal to the combined size of the navies of any two other powers.

But there was more to it than that. As an imperial power with worldwide defence responsibilities, Britain needed a balance of warship types and, within each class, performance specifications different to those of other nations. One outcome of the conference-approved tonnage limitations was the strange spectacle of the two new British battleships, *Nelson* and *Rodney*, with their sterns and rear guns lopped off to compensate for the weight of their main armament. Another was the tussle to retain the number and types of long-range cruisers that Britain considered essential for commerce protection. Even more abject in the long run was Britain's surrender to American pressure to abandon the Anglo-Japanese treaty when this came up for renewal, an unforgivable snub to the Far-Eastern ally that led inexorably to Pearl Harbor, Singapore and, for Britain, the beginning of the end of the empire.

The disarmament in-fighting, begun in Washington, was resumed with tedious persistence at later conferences in Rome in 1924 and Geneva in 1927. It was still preoccupying the naval powers at London meetings in the mid-1930s. Beatty, supported ably by a skilled negotiating team under Chatfield, had fought a valiant rearguard action; and if he did not save for Britain all that he intended, this was due as much to the weak wills and vacillations of his political masters in Whitehall as to the single-minded ambitions of the Americans.

And on the home front there were other problems. Prominent among these were the Royal Air Force's determination to secure control of the Fleet Air Arm, an instrument of growing importance to the Navy. There was also the constant threat to the Navy's viability and morale from the endless chain of economy measures, a reflection of the deteriorating situation leading to the great slump at the end of the 1920s. A quasi-pacifist mood was beginning to take hold of public opinion, which could not bode well for the future of the Navy.

These setbacks notwithstanding, the Admiralty in the inter-war years was still a force to be reckoned with. It administered the Navy's far-flung apparatus, gathered intelligence about foreign navies, planned and directed British naval strategy and operations, and kept in step with military and air force developments. The Admiralty, uniquely among the service departments, was responsible for the design and procurement of all its *matériel,* the support facilities ashore as well as of the warships, some of the latter being built in dockyards owned and managed by the Navy, others under contract with private shipyards.

The chairman of the Admiralty board, the First Lord, was a cabinet minister and a civilian. The chief executive, the First Sea Lord, was an admiral and, while holding the appointment, the professional head of the Navy. The permanent staff of the Admiralty, under the Board's secretary, were civil servants and their job, besides keeping the great machine running, was to smooth the way for their decision-making colleagues, generally naval officers of commander rank or higher on two- to three-year appointments.

Most naval officers, lacking experience of Whitehall or training in the ways of bureaucracy were ill at ease first time round at the Admiralty. Wearing plain clothes, they were shorn of the air of authority that went with a uniform. They missed the simple order-giving milieu of a warship or training establishment. They were often at a disadvantage in an ambience where intellectual discipline, political guile, negotiating skills, fluency in committee or in writing and a temperament suited to endless flows of paperwork were necessary attributes. The collaboration worked partly because of the tact, patience and competence of the civil servants and the cheerful anxious-to-learn good nature of the naval officers. It was mainly successful because all who worked at the Admiralty – officers, officials, clerks and messengers – were drawn together in their determination to do their best for the Navy.

This positive spirit was never more marked than during Beatty's tenure as First Sea Lord. Despite the setbacks, Beatty's sanguine good humour, disdain for slouches and ability to enthuse those who worked with him never faltered. He was that rare naval creature – a vigorous and successful fighting admiral able to trim his sails to the sometimes fickle, sometimes obdurate winds of bureaucracy and politics. For such an active and adventurous man, Beatty's capacity for painstaking progress in negotiations was remarkable. He was 'as effective at the council table as he had been in command of fleets at sea . . . and ministers soon came to learn that they were dealing with a man on their own level, if not above it,' Beatty being 'the only First Sea Lord who could really talk on even terms to the highest cabinet ministers and stand up to them in argument.'[11]

Unlike most of his predecessors Beatty gave staff officers their head. He approved the naval staff college at Greenwich and re-established the war course of senior officers. He encouraged closer liaison between those who designed the ships and those who might have to fight in them. He was an advocate of scientific and operational research. And he was a prime mover in creating the tri-service chiefs

10.) Bored sailors find solace and amusement in open-air dancing parties.

of staffs committee, to prove itself before long as the government's most effective instrument for the conduct of war.

Whereas most of his peers had qualified in gunnery on their way up the promotions ladder, Beatty had remained an all-rounder or, as the Navy had it, a salt horse. Beatty's reluctance to specialize, his professionalism and early successes as a seagoing commander and his dashing manner inspired the younger generations of salt horses impatient to command their own ships and emulate their hero. It would be these officers, led by Beatty's example, who as captains of the smaller types of warship, notably destroyers, would so ably bear the brunt of the Second World War at sea.

After stepping down as First Sea Lord in 1927, Beatty lost no opportunities in the press or on the platform to argue the Navy's case for more resources or in his contacts inside and outside the service to stimulate pride in and loyalty to the Navy. The familiar figure on the bridge of his private ocean-going yacht, albeit off duty, would turn up from time to time and be made welcome at naval exercises, his presence providing a fillip to the host commander-in-chief.

As the pace of his life slackened, Beatty remained ever ready to give vent to one of his characteristic bursts of vigour. Thus, in 1931 he was with reluctance convalescing from a fearful accident which had smashed his jaw, and a nurse was in attendance. Suddenly a pack of hounds appeared and could be seen in full cry streaming across the park. David Beatty rushed out of the room and brushing aside all protests mounted a pony and disappeared in pursuit.[12]

But with his wife's death in 1931 Beatty's spirit and health began to weaken. In 1935, against medical advice, while severely ill with influenza, he rose from his sick bed to attend the funeral of his old comrade-in-arms, John Jellicoe. Four months later, at the early age of sixty-five, Beatty was dead too.

In May 1936, when recommending to parliament that a monument be erected to Beatty's memory, the prime minister, Stanley Baldwin, recalled how Beatty, as Commander-in-Chief of the Grand Fleet during the last two years of the war, 'bore upon his shoulders that almost intolerable responsibility, the chief responsibility for the safety of our country'. This was to be followed by more than seven years as First Sea Lord at a time when, in the hands of a lesser man, it might have been impossible to have accomplished so skilfully what was done when he was obliged to reduce a great force 'to the very skeleton of what it had been'. Baldwin opined that Beatty, 'although a public figure, gifted with all those qualities that attract the admiration of mankind, . . . was fundamentally a shy man, a man who disliked publicity, who never courted it and kept himself aloof from the controversies that have raged since the war.'

Today, in Trafalgar Square, the busts of only three fighting admirals, Beatty and Jellicoe from the First World War and A.B. Cunningham from the Second World War, are honoured with a place in Nelson's shadow. This triumvirate, looking up to their apotheosis at the top of his column, remain 'as witness to future generations concerning the spirit by which they were inspired. It is more than discipline and beyond duty. . . . Such is the essence of the Service and of all heroic tradition rooted in self-sacrifice. As such, Spirit is both the cause and the consequence of civilisation.' Anyone who may be called upon for a superhuman effort requires a beacon – if we fail to reach out to it, its light can still lead us.[13]

* * *

The postwar winds of change having died down, there followed a demoralizing five-year period in the doldrums before a new breeze put the Navy back on track. This turned out to be a pre-war breeze, to build up all too soon to storm force as the nation found itself plunging, battened down, into the roaring forties of renewed conflict.

A pivotal figure during the doldrums period was Charles Madden, Beatty's successor as First Sea Lord. In the aftermath of Beatty's stewardship, the Navy, despite all its vicissitudes, was apparently in fair shape.

Its ships sailed the seven seas, performing their peace-keeping roles, the assured

> manner of their sailors seemingly unchanged; and the world at large, including the British public, saw the Navy only for what it was still trying hard to be: ruler of the waves, immaculate, unrivalled, supreme. . . . Other navies might be edging into the limelight but none could . . . hold a candle to Britain's in showmanship, panache and hospitality. The US Navy, confined to soft drinks at its social functions, its ships stripped down to grey essentials, its officers over-anxious to please within the tightly drawn limits of their rules books, had small talent for pageantry. The Japanese, grim, aloof and devious, were evidently not in the game for fun; while the French and the Italians, despite their ebullience, seemed oddly ill-at-ease afloat. . . . Under the bright and gleaming surface, however, a rot was setting in.[14]

Madden, a former torpedo and electrical specialist, a right-hand man of Jack Fisher during the latter's most innovative period and, after commanding HMS *Dreadnought*, a versatile staff officer and a fourth sea lord, was, from 1911 to 1922, a flag officer afloat with the main British fleet. During the war, he served first as Jellicoe's chief of staff and then, from 1916, as second in command to Beatty, demonstrating once again, under the most arduous conditions, his gift for adaptability. In 1924, having been created a baronet and thanked formally by the Admiralty 'for his services to the Royal Navy and to the Empire', he was promoted to Admiral of the Fleet. In 1927, at the age of sixty-four, having enjoyed a brief spell in retirement, Madden was recalled to duty as First Sea Lord.

It says much for Madden's quiet determination and resilience that, for three frustrating years, a tenure longer than had been intended,[15] he kept the naval ship on an even keel and pointed it more or less in the right direction. At this time the navy lay becalmed in the contrary swells generated by the international politicians as they continued their increasingly acrimonious disarmament debates and the national politicians as they wavered indecisively from one penny-pinching formula to the next. When the government caved in to American pressure to reduce the British quota of cruisers from seventy to fifty, Madden, using the First Sea Lord's prerogative of direct access to the prime minister, had to be dissuaded from resigning. In July 1930 Madden, his integrity intact, was ready to swallow his disappointment and, making way for Frederick Field, resume the family life for which he had long pined.

A year later, yet another cheeseparing Whitehall committee recommended a further pay cut for various classes of public employees which, due to certain accidents of history, seemed likely to hit naval personnel the hardest. When the government changed the following month and their lordships were asked for their considered comments, it was found that most of the Admiralty's top brass were away sick, on leave, about to go on leave or just back from leave. In the view of Lord Stanhope, a junior Admiralty minister, the present board 'is the worst I have ever served with. . . . Pay and allowances for the fleet are perhaps being settled for this generation and heavy cuts are due. Yet the Sea Lords responsible are away!'

In September 1931, with the prevailing economic crisis worsening and the unemployed demonstrating in Parliament Square, and with the Admiralty about to brief the fleets about the impending cuts, the economic crisis worsened. There were now 2½ million out of work, an increase of more than 100 per cent since the previous year and, given the prevailing mood, their lordships urged the government to withhold public announcements about the new measures to allow time for the details to be passed down the line to the lower decks. In the event, however, the Chancellor of the Exchequer made a statement in parliament on the same day as the despatch of the corresponding Admiralty letter to the flag officers of fleets and squadrons. This letter, sent by signal to overseas posts, left London by surface route to its destinations in home waters.

The chain of command being sacrosanct, onward transmission of the letter's contents was meant, properly, to be with the various Admirals' authority and thence with each Commanding Officer's endorsement.

> This needed time, the more so when delicate and complicated matters affecting the well-being of personnel were involved. But the letter did not leave London until the Thursday evening; with most of his ships at sea, the Atlantic Fleet's supremo, admiral Hodges, lay ill in hospital near Portsmouth; and the weekend lull was imminent. The letter duly arrived in the fleet flagship, berthed at Portsmouth, to await its ailing commander-in-chief's pleasure, and was pigeon-holed; and no copy got through to the office of his temporary substitute, admiral Tomkinson, afloat at Invergordon, until the Sunday afternoon. Meanwhile, on the Saturday afternoon, (another copy of) the official order, in its usual unexciting envelope, had reached Tomkinson's office (by another route), where it sat waiting its turn in a pending tray.[16]

But the news was already out, via BBC broadcasts while ships of the Atlantic Fleet were still on their way to Invergordon, and in newspapers, which, awaiting their arrival, were to be read avidly by ships' companies before the official communications were in their officers' hands.

The impact of proposed cuts varied widely. An Admiral's daily rate of pay was to be reduced by 10*s* to £5 16*s* 0*d*. Among some of the lower ranks there was to be an across-the-board cut of 1*s*; for example, a Lieutenant-Commander's and an able seaman's pay, reduced by that amount, might fall to £1 6*s* 8*d* and 3*s* respectively. In the latter case this meant a devastating and, with hindsight, blatantly unjust cut of 25 per cent.

On overseas stations where most ships happened at that time to be on detached service, the official announcement, relayed promptly by signal and conveyed in good time to individual ships' companies by their captains, was received calmly. At home, however, the mishandling of the communiqué and the fact that the bulk of the Atlantic Fleet was concentrated at Invergordon facilitated the work of agitators as the sailors congregated in their spare time in the canteens ashore. While the men's obvious anger caused concern, no one imagined their present outburst to be the prelude to mutiny.

In the forenoon of 15 September 1931, the Tuesday following the fateful weekend, when the assembly was due to go to sea for exercises, several of the crews refused to work their ships. There was no overt organization, no violence and no failure to provide essential shipboard services. Officers who tried to reason with their men were listened to politely, and ignored. The ratings appeared to have no strong animosity towards anyone, least of all towards their own officers. It seemed to be more a case of disappointment that the Admiralty had failed to protect them from the politicians.

As usual when confronted with a public relations crisis, their lordships blundered. At a time when the more said might have been the better, they took refuge in a characteristically terse statement that feeding curiosity and rumour encouraged speculation and distortion.

Public opinion was shattered. It was beyond belief that ships of the Royal Navy, symbol of strength and stability, could be immobilized by mutiny. In the world's money markets, already uneasy about the state of sterling, there was a run on gold and by the end of the week, with the value of the pound falling, Britain was forced off the gold standard.

Meanwhile, after only a day and a half, with the Admiralty having promised to investigate grievances promptly, the mutiny collapsed, and the ships sailed under their officers' orders for their home ports.

While leave was given and committees in the naval barracks went through the motions of attending to complaints, a few heads began to roll. A couple of dozen ratings with subversive tendencies were quietly removed from the Navy. After a decent interval, the Admirals Hodges and Tomkinson having been relieved of their posts, Field was given the rank of Admiral of the Fleet and put on the shelf; Fuller, the Sea Lord responsible for personnel, was retired into obscurity; and Dreyer, the Deputy Chief of Naval Staff, was banished to the Far East as Commander-in-Chief of the China station.

Meanwhile the government, bowing to pressure, took steps to reduce the severity of the cuts they had so recently and clumsily decided to impose; and the offending fleet waited on tenterhooks for the new broom that, inevitably, would be sent to sweep it clean.

BETWEEN THE WARS, 1918–39

CHAPTER THREE

Views from the Nursery

In its interwar heyday, the Royal Navy's best known nurseries for new entrants were the RN College at Dartmouth for officer cadets and HMS *Ganges* near Harwich for boy seamen, the entry ages being 13½ for the former and between 15 and 16 for the latter. Here, first, is the diary and progress report of a cadet who joined Dartmouth in May 1929.[1]

In the late 1920s, when I was eleven, my father sent for me and said it was time to consider my future. Like many men of his generation who, in the First World War, had suffered the horrors of trench warfare in France, my father held a poor view of the Royal Navy's contribution to the conflict. Soldiers living or dying in muddy, rat-infested squalor felt that the sailors in their snug warships lying comfortably at anchor at Scapa Flow between occasional forays into the North Sea in pursuit of an elusive enemy were having it a bit too easy; and the indecisive result of the Battle of Jutland, including an assumption that some of our heavy ships had run away from the fight, did little to relieve the feeling of illwill. For my part, however, I had never forgotten the impression made on me when, as a child of seven, I was invited to a party on board the aircraft carrier HMS *Argus*. The Navy has always been good with children but, on this occasion, excelled itself. The result of clever improvisation and hard work, we were entertained with aerial railways, roundabouts, boat trips, clowns, punch and judy shows, coconut shies, singing, competitive games and enormous teas washed down with barrels of lemonade.

I plucked up my courage.

'Destroyers are always in the thick of it,' I suggested. 'Even in the last war . . . weren't they always at sea fighting the enemy?' This remark pleased my father. He looked out of the window lost in thought.

Much as parties on board one of the bigger ships appealed to me, my greatest excitement had been a visit to a British destroyer. My introduction to these glamorous warships was aided by the romantic nature of my nanny who was much enamoured of a warrant officer serving aboard a 'W' class destroyer at this time. When he came to our house to be entertained in the nursery, I was seated between them on the sofa as a kind of chaperone while they pretended to interest me in a picture book spread across my knees, all of us close enough so they could reach across me and touch each other. I was much intrigued by these goings on, the objects of which were not at that time entirely clear to me, but it was nice to be apparently the cause of so much pleasure to two adults.

But the best of it was an afternoon on board this genial Warrant Officer's ship. There I was put into the hands of a sailor while the lovers were, for all I knew, kissing and cooing in the officer's cabin. Their wish to be alone for as long as possible ensured that I was given the run of the ship in detail; up and down the ladders, all over the bridge, down the engine room, into the mess deck, in among the guns, torpedoes and depth charges. I was so inexhaustibly enthusiastic that I ran through two or three sailors working in relays in a single afternoon. And after all that exercise, tea in the wardroom with buttered toast and jam and, greatest treat of all, spoonfuls of rich brown sugar.

My interest in destroyers was not related consciously to blood and thunder – it never occurred to me that if I joined the Navy I might have to fight in a major war. What appealed about these smaller ships was the informality, the less stereotyped discipline compared to that prevailing in the bigger ships. The camaraderie was more evident. The speed and manoeuvrability, the sense of dash and bravado aboard these ships was very attractive. I could think of no better place to be when I grew up.

'Yes,' I said. 'I have made up my mind.'

My father stood and looked carefully at me.

'Right,' he said crisply. 'I will write to your headmaster and ask him to put you in his Dartmouth tutorial. Any questions?'

I smiled and shook my head. I knew it all. In a year or so, one of several hundred applicants, nominees of schools up and down the country with reputations hitched to their success in grooming boys for a naval career, I would have to endure a very stiff medical examination, an interview board and two days of written examinations in London. Then, with luck, at about thirteen and a half, kitted out with my brand new naval cadet's uniform, I would report for duty and training at Dartmouth.

On reflection, I became convinced that I got through the naval interview because I was not myself. I was stiff, uncommunicative, gaunt with apprehension, bowed down with weeks of rehearsal. To complete the disguise my mother, in a moment of panic, engulfed me in a huge Eton collar and a last-minute session at the hairdresser. The latter cut me to bristle length at the sides and cemented my upper hair with grease. This left a tail-end standing erect at the back of my head which vibrated as I walked, causing me to frown.

My uncle Tom being a serving naval chaplain was presumably an asset on my CV though when the president of the board glared at me and said 'So you're young Crick's nephew, eh?' it was not quite clear to me whether I was being congratulated or accused. A sense of doom gripped me when one of the admirals led me across the room to a map of the Atlantic. No names were shown on his map. The admiral planted a thick forefinger on what I knew to be the Cape Verde Islands.

'Well, my lad, what are these islands called?'

'Cape Verde, sir.'

'Quite sure?'

'Yes, sir.'

The admiral stared at me with a quizzical look and then glanced towards his board colleagues as though seeking support. But all the men seated at the table were carefully studying the documents before them. The admiral returned his gaze to me.

'Now then, my boy,' He sounded gruff, 'You say these are the Cape Verde Islands. What about these?'

His finger moved northwards to the Canaries.

'Those are the Canary Islands, sir,' I said but there was a quaver in my voice. I realized my dilemma.

The admiral hesitated. Then he smiled faintly and placing his hands on my shoulder guided me back toward the table.

'It may surprise you to know,' said the admiral quietly, 'I was always taught they're the other way round. What do you say to that?'

My instinct warned me to remain silent but all the members of the board were now looking at me, expecting an answer. At last:

'Sorry sir,' I blurted out, 'all I can say is, sir, it must have been a pretty rotten school you went to, sir.'

Everyone laughed, even the admiral, and I felt better. So, as it turned out, I was one of forty-four boys who, having passed the tests, assembled at Paddington in May 1929 to board the train that would take us to the start of a stint of nearly four years at the naval college. Of the favoured few, I was listed eighth in academic order, a tribute to my headmaster's diligence, and to a burst of energy on my part never equalled during the rest of my life.

* * *

My infatuation with the Royal Navy was shared with many young British boys of my generation. Those who aspired to enter Dartmouth and gain commissions were to a large extent the sons, nephews or neighbours of naval or military officers and among the boarders of those elite prep schools whose names appeared in *The Times* and *Daily Telegraph* from time to time alongside those of their latest pupils to secure a Dartmouth cadetship. They were impressionable romantically-inclined lads like me who, between periodical exposure to the sight, sound and feel of British warships and their crews, remained steeped in the daring adventure stories of the likes of Percy F. Westerman, Taffrail and Bartimeus.[2]

Ludovic Kennedy, as a child in the 1920s, spent several summer holidays at

Nairn, in Scotland, where his grandfather rented a seaside house with views across Moray Firth. For Kennedy the most thrilling event was the Navy's annual visit to the area. There, out of the blue, in line ahead, 'with their grey paintwork glinting in the morning sun, were the ships of the Home Fleet – battleships, battle cruisers, aircraft carriers, cruisers, destroyers, submarines, almost like toy ships, all slowly and sedately making their way into the Invergordon anchorage. . . .'

One year, 'my cup of happiness brimmed over' when, invited to tea on board the battleship *Nelson*, 'we drove on to the quayside at Invergordon where a picket-boat, its crew holding aloft raised boathooks, and commanded by a young midshipman, came alongside. We embarked, and with a surge of power which left one tingling all over, the boat weaved a path through the crowded waters.' Alongside the battleship, 'I could hardly believe the sheer bulk and height of her. As we stepped from the boat the midshipman saluted, and at the top of the gangway on the quarter-deck other officers followed suit and a man blew a whistle. Oh, it was magic.' After a detailed tour of the ship, 'I thought I would faint with the beauty and strangeness and excitement of it all. I had tears in my eyes as the boat took us away; and as the midshipman saluted for the last time, I thought, I want to be you, I want to wear a uniform like yours, I want to command a boat like yours, to belong to a ship like yours, like you to be part and parcel of the Navy.'[3]

On arrival at Dartmouth, the novices were allowed twenty-four hours in which, as the Navy has it, to 'sling their hammocks' before the arrival of the main body of 400 or so cadets would set the wheels of the college in full motion. That first day of indoctrination was misleadingly calm and gentle – the storm, when it hit us, came as instant shock.

> By the third day, while most of us were adapting stoically, even cheerfully, to the unfamiliar regime, some were more homesick than ever before. We could find no kindness or affection: only constant chivvy, nag and menace. We longed for the end of every day, for the privacy of bed, for a brief escape through sleep from the shouts and threats and orders which right into our dormitories, right up to lights out, still pursued us.
>
> Our hard-sprung iron beds were arranged in two parallel rows beside corresponding lines of wooden sea chests, about a couple of dozen beds to each dormitory. We had to open the windows uniformly each evening, according to the weather: with cold north-westerlies and showers in the offing the order might be, 'Half-open south, quarter-open north, close all fanlights.' Now, with the neat edges of the sheets up to our chins, only our faces and heads showed outside the bedclothes – inside, we were required to lie on our backs at attention, hands clenched, feet the regulation ninety degress apart.
>
> The upper half of each sea chest lay open to inspection, the next day's garments folded carefully on the lowered flap, all to the same pattern; while inside, the clean clothes were arranged in their own neat piles. The stack of

shirts offered a standard model of orderliness – each had to be folded and pressed to precisely the same length and breadth, the rows of buttons centred one above the other in straight vertical lines. Any deviation would invite a reprimand or, if there had been a previous similar offence, the award of a 'tick'.

A tick, the sign entered against an offender's name in the cadet captain's notebook, was for minor misdemeanours. A cadet might earn a tick for having a food stain on his uniform jacket on parade, for dodging a cold bath in the morning, for talking while dressing, for not being fully dressed seven minutes after reveille, for having his blazer collar turned up when it should be down, for not saluting, for not running, for not walking, for not standing to attention, for being where he ought not to be, or for giving a general impression of slackness: the breakable rules were extensive.

When three ticks had been accumulated, the culprit was summoned from his bed after lights out, marched to the wash-room lobby and there, across a taut, pyjama'd backside, chastised with at least three sharp cuts with the cadet captain's cane. The cadet was now in the clear – if he acquired another three ticks in the same term he would be beaten again, this time more severely, but, at the end of the term, any residue of ticks would be erased.

Even 'spare-time' recreation was elaborately over-organized. Every cadet on every workday afternoon had to make up a 'log' of chore, effort or achievement. Performance in an organized game of football or cricket or in a sailing race or a cross-country marathon counted as a log but softer options, such as shooting on the .22 rifle range, a game of tennis, a music lesson or a haircut, counted as only half a log. On wet days, denoted days of 'optional landing', the log requirement was, mercifully, suspended.

On Saturday afternoons there was more freedom except for cadets in competing teams or crews and conscripted supporters to shout encouragement from the touch line. On Sunday afternoons cadets were allowed to roam beyond the college surroundings but the limit was a walk to one of several approved farmhouses for a Devon cream tea. With luck, the preferred farmhouse might be within only 4 or 5 miles of the college and, besides the tea facility, might offer a private parlour with armchairs, a log fire and, the ultimate joy, a wireless set tuned to the latest jazz from Radio Luxembourg. The town of Dartmouth and all public places were strictly out of bounds.

Some of the quaint customs were blindly observed by the cadets. One of these was saluting the college quarterdeck– the main assembly hall. Here were displayed a white ensign, a statue of the King and numerous portraits of admirals, but no one ever explained which of these items, if any, was being favoured by so many hundreds of earnest salutes each day. Some of us understood it to be an imaginary crucifix, some the spirit of Nelson, while others, whose sense of values was

11.) A succession of world-renowned and, in their time, popular monarchs headed the Royal Navy during the period of this book. Queen Victoria in the last days of her reign at the turn of the century in procession on the Isle of Wight.

12.) Victoria's son, Edward VII, and his son and grandson, due to become George V and Edward VIII respectively, on board the royal yacht.

13.) George VI, who succeeded his brother Edward upon the latter's abdication, on duty with the Home Fleet during the Second World War.

gradually taking shape, liked to think it was the anonymous cohort of cleaners who kept the great wooden floor in such a brilliant state of polish.

Incongruously the college band played for dancing on the brightly-lit parquet-floored quarterdeck most evenings in the short interval between prep and bedtime. Cadets who felt so inclined would take to the floor in pairs, to practise their foxtrots and waltzes – all good training for showing a decorous flag in far-off imperial outposts in the years ahead; and in that spirit, while small talk was in, body contact was definitely out.

On Saturday nights the band played all evening and, besides the throng of cadets, there would be a few officers, masters and, the sole concession to heterosexuality, a sprinkling of nurses from the college hospital. Even so, the unit-norm on the dance floor was still two cadets, each pair invariably from the same age group – to quench homosexual appetites, older boys were not allowed to partner younger boys. With an awkward show of duty, however, an officer or a master would occasionally commandeer a cadet and steer him a couple of times around the arena or, the ultimate in ecstasy, one of the prettier nursing sisters might succumb to an older cadet's tentative approach and, for once, briefly, allow him the feel and aroma of a nubile, female body.

* * *

The motivation at Dartmouth was fear. The Navy had been savagely cut down and the officers dreaded another axe. Cadets were drilled and toughened into faceless squads of precision instruments to earn good marks for their officers on parade. Even between classes or into meals, it was impossible to move without first being fallen in, inspected, formed into fours and despatched at the double.

The curriculum was heavily loaded with rifle drill, the seamanship manual and elementary engineering, inculcation consisting mainly of toneless repetition by retired petty officers, with the technicalities committed to memory parrot fashion. How and what were explained at monotonous length, but seldom why.

The school syllabus was otherwise in the hands of civilian masters working to a brisk timetable and under pressure to introduce a naval bias, distortion being specially evident in the treatment of history. Besides the usual slog down the reigns of English kings and queens, cadets had to wade painstakingly through sycophantic appraisals of famous British admirals. Their battles were splendid victories attributable to infallible skill and courage, the only exception being the unfortunate Byng and he must have been included to show all the others in a relatively glorious light.

The masters had no responsibility for the welfare, discipline or overall development of the cadets. All this was the prerogative of the naval officers, most of whom served only two years at the college and regarded their appointment there as a form of penance. They pined to get back to sea where they could be men of action and, maybe, earn promotion; and meanwhile, they looked upon their landlubber colleagues with pity and condescension. Thus the masters occupied second place in the college power game. They were an unseamanlike lot in their sloppy civilian clothes, reluctant messmates, seldom good for a round of gin.

* * *

During his first two years, a cadet might be taken aside for a private talk with his officer.

> When the unexpected summons came I could only assume it meant trouble; and as I proceeded at the double to this officer's cabin, a catalogue of recent misdemeanours formed quickly in my mind. There were plenty of these but at such short notice plausible excuses were in rather short supply.
>
> The officer remained seated at his desk while I stood at attention before him.
>
> 'Well, Owen,' said the officer sternly. 'I wanted a yarn with you about . . . well,' he faltered, 'about one or two things, about things concerning your future.'
>
> 'Yes, sir,' I replied, with a feeling of relief. The future was likely to be a more congenial subject than the past.
>
> 'As a matter of fact your father wrote to the captain asking him to deal with the

matter. And the captain's passed the baby on to me.' The officer allowed himself a thin-lipped smile and a nervous grunt, which I took to be a tentative gesture of cordiality. On the other hand, intervention by my father sounded ominous.

'Well, baby's not far off the mark, as it happens.' The officer seemed to be enjoying a private joke, but he caught my eye and stiffened. Then he half turned his back on me and glared out of the window.

The rest of the conversation comprised a series of rapid flashes, like salvoes from a gun.

'How old are you, Owen?'

'Fifteen, sir.'

'Soon you'll be grown up, eh?'

'Well, yes sir. I hope so, sir.'

'And you'll start going around with, ah, women.'

'I suppose so, sir.'

'Do you know much about women?'

'I think so, sir.'

'And babies?'

'Yes sir.'

'I mean – you know all about sex and all that?'

'Oh yes, sir. Well, enough to be getting along with, sir.'

'Good man.'

'Thank you, sir.'

'You're quite sure there's nothing more you ought to know about that sort of thing?'

'I don't think so, sir.'

'If you ever need advice you can always come to me. Or to the padre.' The officer suddenly brightened. 'Yes, he's a good chap, the padre. Sex is really part of *his* job, don't you think?'

'It could be, sir.'

'Well, have a word with him if you're worried.'

'Thank you, sir.'

'All right, Owen?'

'Yes sir, thank you, sir.'

'That's all.'

'Aye, aye, sir.'

A week later I was stopped in a corridor by the padre.

'Oh, Owen. I gather there's something you might like to discuss with me.'

'Well, no sir. I don't think so, sir.'

'Not necessarily anything religious.' Pause. 'Sex, for example.'

I smiled. 'My officer told me all about that, sir.'

The padre looked disappointed. Then he put on his man-to-man smile and laid a hand firmly on my shoulder.

'You know about the ladies in Leicester Square who carry red umbrellas?'

'Yes, sir.'

'And you must always steer clear of people like that?'

'Yes, sir.'

'And that you owe it to your future wife to live cleanly as a bachelor?'

'Yes, sir.'

'Good lad.'

'Thank you, sir.'

'Well now, if you ever have any private worries it is your duty to take them to your officer in the first place.'

'I understand, sir.'

'But do not hesitate to come to me if it's something really important.'

'I won't, sir.'

'God bless you, Owen.'

'Aye, aye, sir.'

* * *

The eleven terms at Dartmouth were the first phase of a lengthy regime of indoctrination. The next step was six months of drill, discipline and seamanship in the training cruiser, HMS *Frobisher*. Here, instead of iron beds, the cadets slept in hammocks slung cheek-by-jowl above their 'broadside' mess tables in living conditions the same as those endured by the lower deck sailors, alongside whom the young gentlemen now worked on their daily ship-board duties.

Frobisher being a new venture, several brass hats came to Chatham to see the ship sail. The press had a field day. The *Daily Telegraph* reported a typical daily routine 'Rise at 0530, stow away hammocks, scrub decks. Breakfast at seven, clean ship and messes, attend divisions. From nine, school work or various on-deck chores, with dinner break at twelve. Around four, drills, evolutions, followed by tea. Then, time for deck games at sea or shore leave in harbour and, at seven, supper. Into hammocks and pipedown by 2100.' There were numerous photographs of cadets looking self-consciously nautical.

The cruise programme covering the first three months of 1933 seemed exotic – Azores, Trinidad, Grenada, Barbados, St Lucia, Antigua, Bermuda; but on a pay scale of 1*s* a day and such an early curfew, temptations were safely out of reach.

The best time was at night, sleeping on deck beneath the stars. I contrived a slinging billet for my hammock from one railing to another on a searchlight platform and when it rained, my oilskin, supported by a rope jackstay, provided cover. Years later, I recall clearly the warm scents and sounds wafted across the water from nearby Caribbean shores.

The Dartmouth group shared the *Frobisher* experience with two batches of newcomers straight from public schools. The 'old hands' from Dartmouth, although outnumbered, were soon the top dogs. The first taste of naval drive and discipline must have been shock enough to the bemused public schoolboys without the extra strafing meted out by the already sea-wise Dartmouth gang. One object of the strafing was to dampen the new boys' eagerness to please. By now, the Dartmouth code was to give only the inch, gain comforts by bending rules, go slow or act unruly when out of sight of officers, know when, very occasionally, to make that special effort.

The friction continued off and on into the second *Frobisher* cruise that summer, when the ship called at various ports in Scotland, Norway and the Baltic. At one time, it got so heated that the captain, in a quiet man-to-man chat on the mess deck, said he might have to take the cruiser back to Chatham unless the quarrelling stopped. He appealed to the Dartmouth group to give a helping hand and share more of their professionalism with the newcomers. The Dartmouth lot were so impressed by the old man's courtesy, by the absence of any 'or-else' threat of disciplinary action, that they succumbed. So quite soon, the two streams merged, their origins no longer discernible and all were, once again, one Navy.

The most stimulating part of the *Frobisher* regime was that emanating from the cadets' daily contact with lower-deck sailors.

> My own favourite sea daddy was the veteran matelot whom I partnered at brightwork stations. He was a deceptively mild-mannered able seaman, a stripey, caustic, sardonic, a veteran of many ships and climates, a man wise in the ways of officers, experienced in avoiding their attentions.
>
> Our baby was in a quiet corner of the quarterdeck where the ship's builders, as an afterthought, had grouped together a cluster of ventilators. These were vertical steel pipes crowned with fat round heads, like petrified mushrooms planted in the deck. They were of varying height and girth. Some emitted strange hot smells, others sucked fresh air to remote places down below. All were painted in grey except at their aperture. Here gleamed a large brass mouth, agape in a square-shaped grin of imbecility.
>
> The many hours we spent polishing those brass mouths was an invaluable part of my education. The first lesson was in perks, protocol and precedent. This was easy and based on simple justice. The older hand cleaned the shoulder-level mouths except those which were really dirty. I, the apprentice, cleaned the tall mouths, the short mouths and those mouths in my mate's territory requiring a strong application of elbow grease. While I stretched, bent and sweated under my mentor's approving eye I was treated to a running out-of-the-corner-of-the-mouth commentary on the characters and habits of the parading officers. This was the main part of the syllabus, the philosophy of the seagoing underdog.
>
> 'Now see that one over there. 'Is dad's an admiral and 'e don't ever let you

forget it. But look at 'im. All flannel and kiss-me-arse. Why, 'e couldn't tell a figure-eight knot from an 'arlot's navel.'

'An important admiral?'

'Only a pusser, as it 'appens. Mind you, pussers are all crooks and that makes them 'uman.'

'Harlot's navel, I think you said.'

'That's right. Seen one?'

'I'm afraid not. Are they different from any other woman's?'

'Oh yes. They're bigger.'

'Bigger?'

'Naturally. Everything about an 'arlot's bigger. And the black ones are the biggest of all. Why, in Trinidad last week . . . '

'Yes?'

'No. There's some things you best find out for yourself. Now take that one. E's a proper sentimental do-gooder. Thinks all men should be equal. Except that poor bloody ignorant sailors mustn't expect to be quite as equal as officers: not in this world that is. But we will all be saved in the end and join 'ands and skylark together in 'eaven and see the glorious light.'

'Perhaps he's missed his vocation.'

'I'll say. 'E should've been one of them psalm-singing padres, 'assock, cassock, 'alo and all. 'Ere, look out.'

My mate's sixth sense warned him we were under observation. We stopped talking to concentrate on our work with industry and devotion. An officer approached, glanced critically at our unwelcoming backs, could find neither fault nor reason for praise, and walked on reluctantly in search of other victims.

'Now that one, 'e's the prizest pig of all. Red-faced bastard. Lash us to the mast and flog us to death if 'e could. Ever seen the wife? Battle-axe. When 'e comes aboard you see the worm turning. Impotent, probably. The rough ones often are. The louder the mouth the bigger the flop. Drinks, too. 'Is liver's the trouble. Barnacled and blistered. Early morning's the worst time. Gets a little quieter after breakfast. Kill you before breakfast, 'e would, but afterwards, just maim you for life.'

* * *

As midshipmen later that year, pay went up to 4*s* 6*d* a day and the young officers could no longer be on familiar terms with the lower deck. They slept in hammocks but were now members of the junior officers' 'gunroom' mess. Although still nagged and chased by their seniors, they were expected at times to perform and give orders as an officer.

At just eighteen, I was appointed to the battleship HMS *Barham* in the Home

Fleet. Our ship's routine in harbour was generally drills, ceremonial and cleaning ship. At sea the order of the day (and night) was mock warfare, largely unexplained – squadron manoeuvres, weapon trials, target practice, equipment exercises. Most of this work took place in home waters – more often than not in uninviting weather in and around Scotland. Early each spring, however, the ship edged towards the sunshine as one of many units in a vast ten-day exercise in the Atlantic. The Home and Mediterranean Fleets took part in strength, representing two imaginary powers at war with one another. The gales were often atrocious and the results of the war-game inconclusive, but it was quite an event to foregather for a few days in Gibraltar *en masse* and, in a haze of alcohol, be reunited with old friends.

My most exhilarating duty was in command of the steam picket boat. This had a crew of five 'petty officer coxswain, and two deck and two engine room hands' and a single propeller with a powerful thrust. The boat had an oil-fired boiler and a tall brass-topped funnel. The wheel and control position were in the open air, behind a dodger, just abaft the engine room. The accommodation for passengers or cargo at the rear end was small, occupying only a third of the boat's length – an enclosed cabin and an open cockpit, each with facing bench seats. On ceremonial days and in foreign ports we flew a large white ensign; and my own badge of authority was that smart miniature sword, the dirk.

In harbour I was on call with my picket boat at ten minutes' notice on alternate days throughout the twenty-four hours. On the other days I kept watch on the quarterdeck under a lieutenant, four hours on and four hours off, another midshipman taking over my boat. Over a two-year period I ran my boat in all manner of ports, harbours and roadsteads, in fair weather and foul, ferrying officers, mail and express parcels from ship to ship or ship to shore.

We were always under observation and the slightest lapse was cursed or punished. When I was one minute late on watch at 0600 one cold, dark winter's morning in Portsmouth harbour, I was sent up the mast to the empty crow's nest for a pointless, freezing two-hour vigil. If the midshipmen as a whole were judged to be slacking off, an hour's gun drill before breakfast and curtailed shore leave would be our lot for a week at a time.

I was nineteen when I received my last caning. This was for failing to spot a senior officer approaching the ship when I was midshipman of the watch. The punishment was given by the president of the mess, a sub-lieutenant two or three years older than I, who ruled the twenty of us with a firm hand. Ours was a tough but genial bloke, a rugger player of distinction and not to be trifled with. Down in the bowels of the ship, in the midshipmen's washroom, I was required to lower my trousers and bend over the bath.

'By command of their Lordships, in the name of His Majesty, and in the interests of the Service, you are hereby awarded six cuts.'

The first five would be fairly light but the sixth was meant to hurt, and did, and made me wince. I knew the weal would need several days to mend. When I was dressed, the sub proffered his right hand.

'Slate clean. No ill feeling. In the mess in five minutes, a gin on me.' A bit of *badinage* over a drink and the incident was closed.

At Portsmouth, the ship's home port, when allowed ashore, the midshipmen drank beer at the Goat and, when they could afford it, ate steak in the Queen's Grill. There were cinemas, a straight theatre, a variety theatre and, for dancing, the Assembly Rooms on Southsea sea front, known to the cognoscenti as the Arse-n-belly Rooms. Some of the girls there worked in shops and offices in the day time and were out to catch an officer and marry him. The sailors, in uniform, were much better dancers and much sexier than the officers in their off-the-peg mufti – thus the sailors invariably got the bird if not the bride.

In harbour on detached service, if not on call for social duties, the midshipmen dressed for dinner – bum-freezer, stiff shirt, butterfly collar. They ate off a polished table, served by white-coated stewards. At the end of the meal the port was passed and they drank a formal toast to The King. On special occasions the ship's band played for them.

Several of these evenings, having begun so decorously, ended in a rough house. In the worst case the ship's commander would be kidnapped and tied to a stanchion on the quarterdeck. Or the junior midshipmen would be discharged into the sea through the gunroom portholes. Or they would cross the water to sack and pillage the equivalent mess in another ship. Many of the harsh rituals that had been disclosed quite recently to a startled world by Charles Morgan lingered on.[4]

These macho rituals were akin to those practised as part of the maturing process in other civilizations. Instead of duelling, hunting big game, enduring circumcision or waging war on the next-door tribe, British admirals in the making drank a lot of beer and beat each other up. However, only a small minority of frustrated bullies instigated and actually enjoyed the violence. The football hooligans of more recent years are of similar ilk.

Was the cadet-midshipman moulding process of that era effective? The contradictions were an essential element. It was accepted that these young officers-in-being were to be harried relentlessly yet, as midshipmen, when they buckled on a dirk and went smartly away in charge of a ship's boat, on watch or on parade, ratings would leap willingly to their commands.

> The lower deck, through fellow feeling and a fascination in the moulding process taking place before their eyes, having enjoyed the Roman holiday, were well satisfied with such a 'democratic' officer-making ritual. More important, they were able to be their own judges, through close observation, of the calibre and staying power of the toughened young 'warts' whose orders they would have increasingly to obey and who, later on, might lead them into battle.

To say the least, what emerged was a definite breed of fit, tough, daring, highly trained but sketchily educated professionals, ready for instant duty, for parades or tea parties, for catastrophes, for peace or war; confident leaders, alert seamen, fair administrators, poor delegators; officers of wide interests and narrow vision, strong on tactics, weak on strategy; an able, active, cheerful, monosyllabic elite.

All too soon, in the tough, arduous and prolonged naval war of 1939–45 they would be put to the test.

* * *

In the meantime, at the start of 1936, the May 1929 Dartmouth intake, after being scattered worldwide on their midshipmen's duties, were reunited at the naval college at Greenwich. Here, as acting sub-lieutenants in a relaxed, quasi-university atmosphere, they were, at last, emerging from the nursery. Besides the splendour of Wren's creation, there was the luxurious accommodation. Instead of cramped quarters on board ship, each now had a spacious bedroom, shared with one other officer, furnished to the standard of a London club.

The public rooms, used by officers of all ranks, including staff course high flyers, were palatial. On mess nights the restaurant, with polished tables, gleaming silver, white-gloved stewards, attendant orchestra and everyone in evening dress, looked fabulous. An invitation to these functions was much sought after, not least because of the *cuisine*, reputedly the work of the Navy's keenest cooks under a former Ritz hotel chef. And as the guests invariably included a sprinkling of public figures, politicians, tycoons, top Navy brass, the newcomers felt themselves admitted, for the first time, into one of the ante-chambers of imperial power. Naturally this flattered their egos while reinforcing their belief in the permanence of Empire and of the Navy's unique place in its scheme of things.

But this was also academe, a place of higher learning. The curriculum had a naval bias, with Trafalgar and Jutland never far away, but it was broad-based in both science and the humanities and interpreted mainly by civilians. The officers wore uniform at work but there were no parades, the only disciplined chore being a twice-weekly physical-training class.

And all the joys of the West End were close by. The double-deck trams ran from outside the college gate to Westminster Bridge and the trains from Maze Hill to Charing Cross. Evenings up the smoke would usually begin at one of the service clubs – in Piccadilly, at the Naval and Military club, the In and Out, the least formal and most naval of the clubs; the United Services, the Senior, known also as Cripplegate, which tended to attract the higher ranking officers; or the Army and Navy, the Rag, which seemed more military than naval, but second-best military, it was said, the cream being skimmed by such as the Guards and the Cavalry.

14.) Lord Charles Beresford, seen here with Cora, believed he was the right man to lead the navy into the future but John Fisher, his ruthless and quicker-minded rival, beat him to it – the fleet that sailed confidently into battle in 1914 being known as Fisher's Navy.

15.) Like father, like sons – in the best tradition, Admiral Sir Michael Hodges was happy to give all, including three of his sons, to the naval service.

16.) In the early 1930s, the midshipmen and sub-lieutenants forming the gunroom mess of HM battleship Barham, *imbued with zest and self-assurance, were clearly rarin' to go.*

These gradations were important to us as we clung hopefully to our new-won perches on the social ladder. If there was nothing else on offer my clique might stay at the club for dinner or go to a cinema and back to the college by midnight. When we were in funds we would remain in the In and Out until eleven before making tracks for a nightclub. But money was tight. A sub-lieutenant's pay was 9*s* a day, supplemented in my case by an allowance of £1 a week from my father who also paid the essential bills at Gieves, the naval outfitters. Lodging at Greenwich was gratis but we had to contribute to the cost of our board. We could imbibe and smoke fairly cheaply because drinks and cigarettes were at cut prices thanks to the supplies in bulk to officers' messes by the appointed wine merchants. The main expenses were eating out, getting about, celebrations and hospitality. And at parties, style and quality were important, the accepted upper-class standards being the bench mark, the rules for dress and etiquette clearly set; and it was possible to take a girlfriend to dinner, theatre, dance and cabaret in the West End, including drinks, front stalls and taxis for two, for less than £5.

When I began to question this array of pointless dissipation, salvation arrived in the shape of the college commander. I was dozing quietly in the back row of a lecture room, oblivious to the instructor droning on about celestial navigation, when the door opened and in strode the commander. 'Four volunteers,' he barked. 'I need four volunteers for Lady Goode-Ferguson's dance. Sixteen Bruton Street. Tonight. 2130. Tails.' Eyes downcast, the assembled sub-lieutenants made no move. The occasion was a deb dance short of young blades, a flop, obviously, the hostess having resorted to this last-minute press-gang trawl in Greenwich.

'Right,' said the commander, pointing at me and three others. 'You there. In the back row. Names.' These having been noted on a list and on four blank invitation cards which were then handed out to us, the commander withdrew. Volunteers, indeed! During the break that followed, we four conscripts were muttering among ourselves when the commander approached us. He had quietened down and was almost genial. 'Sorry to have lurked you lot,' he said. 'I know you won't let us down, but remember. Duty first, Keep it ship shape. Take your share of the free booze, by all means, but don't get plastered. Be nice to the mums. Be even nicer to the wallflowers. Dance with them and no funny stuff afterwards. Right?' Then, as he turned away, 'And, for once, you will have earned your zizz in the back row of the class tomorrow.'

When the Greenwich contingent arrived the place was already humming. It took time and perseverance to get through the scrum to the bar. Most of the people jostling around us were loud-voiced young gentlemen-about-town – guards officers, stockbrokers, Oxbridge undergraduates, the sons of wealth and privilege. These were the regulars, the debs' delights, the eligibles, known largely to each other, their hostesses and, of course, the girls, united exclusively by dropped names and languid, top-drawer gossip. Beyond the immediate hubbub was the sound of dance music. Some couples were fox-trotting in the main reception room. Later arrivals, from dinner or theatre parties, joined the throng. At around eleven, there would be the supper interval at tables for eight or more, new pairs and groups would form and, with the main dancing session to follow, the show would be well along the road.

The music stopped and the band leader announced the break. Some of the people made towards the supper room, in search of pre-booked seats or partners, the rest following slowly, to be distributed among the gaps at the less popular tables.

As I paused on the threshold of the gathering, a smartly gowned lady came up to me. 'I am your hostess,' she said. 'Susan's mother. You're one of the naval officers from Greenwich, I think?' I nodded and gave my name. 'I'd be so happy if you would join my table.'

I was shown to a vacant chair beside a rather plain girl who, already seated, was exchanging *badinage* with some of the other guests. When I sat down she turned to me. 'Bad luck,' she said cheerfully. 'I get the best-looking sailor in the room and you get the ugly duckling.'

'Oh, I wouldn't say that,' I began.

'I'm Susan Goode-Ferguson,' she broke in. 'I'm tonight's star turn. Just for once, men queue to dance with me. There's about a dozen of us this season – the wallflower debs. Awful waste of money but mummy insisted in initiating me.'

'Sounds like some tribal de-flowering rite,' I said boldly.

Susan put down her knife and fork and turned to face me.

'At last,' she said. 'Someone witty.'

'At last,' I responded. 'Someone unconventional.'

'Even so,' Susan countered. 'I think there's scope for a mutual improvement society. Will you join?'

One consequence of promotion to the Goode-Ferguson top table was inclusion in other guest lists. If Susan might be there, I would aim to go. Sometimes we kept an early evening date together in the West End where we might meet for tea at the Criterion, attend a cinema, eat cheaply at the Brasserie Universelle in Piccadilly Circus or Lyons Corner House in Coventry Street.

Susan had an important effect on my attitudes and ambitions. Hitherto the chief emphasis in my life had been of obligation rather than opportunity. I knew little of the world at large, of the way it worked, of who made it work. 'You should be pitting your wits against sharp and flexible minds instead of marching in step at the speed of the slowest naval dimwit,' Susan insisted. 'Wouldn't it benefit the Navy to have a sprinkling of better-educated, broader-minded talent in its officer ranks?'

According to Susan's analysis, the peacetime Navy allowed its officers ample spare time. Instead of squandering this on sport, *bonhomie* and banal social activity, why not cultivate potential high-flyers in the outside world; share some of their intellectual pursuits; form and develop non-naval skills and interests? The present period at Greenwich and the next two terms at the technical schools in Portsmouth offered a starting point; and Susan would help open a few doors.

But it was already high summer and soon we would part for the holidays. Meanwhile, one big event remained on our social calendar. Lady Goode-Ferguson was to host an end-of-season supper-dance at the Savoy for her daughter and, at Susan's behest, I was to be the number one guest.

'This time,' explained Susan, 'you will sit at my right hand, and you and I will open the dancing. Can you bear it?'

'You can be improving my mind as we waltz around,' I said. 'And in the autumn, you come back to tutor me?'

'Certainly.'

But that, alas, was not to be. In Scotland, after the Savoy party, Susan met and fell in love with a leading laird and, the following spring, married him in great style and lived happily ever after.

* * *

At Portsmouth, although truer to naval form than life at Greenwich, the regime still provided a club-like ambience and every weekend off.

Socially, following our two scattered years at sea as midshipmen and, more recently, the chance to make new friends beyond the naval environment, we still depended on our fellow-trainees for day-to-day company. Sad to say, my attempt to follow Susan's instructions proved somewhat half-hearted, the lure of more sybaritic temptations overriding my good intentions. So, in the spring of 1937, aged twenty-one, we were fully-fledged sub-lieutenants, candidates for the King's Commission; and like many of our peers out of the public school system, we were ready and eager to go out into the great British Empire and do our bit.

Abroad for a naval officer meant a 2½-year appointment, while for others, for colonial administrators, Indian civil servants, tea planters, it could mean five, or seven, years without home leave. The Navy in its worldwide policing role was the imperial cement, the white ensign bringing to outposts their only tangible link with England. With his deceptively affable manner, his readiness to lay down the law or quell a riot, his steady measured tread, the Briton abroad in his empire was a reliable and generally welcome figure.

Now, in our turn, we were to be of that ilk. We were far from solemn about the new role but it was, at least, a challenge, an opportunity and, of course, a duty. Marriage being frowned on for officers under thirty, none of our group had wives to weep at our departure, few even had a steady girlfriend and all of us, still based in the parental home, were becoming restless. To go to sea, and preferably abroad, was our outlet. The girls in our circle were, usually, mother-supervised virgins – some of the mothers might be willing, but the daughters had no choice. So, if most of *us* were no longer chaste, our route to emancipation was seldom one to write home about, our sexual outlets being mostly dance hall pick-ups, servitors or, more likely, paid prostitutes. Of course, homosexuality existed, but only furtively among a small minority – it was not respectable, let alone feasible, least of all in a setup where privacy was at a premium and sodomy a punishable offence and, in an officer's case, ruinous to his career.

At Dartmouth, in particular, despite our shut-in existence, the forbidden fruit among ourselves had been hard to come by and, if suspected, looked down on if not stamped on. One careless member of our group had been sacked for writing a 'love' letter to a fellow-cadet. To atone for his sin the rest of us were strafed over a two-week period with, as we saw it, a grimly hilarious blend of early-morning physical training and full-length services of holy communion, sermons and all. After that, for a while, the three prettiest members of our term held giggly court in the cubicled long baths for twenty-minute masturbation sessions with any of us who wanted it. When the captain, hugely embarrassed, gave us a weighty lecture about the evils of tossing off, we decided to go straight, if only to spare the old boy further awkward displays of man-to-manliness.

In pursuit of one's first appointment as a sub-lieutenant everybody was allowed unofficially to wait on a civil servant at the Admiralty called Mr Dye. Although it was accepted that one had to go without question wherever one was sent,

> I was permitted to ask politely whether I could, perhaps, be appointed to a small ship, if possible a destroyer, on the China station. Mr Dye smiled kindly and said, let's see what can be done. So, a fortnight later, when I received an appointment to a very large home-based battleship, HMS *Nelson*, I could only bite my lip.[5]

* * *

A blind spot in the nursery curriculum had been the failure to provide the young officers with insights into the quality of life of lower-deck ratings. That the latter lived on board ship in overcrowded and, for the lower ranks, often squalid conditions, in marked contrast with those of the conspicuously more civilized officers' quarters, was obvious. However, the struggle to make ends meet, let alone keep up appearances, at levels below that of petty officer was barely understood. This myopia was, of course typical of the general lack of concern of the upper and middle classes for the lower classes of those days, but in an 'all of one company' service like the Navy it was inexcusable.

Thus, in the interwar wardrooms (as in the Admiralty, as we have seen, at the time of the Invergordon mutiny) there was little, if any, appreciation of the effort required by an able seaman on a basic pay of 4*s* a day, in debt for mortgages to building societies, for rent to landlords or by 'easy' payments to household suppliers, to look spruce and confident, to perform afloat and ashore, at home and abroad, as though he had hardly a care in the world.

Some aspects of his early training in his corner of the nursery in the interwar years echoed those experienced by the relatively cossetted, but equally hard-driven, cadets and midshipmen. The joining age for a boy seaman was fifteen to sixteen and his first taste of naval life was usually in HMS *Ganges*, the shore training establishment near Harwich. There was no shortage of recruits – to have a son in naval uniform, and in a steady job, at that, was a feather in the cap of a working-class family. Tom Cable recalls:

It was dark when we arrived (in HMS *Ganges*) and after being shown into a large messroom we were served with a meal I remember as vividly today as the day it was served. As much cocoa as we could drink, herrings in tomato sauce and all the bread and butter we could eat. We felt we had arrived in heaven!

All new boys were sent to the annexe which consisted of a mess hall and a number of huts containing beds and kit lockers. A class of boys were allocated to each hut and became the responsibility of a Gunnery and Seamanship Instructor. The first morning was spent at the swimming baths where we had to take a test swimming two lengths of the bath followed by staying afloat for three minutes clad in a stiff canvas suit. Although the water in the bath was heated, the changing passage was bitterly cold. The wet canvas suit made us feel even colder.

The main part of the establishment contained vast playing fields and a huge parade ground on which stood the legendary 120 ft high Shotley mast. After being kitted out, the breaking-in period began with days on the parade ground and in the seamanship room there were periods for furthering our academic training. The pay for boys second class was 6*d* a week and for boys first class 1*s*.

On receipt of this massive sum it was a mad dash to get in the queue outside the canteen and there to blow it on a long cream filled doughnut in which was placed a bar of chocolate, known as a quim (a boy's idea of a female's private parts). The rest of the money was spent on a bottle of ginger pop and a postage stamp. The latter was a standing order at *Ganges* and enabled us to send regular letters home.[6]

As John Douglas has recorded, there were kit-musters once a fortnight and the only shoes that were allowed were the canvas, leather-bottomed type, which a boy had to change into if he needed to go to his bed or locker on the polished deck.

No talking after lights-out, nine fifteen; 'tuppeny bloods' were comics and if an Instructor caught a boy reading one and he couldn't answer a question pertaining to his trade, he was sentenced to two hours reading the Seamanship manual or Communications Instructions and Flag meanings. To compensate these humilities boys were given half a pint of milk at the forenoon stand easy and a sparse-curranted bun to allay the hunger pains as the midday meal-time approached.

One of their last tasks before leaving the Annexe was to climb the mast. Some went over it easily and without any urging from the 'gogger', a yard of rope with a knot in the end as big as a monkey's fist and wielded by two G.I.'s who were trying to see which one could hit the most boys. At the bottom the rigging, the square-meshed foot-holds, were wide and easy to climb but the rigging bounced and swayed alarmingly with relays of ten boys at a time swarming up it; as they neared the devil's elbow, an elbow-like protrudence half-way up the mast, the hand and foot-holds became smaller, and to traverse the devil's elbow a boy had to suspend momentarily over empty space, looking down at the safety net and tiny figures below, before going on up to the half-moon, a small platform almost at the top of the mast. Above the half-moon was a Jacob's ladder about ten feet up and another ten feet of bare pole upwards, at the top, was the 'button', a circular platform about three feet in diameter and topped with a metal lightning-conductor. Few were brave enough to climb onto the button, hanging on to the lightning conductor as their only support from falling off. It wasn't getting onto the button that was difficult, it was getting back off it again onto the mast, trying to wrap plimsolled feet around the top of the mast, over and under the three-foot button. On any day when *Ganges* held a big parade the hand-picked Button-boy was, naturally, the star turn.[7]

Some memories were rather less benign:

What can one say about *Ganges* in the 1930s? It seemed to be staffed by some of the most sadistic and bloody-minded chief and petty officers in the Royal Navy although there were a few good ones amongst them.

So wrote Eric Smith who was not surprised to learn of a home secretary's proposal to use the daily training routine of the *Ganges* boys as the model for a system of short sharp sentences for young offenders, but excluding the boys' daily 0500 hours call followed by boat pulling or mast climbing, this early start being considered too hard on young criminals.

Some of the lads found it hard and bewildering to be shouted at all the time. It served to align the physical training instructors, in the minds of the boys, with the 'Gate and Gaiter' branch of the gunners' mates, probably at that time the most hated branch in the Navy. [One of the instructors] always carried a length of rubber hose around with him which he used frequently and with relish on any unfortunate boy who he considered was not paying sufficient attention to his instructions. Our seamanship petty officer on the other hand was a different type of man. . . . Any boy not paying attention to 'Tubby' was rewarded with a slap from his hoary hand on the nape of the neck which stung for a while but was not done viciously, and he was popular with us boys.[8]

Tom Cable relates what befell him after HMS *Ganges*:

I passed the final examination on the 26th of May 1927 and was rated up to Boy First Class. I was then transferred to Gosport in Hampshire to a new boys' training establishment called H.M.S. *St Vincent*. The four months spent there seemed interminable as it was the longing of every boy to get to sea as soon as possible. On the 28th of October class 54 left Portsmouth Harbour for Plymouth to join the 3rd Battle Squadron. They were coal-burning battleships which had taken part in the Battle of Jutland during World War I and it was to H.M.S. *Benbow* that I was sent for my first taste of life at sea.

Before leaving port it was necessary to transfer 2,000 tons of coal from barges moored alongside. With the exception of the Royal Marine Band, ships' cooks and essential watchkeepers, everybody, including the officers, was employed. The band played all day and the ships' cooks provided gallons of tea and corned beef sandwiches. Within an hour the ships and crews were coated in coal dust, with handkerchief face masks to help protect the lungs. As the last bag of coal went into the bunkers a flag was hoisted on the yard arm and the first ship to finish was awarded the Coaling Trophy. The task was then to clean the ship from truck to waterline. All paintwork had to be washed down and the decks scrubbed, the boys being the last into the bathrooms and once there they had to be content with what was left of the cold grimy water. Tom Cable:

> I was allocated to the quarterdeck to be responsible to a long serving petty officer who remembered the days of sail. On the first morning at sea, he told me I need not take my boots off and scrub decks as the other boys had to but to go up to his caboose, part of the ship's storeroom, to serve out scrubbers, brasso, cotton waste and other cleaning materials. Unwittingly, when he gave me a bar of chocolate, I thought how kind he was, however, when he put his hand up the back of my trousers and felt my behind, I kneed him in the crotch. Therefore, for the rest of the cruise I had every dirty, cold job he could find. Such was the price of retaining ones virginity.

Eric Smith a few years later in a more modern battleship:

> The boys were crowded into messes in the casements of the secondary 6" armament. They were still roused at 0500, and by 0530 hammocks had to be lashed up and stowed in the nettings and ship's cocoa drunk, after which, wearing duck suits and bare-footed, they were scrubbing the acres of *Ramillies*' quarterdeck while the remainder of the ship's company were being called.
>
> Boys were not allowed to wear boots or shoes during the scrub-deck period and few, if any, could afford sea-boots. As the ship's company seamen were not called until half an hour after the boys, it fell to us to commence hosing down the decks with the help of a few men 'under punishment' who were also called early as part of their punishment. We boys were given a holystone each, about the size of a house brick weighing about one-and-a-half pounds, and starting from the stern we holystoned forward until reaching the after superstructure on the quarterdeck. In bitter winds and half an hour of this work we were left cold and with painfully sore knees. In wild places like Lamlash, Stornaway and ports in the north of Scotland, it was a wonder no one went down with frostbite.

F.B. Coombs, a boy seaman serving in the battlecruiser HMS *Hood* in the mid-1920s, takes up the story:

> Our long troubled night, broken by odd bumps underneath as passersby headed our, perhaps too low slung hammock, was ended by the switching on of all the lights and the raucous shouting of the ill tempered, through being shook himself before the normal time, Petty Officer, who was on duty, the time being 5.30 a.m. On mustering, we were all reported to the Duty Officer, who gave the usual order to scrub decks, the only difference that morning was that in the unusually cold weather for Portsmouth, when the sea water was pumped and hosed on the decks, the water froze and turned to icy slush as it ran on deck and over the side.
>
> The lower end in the pecking order, those with no rubber boots, rolled our trousers up and were told to grab a long handled, heavy scrubber and 'Scrub Aft', the icy slush felt on bare feet being enough to set us all hopping and heading for a dry part of the deck. The Duty Officer, still wearing his uniform jacket and trousers over his pyjamas, was sat in his nice warm Cabin, sipping nice warm tea as he waited for his nice hot bath to be run for him. Don't know how long it took him to get back on Deck but when he did all he could find there was his Senior Ratings, and those few wearing Sea boots, still washing the Decks but, instead of scrubbing them, trying to broom the slush over the side before it froze solid. After that fiasco it was no surprise to find that our lives were to be spent in endless, meaningless jobs such as chipping paintwork, washing it and any time-consuming job that could be easily monitored.
>
> The first time we were both rattled for a very minor offence, was by one of the Midshipmen, of about our own age but educated. Such as us, with no ambition and very little interest, were thought to be good food to feed on. We went to build the mound of their ambitions. It was explained to us by the older members of the Crew, a lot of whom were survivors of the War Time Fleets, they only put up with the poor conditions and pay to avoid the mass unemployment that awaited them.
>
> Soon came the day that we had been waiting for, when, for the first time for a lot of us, we went to sea, fell in, stood at ease and waited to be brought to attention in our extended lines, to salute any passing Flags. The pride we took in our first appearance as part of the crew of the 'Mighty Hood' as she slid quietly and quite close to the Fortifications guarding the entrance to Portsmouth Harbour, with cheering crowds waving their farewells, was soon watered down. Instead of getting a close and interesting view of the Warner Light Ship and Nab Fort, with the Isle of Wight in the distance, all we had was a close look at our decks as, on hands and knees, we rubbed the grime of Portsmouth away to reveal the near white wood.
>
> The Ship's Commander, Rory O'Conor, was, like all who had ambitions for promotion, trying to make a name for himself by showing that he ran an

efficient War Ship. One way was to be 'Cock of the Fleet' in the Fleet Boat Pulling Races to be held in Scapa Flow, which he intended to win. Much to our dismay we found that, on looking at the Mess Notice Board, we had 'volunteered' for the Boy's Cutters Crew and were to report for training each day, at a set time, in working hours, and for half an hour each evening, for both boat pulling and physical training.

There was a reward in seeing a spotlessly clean pulling or sailing boat, with its sun bleached thwarts and non-painted wood work contrasting with the brilliant white inside paintwork. The standing rigging and sails was our responsibility too, even to washing the sails with soap and warm water to soften them to try to make the canvas look like duck to suit the Admirals and Captain's Gigs and Galleys, though we always rinsed them in salt water before rigging them in a light breeze to get the wanted set of sail shaped in them. By learning how to tend and rig sailing boats and making a good job of it, we were soon invited to help different junior officers and some keen non-commissioned senior ranks to form part of their crews and enjoyed it all, a far cry from the days when it seemed that we could never keep out of trouble. In harbour we spent a lot of time in boats that were in the water, mopping, drying and cleaning. At sea we did much the same job, cleaning the inside and outside of the boats as they sat in their cradles, though we had a large sail and rigging store to work in in inclement weather which was handy as we were out of sight to onlookers.

Come the 31st March 1937, we were rated up to Ordinary Seaman, a milestone for us as it meant that we, at last, got away from the hated boy's division, were left more to our own devices and learnt that if we mucked in and pulled our weight, everyone did the same. We never looked back, feeling better for just being treated as equals if still junior. Soon after being rated Ordinary Seaman we were moved through the basic skills of preparing paintwork to enamelling where a hard gloss, highly polished surface could be achieved. This, naturally, was only in places of special importance such as the Commander's lobby with its Trophy Award show cases and where his request men and defaulters were interviewed and the Captain's lobby which, besides his Royal Marine guard, sheltered his defaulters. We looked on this as privileged work and kept our noses clean with the advantage of being out of sight.

The *Hood* paid a visit to Juan Les Pins on a couple of occasions and our understanding of humanity was improved upon even if it was only the fact of how little we knew. The Duke of Windsor as he was now, gave us something to think about by coming out and circling the *Hood* where we lay at anchor, one Sunday afternoon. Stood on the bridge of a gleaming white large Motor Yacht, he was soon spotted by the Duty Middy, full of his own P and importance and with his looking stick tucked under his arm. He belted to the ward room to tell the duty officer but he was too late as the duty signal men on the bridge had already seen the Ex King and passed the buzz down the lower decks. The Prince of Wales, who had always been a favourite with the Navy lower deck, was given proof of this when some small group started cheering which spread like wild fire throughout the ship to be heard by our senior officers who promptly gave the order 'Clear the Upper Deck'. Whatever the rights and wrongs of all that, the common sense that normally ruled the lower deck was right, it being pointed out he had paid for doing his duty as we were, and while the smallest amounts that we were paid did not allow us to pack it all in when and how we wanted, he could do what he wanted to do having been paid enough to cover the enormous amounts that he was supposed to have spent on jewels for his Mrs Simpson. We were given a lot to think about on that our first visit to the holiday resort of our monied class, being now O Ds allowed us the privilege of going ashore in the evenings instead of the few hours Saturday and Sunday afternoons as previous, though 14 shillings a week did not go far in a place like Monte Carlo.[9]

* * *

Here we will leave our two apprentices, each in his own sphere having gained the lowest rung of the grown-up ladder – the officer, an executive Sub-Lieutenant with a career to at least the rank of Lieutenant-Commander to look forward to, and retired pay to follow; and the rating, an ordinary, soon to become able, seaman with ten years to serve, then the option of a further twelve, to about the age of forty, yielding a modest pension (up to £2 a week) by way of compensation or, as some might say, recognition.

To remark that these two life styles were poles apart, implying a critical lack of common ground, is to read only the obvious signs. In practice the bonds that drew Royal Navy officers and ratings together were substantially stronger than the differences that tended to separate them. An effective ship's company, the leaders and the led, was united by cause, bound by tradition, inspired by their own professionalism, drawn together by the hardship, camaraderie and, at times, dangers of cheek-by-jowl life in a man-of-war at sea and, in the last resort, upheld by that distinctive British trait, a cheerful, dogged mock-sardonic capacity for endurance in adversity.

CHAPTER FOUR

Med Fleet

If *esprit de corps* is the driving and unifying force of a successful organization, leadership is the mainspring; and if leadership at the top can inspire eager compliance down the line, all things are possible. In the first half of the twentieth century the Navy's top ranks were not short of men with that capability. The styles, methods and personalities of these leaders varied but were united by a common purpose – to enhance the fighting efficiency of the service they revered.

First among the incentives that motivated them was the idea that the spirit of Horatio Nelson lived on – to emulate that icon's example was the surest route to perfection. On the fringe of battle this meant steering towards the sound of gunfire; on sighting the enemy to close the range and hit him hard; to fight on, whatever the odds. In these respects, in two world wars, the Royal Navy met its match only with those other exceptionally tenacious island people, the Japanese. The Germans, a continental race for whom the sea was not a natural battleground, with naval leaders hamstrung by orders from their headquarters not to take unnecessary risks with their ships,[1] nevertheless produced valiant and highly-trained sailors, while the happier-go-lucky though technically proficient Italians lacked the experience and bellicosity for sustained combat at sea.

The Royal Navy's brass hats were buoyed up also by another factor peculiar to a confident, long-established maritime force – the sense and sentiment that in moments of danger we, officers and men together, are literally all in the same boat, but that *in extremis* it will be the admiral on his bridge and then the captain on his who go down with the ship rather than abandon it before every other surviving member of the crew has had his chance to get away.

* * *

In May 1925 Roger Keyes took over as Commander-in-Chief of that great testing ground of up-and-coming admirals, the Mediterranean Fleet, England's main battle fleet. As the largest fleet in the world it was 'based on what was then the strategic nerve centre of the British Empire'[2] and Roger Keyes soon made it his fiefdom.

> At this time the Mediterranean sea, from Haifa to Tangier, was *mare nostrum* to the British fleet, before Mussolini publicised the phrase. Sir Roger would accept no interference from others, not even the Admiralty, and when on his own initiative, he sent the (battleship) *Resolution* to Alexandria to help pacify the populace he was letting it be known that one man gave the orders for these waters. It was not so much *mare nostrum* as *mare meum*, in Keyes's time.[3]

Keyes had got off to an unlucky start by being nearly killed in the crash of a naval aircraft in which he was a passenger. Some of the condolences were illuminating. His predecessor, Admiral O. de B. Brock, wrote 'I wouldn't go up in an aeroplane when I was C-in-C. I said my place was on the bridge of the flagship, and that was quite high enough to see what the fleet were doing.' Another Admiral, de Robeck, sympathized, 'These aircraft are bad mounts: they are as bad as an unbred horse, fall into the middle of a brook, and then they try to drown you. You stick to the polo pony.'[4]

Keyes needed no prompting. Polo was already flourishing in Malta, the Mediterranean Fleet headquarters, and Keyes had had three ponies sent out from England for his own use. All officers with any bent for the game were encouraged to play. If polo tended to be an obsession with Keyes, this was in line with the custom that individual idiosyncrasies were allowed, even encouraged, among senior officers provided these leaders conformed in essentials and, overall, achieved the desired results.

In 1926 when Louis Mountbatten was appointed assistant fleet wireless officer he had his own ponies sent out separately to Malta by sea. 'He practised polo more assiduously than ever, knowing that his new chief considered that it brought out all the qualities he looked for in an officer.'[5] In due course Mountbatten would captain his admiral's team. Lady Keyes and her three daughters 'made up another team, the "Bunch of Keyes", and ladies and guests of the household a third,' the last-named being out most mornings before breakfast playing against teams of midshipmen and novices. . . . In Portsmouth or Pall Mall, Bermuda or Hong Kong when someone spoke of a polo promotion every sailor and everyone who had recently been to Malta knew what he meant.[6]

Not everyone was impressed. David Niven, at that time a young army officer stationed in Malta, was scornful.

> The Marsa Polo Club was the smart place to be – smart in the most colonial sense of the word; it was mounted suburbia. It was parasols and fraightfully refained voices. It was 'Boy, bring me a stinger', and naval wives who announced with a smirk – 'We're going in to have our bottom scrubbed next week,' but it was still heady stuff compared with what I had been exposed to before (coming to Malta)

and I thrived on it. Girls there were in plenty. Apart from the resident ones, daughters of senior officers and officials, there were also for several months a year hundreds of young and lonely naval officers' wives. There was in addition the 'Fishing Fleet', a motley collection of passed-over debs and pink-cheeked country cousins who annually timed their arrival to coincide with the return, after many months at sea, of several thousand sex-starved mariners.[7]

Clearly there was more to life in Malta than polo, though not enough to satisfy every taste. Between exercises at sea Mountbatten was allowed to live ashore.

He found a villa 'with a garden and a flat roof for sunbathing and . . . while he waited for her (Edwina) to join him, he organized the servants, settled the ponies and worked out a routine for his work.' Later, 'he fitted a new gramophone and amplifier' to help entertain the constant stream of visitors. Edwina, having joined her husband, 'disposed of duty calls – people she had to know but did not wish to see found her cards when they woke from their afternoon sleep – and had the Governor to dine.

It was not difficult for Edwina to look after her visitors, although she had less room and fewer servants than she was used to but 'the weather was warm, so clothes and meals could be simple, the pace was slow . . . and the amusements unpretentious: dances at the Sliema Club, supper at the Union Club, parties at Admiralty House and the Governor's Palace, polo;' while in the harbour, below the villa, lay their yacht, *Shrimp*. Dickie enjoyed it all but, 'Edwina could not settle to being a junior officer's wife' and 'a month after she arrived in Malta, she left to shop in Paris . . . and return to London.'[8]

On the other hand, as Barbara Blunt, a naval captain's wife, recorded:[9]

We have taken a place in Floriana over-looking Grand Harbour. It belongs to a Maltese nobleman, who rejoices in the name of The Most Noble Filipo Malia Gotto, Count of Birzebuggia. The house is in a Chelsea-type terrace in a small square called the Piazza Miratore and has three storeys, up narrow winding stairs made of stone. The drawing and dining rooms are on the first floor, the kitchen and maid's room are on the ground floor, and the main bedrooms, three of them, are on the top floor. It's within walking distance of the Customs House where Charles' boat picks him up every morning.

We wake up to the sounds of the harbour: dghaisa men hailing each other, the occasional bugle call or pipe, the throb of boats plying to and from the ships. We can see it all from our bedroom. The sun floods the whole scene and shimmers on the calm waters. It is warm enough to go on the balcony in our dressing gowns, and many a time I have seen through Charles' binoculars a telescope turned on us, usually by a signalman, sometimes by an officer on watch.

At five to eight a warning flag goes up and the guards and bands start parading on the quarter decks. At first, each ship seems to play a different tune and the air is filled with a lovely mix of martial music. At eight o'clock down comes the signal, the bugles sound, and the ensigns and jacks in every ship are hoisted as all the bands play the National Anthem. It is a fabulous sight and never fails to bring a lump in my throat. All the Maltese dhgaisa men stand up in respectful silence in their little boats and every sailor, whether on shore or aboard, stands strictly to attention. Even Charles, believe it or not, stands to attention in his pyjamas. I asked him if he thought that I should do so in my nightie, and he actually said, 'Well, it would be nice, but even if you don't come strictly to attention, I'm afraid you must stand up'. A bit Ruritanian, but I love it all, and I am so glad I married a sailor.

In those days the paths of a noble Maltese landlord and his naval tenant were unlikely to cross, each being in his own opinion a cut above the other. Barbara Blunt:

Although our top people occasionally invite high-ranking Maltese officials to dinner, one almost never meets the locals socially. However, when Charles and I were bidden to dinner by the commander-in-chief at Admiralty House, a mansion in Strada Mezzodi, we found there were twelve of us: Sir Roger and Lady K, a visiting MP and his wife, the Chief Justice of Malta, a Maltese couple, he some sort of civil servant, she sweet, dark, rather fat. The Captain of *Q.E.*, his wife and Flags made up the party.

I found Lady K rather formidable but the commander-in-chief was charming and an excellent host. I sat next to the Maltese civil servant, who spoke English perfectly and was immaculately dressed in tails. They have six children. He told me he is descended from a French family and his wife from an Italian. He said he could speak four languages: English, French, Italian and Maltese. He asked me what languages Charles spoke and I had to reply, 'Only English'. He was most interesting and friendly and so courtly.

After dinner his wife told me a marvellous story about a scandal of a few years before. Unusually, an English N.O. kept a Maltese mistress in Gozo, the neighbouring island, and his English wife in Valletta. The Maltese was from one of the island's noble families and was extremely beautiful. The man had to visit Gozo frequently to inspect the harbours there, or so he told his wife. One day she was talking to her husband's Captain and said, lightly, that she wished it wasn't necessary for her husband to be away in Gozo quite so often inspecting the harbours. The Captain, unthinkingly, remarked that it was not he who sent the husband to Gozo. Then, a little later, he asked if her husband's health was improving: he was so sorry the chap had been off sick so much recently.

The wife put two and two together, taxed her husband with infidelity, and went off to Gozo to confront the 'other woman'. There was a terrific scene and, the Maltese girl having admitted it all, the wife told the naval authorities, whereupon the husband was sent home, not for keeping a mistress, but because the mistress was Maltese. The husband promptly resigned from the Navy. He now lives in Gozo, in the height of luxury, and runs his noble lady's farm there.

* * *

In 1928 Admiral Sir Roger Keyes, a First World War hero, and now Commander-in-Chief of the world's most prestigious fleet, was in his mid-fifties, a man 'short of stature and brisk of temper, wiry, vigorous, nimble as a cabin boy and alive with ambition'. According to his biographer, Aspinall-Oglander, he 'had become a legend even while he was still alive . . . a passionate exponent of the value of the offensive in war'. He was a leader 'for whom the intellectual clique, however, had no time: a "fighting blockhead", Admiral Richmond called him . . . – courageous, independent, but with very little brain'.

Of similar ilk, as commander of the first battle squadron and second-in-command to Keyes, was Vice Admiral John ('Joe') Kelly, 'one of those bluff and breezy seadogs

17.) The Royal Navy's gift for showmanship was ever well expressed by its readiness to form a guard of honour or join a procession. On 21 October 1905, the first centenary of Trafalgar, a ceremonial march in Malta.

19.) Later, a royal salute in the same veuue.

18.) Meanwhile, the dignitaries disperse outside Valletta's cathedral.

20.) Mass parades of seamen were a not uncommon sight.

whom anecdotes stick to like burrs' who, when addressing ship's companies, 'was garrulous, unaffected and worth listening to. For civilians he had no conversation whatever and he made an embarrassing hash of speeches at functions ashore. Keyes was the same – a toastmaster's gavel and a row of stiff shirt-fronts frightened the hero of Zeebrugge to death. . . . Reporting on one occasion of state when he saw Roger Keyes, as usual, fail to string three coherent words together, another famous admiral wrote quite sincerely, 'He could hardly speak today. I liked him for that.'

If the articulate spoken word was in short supply this was not the case with the written word. Orders for a fleet exercise 'went into volumes of closely printed instructions' stating 'at exactly what hour, in what direction, what order and what distance apart, ships would enter harbour twenty days ahead' with 'squadron dispositions and alterations for every moment of the passage'. In harbour leisure pursuits were the subject of comprehensive reports, 'ships had to send details of football teams and spectators landed daily; and when the officers went shooting, even the size and description of the bag was required by the flagship.'

The follow-my-leader fetish was long established; it was a tradition that when it came on to rain no ship's captain would 'allow his officer of the watch to slope awnings until the flagship ordered all ships to slope awnings; when the rain stopped, before any ship made a move to dry up decks she waited for the flagship to signal "Dry up decks"'. The over-staffing, clearly, was monstrous – in the fleet flagship alone there were thirty-one officers with no ship's duties, being engaged solely on staff work for the Commander-in-Chief, besides which Kelly had a staff of twelve just to administer his battle squadron.

Within the framework of conformity, however, seethed a frenetic competition cult as each key officer struggled to be noticed for promotion. The ensuing 'almost vicious spirit of rivalry, diffused through every phase and sphere of the fleet's existence not only failed to bring together, but actually held apart, squadron and squadron, ship and ship'. Thus was the high command's purpose, to blend together a modern version of Nelson's band of brothers, frustrated by the commander-in-chief's inability to delegate initiative.[10]

But the fact remains that Keyes, fashioning his fleet to his liking, was in his element. Many of his best qualities were to the fore. With few exceptions his officers and men responded to his enthusiasms as well as to his eccentricities, spurring him on to ever rising heights.

Then, in the early spring of 1928, as Keyes neared the end of his tenure, a dark cloud gathered. Following a series of incidents 'so petty in themselves as to be shamingly ridiculous' and culminating in a hastily convened court of enquiry, Keyes relieved of their posts and sent home the captain and commander of the battleship *Royal Oak*, as well as the rear admiral whose flag as second-in-command of the battle squadron (under Kelly) had been flying in their ship. The strained relations among these three officers, of which Keyes had more than an inkling, had been most dramatically expressed during an evening dance on board the battleship at which the admiral, disliking the music offered by the Royal Marines orchestra, allegedly told the bandmaster he had 'never heard such a bloody noise in his life' and the commander, in the bandmaster's hearing, that he 'wouldn't have a bugger like that in his ship'.

The timing was unfortunate. To hold the ensuing court of enquiry, the fleet's sailing to keep an important rendezvous off Gibraltar had to be postponed and this delay was the greater because Keyes had stuffed into his pocket, and forgotten, a warning message delivered to him when he was busy on the polo ground. In any case the press was soon on the scent. At first Keyes appeared to have the approval of the Admiralty for his decisions. However, after a while, dissenting voices were heard, among them the King's who, according to Admiral Madden, the First Sea Lord, after spending a night at Windsor, 'would talk of nothing else', being sure 'that Keyes had done the wrong thing', there being apparently 'no precedent in the history of the Navy of one Flag Officer hauling down the flag of another'.

As Keyes recorded in his journal, 'the King had evidently been told that I took more interest in polo than in the conduct of a Fleet.' Later Keyes set out to reassure his monarch, asserting that 'the horse was an excellent trainer' and 'I had never met a keen, dashing polo-player who was not also a good officer.' In the end the King was inclined to agree 'and told me about his own polo days in Malta.' Even so it is generally held that what became known as the *Royal Oak* affair cost Keyes that most coveted of all posts, for which he had long been tipped, the First Sea Lordship.

In general Keyes's undoing was his belief in his own infallibility. A period as supremo of Britain's most important fleet inflated almost to bursting point an already swollen ego. The product of a narrow, vocational education, he had evidently reached the plateau of his intellectual development. Among those under his command in that energetic environment, however, his vigour, charisma and boyish determination had worked wonders.

But, as First Sea Lord, Keyes's conceit and his impatience with the ways of politicians would have been a serious, perhaps fatal, handicap. In Madden's words 'they had to choose a man who would be more amenable to political requirements' and not one who, upon disagreement with government policy, 'would not hesitate to resign and carry all the sea lords with him'. As his supporter, Sir George Lloyd, put it, 'I suppose this miserable Government were afraid of appointing you, because they knew you would fearlessly stand up for the Navy.'

In due course, after a spell as Commander-in-Chief in Portsmouth, he became a respected MP. He made persuasive speeches on naval matters, but on other topics and in debate he continued to be 'very inarticulate, and I find it difficult to marshal my ideas and put them into words.'

Even so, under the spur of the Second World War, Keyes was to find his tongue as well as his markedly more fluent pen in his bombardment of Winston Churchill with schemes for offensive action leading to the development of the commandos, of which combined operations embryo Keyes was the first effective director. In October 1941 after a successful trial-run raid on the Lofoten Islands Keyes, whose implacable single-mindedness had by then irked more Whitehall warriors than was good for him, was shunted aside to be replaced by Louis Mountbatten.

Destined never to hold high executive office again, in December 1945, aged seventy-three, Admiral of the Fleet Lord Keyes of Zeebrugge and Dover died, to be brought in state through the streets to Westminster Abbey for a funeral 'where all the world had sent their representatives to pay their final tribute'. In the words of his fellow admiral, Walter Cowan, Keyes was 'the nearest in characteristics to Nelson of any other sailor in my life time'.

Maybe. In energy and fighting spirit, yes. But in the ability and readiness to calculate, in humanity and in vision, no. For the practical role in which he excelled, however, that of hands-on Commander-in-Chief of a large, balanced, rarin'-to-go fleet, impeccably honed product of the prevailing technology, the whole prepared for win-all set-piece battles which, sadly, were never again to be, Keyes was well qualified. He was, after all, a fully paid-up member of a brotherhood which was tending over much to value bravado above forethought.

Thus to cope with the complexities of top-level command that were to evolve something was lacking, Keyes's failing being shared by others who were soon to prove themselves great sea-going commanders in war. Even A.B. Cunningham, having managed the step from fiery boss of his own fleet to cooperative partner in allied interservice high commands, seemed to lose some of his aura as First Sea Lord.[11]

* * *

Was there life in the Med after Keyes? Indeed, but at a less frenzied pace, until the Italian-Abyssinian crisis of 1935 when, under another dynamic leader, W.W. Fisher, the 'Great Agrippa', an augmented Mediterranean Fleet was being prepared urgently to do battle with Mussolini. As it turned out this was an invaluable rehearsal for the greater war that was soon to come.

In the meantime zealous officers were hastily abandoning the skills of the polo field for sleight-of-hand trickery, their new Commander-in-Chief, Frederick Field, being known as an accomplished and enthusiastic conjurer. But they need not have bothered – as admirals go their new boss proved to be among the most complaisant and innocuous of his kind.

Under the new command the fleet resumed its traditional routine. In the early spring there were the combined manoeuvres in the western Mediterranean or the Atlantic with Britain's home-based fleet, followed by the annual lessons-learned jamboree in Gibraltar. A summer cruise, largely to show the flag, dispersed the fleet around the Mediterranean, with visits to the Côte d'Azur and the Levant as the social highlights. The autumn, including periods in the quieter reaches of the Greek islands, was given over to sporting events involving teams and crews from all the ships and all the ranks, notably the fleet sailing and rowing regattas. Between whiles, based on Malta, the ships were at sea locally for exercises or in harbour for drills, training, repairs and maintenance. There was the opportunity for regular shore leave with emphasis on intensive garrison-style social life for the officers; on somewhat more robust pleasures in the numerous bars, clubs and bordellos for the lower deck. Time was also spent on sports, training for sports or recovering from sports of every variety commensurate with the facilities of a parched, rocky and congested Mediterranean beehive.

Every return of the Mediterranean Fleet to Malta was a memorable occasion. On the approach:

> From seaward, as the main island and the harbour breakwater take shape, the unfolding scene is dramatic. Valletta, the capital, rises theatrically out of the water, with its tiers of neat houses and dignified buildings above massive ramparts, a pale golden tapestry set in the brilliant blue of sky and sea. Across Grand Harbour from Valletta, deep-water creeks shape and divide the ancient cities of Vittoriosa and Senglea, each poised serenely upon its promontory. The main port, steep-sided, impregnable, a glorified moat, is lively with shipping, and its quays with people and their traffic; while, high above the bustle, the onlookers gaze down from terraced gardens and watch discerningly the berthing of the newly-arrived ships. The harbour vistas, with their strong flavour of history, reminiscent of Venice but loftier, sterner, less fragile, are among the finest of their kind in the world.[12]

The onlookers, keyed up for the event, never failed to be moved by the precision and elegance of the manoeuvres as squadron by squadron, flotilla by flotilla, the stately mass of white-ensigned men-of-war crowded their way into harbour. No other navy could match this spectacle or create the same sense of occasion. To the Maltese the fleet's arrival, the martial music, the eloquent ceremonial and the burst of life as picket boats and pinnaces fanned out towards the landing stages brought new purpose, a sense of renewal and, of course, the welcome clatter of money in the island's tills.

* * *

Ashore, in their spare time, there were three main clubs for officers. In Valletta's main street was the Union, a sombre pile on the lines of a gentlemen's club in Pall Mall; the Marsa, with provision for most sports in a country club atmosphere; and the Sliema for eating, drinking and socializing on airy verandas overlooking the sea, venue of the week's star event, the Saturday night dinner-dance. Unless invited to a formal ball or reception at Government House or one of the other official residences, or to cocktails or dinner in the house of a married officer, there was nowhere to go in the evening other than the clubs, Malta's leading hotels being hardly above boarding house standard and restaurants or cafés of quality or sophistication almost non-existent. Thus, an unattached officer at a loose end would return to his own mess for dinner, sometimes with an officer-friend as his guest, or, if so invited, accept hospitality in someone else's ship.

On-board parties, ranging from dances on the beflagged quarterdecks of the larger warships to mixed cocktail parties in the officers' quarters of smaller ships, although popular with the guests and, thanks to the low duty-free prices of drinks, affordable by the hosts, were less frequent occurrences than might be supposed. This was largely due to the scarcity of single girls, the available wives being usually the fairly staid spouses of relatively senior officers, a second-home life overseas being beyond the means of most married officers below the rank of commander. Besides, the protocol and, uniform being worn, the rank differentials did not make for letting-the-hair-down conviviality. To watch unaccompanied wives jockeying for position as they waited on the quay for a picket boat to fetch them was enough for any officer with misogynistic inclinations to give up on-board mixed parties for good. Woe betide the wife of a more junior officer (and, by association, her husband) who, thinking it polite to let the older woman go first, boarded the boat after the wife of the captain.[13]

* * *

The forms of enjoyment available to the lower deck in Malta may have been less varied and colourful than those indulged by the officers but, as Tom Cable relates, they had their moments. In 1933:

> Little did I realize that my first sight of Malta, known to the Navy as the land of hells bells and nanny goat smells, was to become as familiar to me as my own home. Its people became as well known to me as my own people and during my last year of service there I was able to repay some of the trust and kindness they had shown to all those who were based there in pre-war days.

The Mediterranean Fleet was comprised of battleships, cruisers, three flotillas of destroyers, minesweepers, submarines, shore bases and a large hospital. The vast dockyard stores and offices, property owners, the public conveyances, taxis, dhassas, gharrys, farmers, fishermen, hotels, lodging houses, bars, restaurants, shops, brewers, the rich and poor and even the church relied on the money poured into Malta by the British Navy. If they were dependent on us, we were even more dependent on them.

While the big ships swung around their moorings the boats (destroyers) were out at sea becoming efficient in the vital roles they would have to play in time of war, practising what the Navy has already preached 'in time of peace prepare for war'. The only respite came at weekends when we were able to enjoy the beer and bingo at the Fleet Club, hoping for a big win to finance the pleasures of Strada Stretta, affectionately known throughout the whole of the British Navy as 'The Gut'. The long steep narrow street provided bright lights, music, doubtful cabaret turns by ladies from as far afield as Hungary and Huddersfield. Female company at the price of a sherry or champagne, the proceeds of which were shared by the Hostess and the Owner. As one walked its length there would be the familiar cry from the lady at the wild west style double door, 'Come inside Jack, all your ship's company inside'. In the largest cabaret at the bottom of 'The Gut', apart from the usual cabaret acts, there was a homosexual West End concert pianist who, if in the mood, would give a wonderful rendering of Grieg's or Tchaikovsky's piano concertos.

Contrary to the general belief, very few of the girls were of easy virtue. Many of them were Maltese who had married sailors and had refused to leave their families when their husbands returned to 'Blighty'. The frustrated husbands would stop their allowances and so, to earn money to live and perhaps keep a small family, they became Hostesses on 'The Gut'. This desperate step meant being disowned by their priest and their church. There were also restaurants where one could be served with steak, eggs and chips or the favourite roast potatoes, peas and roast pork with a big helping of 'The Gut's' pork crackling. If it was the third week of the month everything would be had on tick. 'Pay you pay day', was accepted as a word of honour and to my knowledge was never ever broken.

On Sliema front (near the destroyer berths) a regular sight was a twenty-two stone lesbian, affectionately known as 'Big Mary', with her barrow load of fresh bread rolls. We were her favourite boys and heaven help anybody who tried to harm us. In the late morning the front would be lined with bins of swill collected by contractors from the boats and sold to the very poor Maltese with their tins, at a penny a dip. The dhaisa boatmen, the gharrys and taxi drivers had memories like elephants. No matter how many years passed between visits they would remember your face and the destroyer you served in. . . .

The spring cruise of 1934 took the whole fleet into the Atlantic under war conditions to do mock battle against the Home Fleet, an exercise which lasted ten days.

We had on board (our destroyer) a passenger in the figure of a *Daily Express* reporter, who was to report on the efficiency of the Navy. The second day out we ran into a real snorter which worked up to force nine, then ten and eventually stayed force eleven. Once again we experienced a flooded, stinking messdeck, everybody wet and cold, living on oxo, biscuits, kai and the warming daily tot. One moment we would be sitting on top of a mountain, the next catapulted on a frightening plunge into a deep valley.

On the third night out I had the middle watch and spent the first two hours on the wheel and the second on the quarterdeck. The timing of the dash aft was essential. I followed the laid down routine, waited for a sea to come in and pour along the upper deck, then I grabbed a lifeline and ran like hell behind it. Before I got half way it (the wave) picked me up and swept me aft. I felt something catch my legs, I instinctively crossed them, hung on and was left hanging on the wire jackstay like a piece of washing out to dry. For the next forty eight hours nobody was allowed on the upper deck, the exercise was called off and thankfully we returned to Gibraltar. It was later estimated that one million pounds worth of damage had been done to the big ships of the Home and Med. Fleets. The boats (destroyers) came out of it practically unscathed. Our reporter laid in his cabin all through the exercise wishing he was dead and only surfacing just before we got to Gib. He said, 'Never again, how the hell you chaps stick it, I'll never know'.

In Gib., one run ashore was enough, with the bars and shore canteen packed with ship's companies of two fleets. From there it was back to Malta and our buoy in Sliema Creek. On the first night in port (a Saturday) it was off to the Fleet Club. Then down to 'The Gut' and enough bottles of blue label beer to wash the salt out of the system, a belly full of roast pork and a full night's sleep in a dry, stationary bed. Lime and lemon in the morning to clear the throat and head, Sunday divisions, the tot, big eats and crash down on the mess stool, with the tin of ticklers for a pillow. It was good to be back.[14]

For many sailors the chief consolation ashore in Malta was one or other of the numerous small, owner-run bars near the landing stages. At their simplest these were little more than caverns, dark holes in the quayside walls, the speciality of the house being often the locally brewed ale. Although open to all, as pubs are in England, some of the bars, finding themselves adopted by individual ships, were effectively clubs for groups of men who were already well known to one another and off duty preferred the company of their own shipmates. In such cases, a bar prospered when its ship was in port but between whiles might have a thin time of it.

A friend of the author, a retired naval captain, recalls the mood and some of the tastes of lower-deck ratings in the interwar years:

When I went to sea in 1929, men were joining the Navy to get a roof over their head. Few were really ambitious. Considering the hours they worked, the long absences abroad and the discomfort of shipboard life, they were under paid even though they were fed, clothed and accommodated. They were generally well led by officers who were dedicated to their Service and were in it, not for the pay, but for the prestige, to serve their country and to enjoy an extraordinarily varied life. Destroyers were the star turns. You had to be a mature sailor. No boys, ordinary seamen or stokers 2nd class were admitted. Anyone who got V.D. got an immediate draft to a big ship.

Sport was a great safety valve. I recall the value of boxing in those days. In the large Fleets they staged open events, officers, midshipmen, novices, boys and so on. An open event was free for all i.e. an officer could box a rating. But there were also professional fights because many sailors on 3/- a day pay would fight in the boxing booths all round the UK for a £5, £15 or £50 purse. The Inter Fleet Boxing each year at Gib was a wonderful event, a huge party for the sailors. They could meet old ships and enjoy first class entertainment, ended by the senior C in C getting into the ring to present prizes and put in a punchy word for the fighting spirit of the Navy.

The combined fleets sailing regatta for 1930 comprised races for all ranks and classes from ten battleships, three battle cruisers, fourteen cruisers, three aircraft carriers and over fifty destroyers. A regatta tote was introduced at about this time, very popular but controversial: a sailor on the make cheered a crew where his money was instead of his own ship's crews.

Of course, soccer was popular but rugger was largely an officers' game, and it was not easy to get enough volunteers from the lower deck for the inter-ship Arbuthnot Trophy cross-country marathon.

Somehow or other one had to keep large ships' companies fully occupied. Ceremonial played its part. Divisions and prayers every day, with church and divisions on Sundays followed by inspection of the upper deck by the captain. On the King's Birthday on 3 June 1930: dress ship at 0800, divisions with guard and band at 1130, 21-gun salute at 1200 followed by National Anthem and three cheers for H.M. . . . And as a last resort, periodically: air bedding, all in orderly lines along the guard rails, and no holidays (gaps).

The one black spot, the Invergordon Mutiny of 1931, shook the world, the Navy and everybody serving. It was quite remarkable how we had recovered by 1939.[15]

* * *

The base in Malta being an essential prop of the world's greatest fleet, one would suppose that the authorities were at pains to be on the best possible terms with the locals. But the habit of aloofness by the rulers was as prevalent in Malta as elsewhere in the great British Empire. Buttressed by the usual pomp, ceremony, bugle calls and sentries, the governor of this small island went about his monarch's business with benign and stately calm. Malta was unusual in garrison terms in that the senior military commander was not a soldier – he was a sailor, an Admiral, the visible head furthermore not only of a famous fleet but of a complex technical and economic infrastructure, the naval dockyard and support services being the vital ingredient of the island's well-being and *raison d'être*.

This was fortunate for Malta where the sailor was a more popular creature than the soldier. Soldiers lived and worked among the populace in a crowded environment – they were all over the place, a constant reminder of the occupation by alien forces. The Maltese, an island people, understood the sea and the ways and whims of sailors. Sailors lived in ships and were often away. When they returned they had stories to tell and money to spend. In particular the ordinary Maltese had a soft spot for the Royal Navy with its professionalism and gift for showmanship and for the individual British sailor with his happy-go-lucky nature and his inherent kindliness and decency.

At the higher social levels, however, apart from formal contacts the rapport was less evident. To the better educated and politically more sophisticated classes in Malta the British were merely the latest in a long succession of unwanted occupying powers. This lot may have more *savoir-faire*, better humour and greater respect for law than previous conquerors, but behind the mask lurked the patronizing and sometimes uncouth indifference to the culture and susceptibilities of a proud and distinctive nation.

On the Maltese side there were two deeply entrenched influences, survivors of many wars and occupations – an old-established aristocracy and, under its own archbishop, a strong branch of the Roman Catholic church. As both of these were linked historically with Italy neither was a natural bedfellow for the British, least of all in the troubled 1930s. All the more reason one would think for the British leadership to get off its high horse and try harder to bridge the gap.

For a last word on this matter, here is Ernle Chatfield, Commander-in-Chief in the Mediterranean, 1930–2. In his view:

> the Maltese were long looked down on and treated as an inferior race. Although this was not palpably resented by the people generally, for whom the British had a real friendliness, it was deeply taken to heart by the Maltese cultured classes. No Maltese person could join a British club, 'even if he were in His Majesty's service as an officer in a Maltese regiment, had been educated at an English university and had an English wife or a son in the Royal Navy.' Many efforts had been made to induce the Union Club to admit Maltese to membership but the blackball invariably prevailed. When the club rules were changed in the early 1930s, 'I do not think the Maltese ever made use of it but an impossible situation in the social life of Malta was changed.'[16]

The award of the George Cross to Malta in recognition of the bravery and endurance of its inhabitants during the Second World War was a noble and well-deserved gesture but, to a colonized people, essentially beside the point. When independence from Britain, the last of the conquerors, followed later, that was the accolade that mattered.

CHAPTER FIVE

Bases and Playgrounds

During the 1930s the British were at their most peripatetic[1]. The middle classes, when not party-going, were travelling. Maps of the period depict the lion's share of shipping routes from Europe to north and south America and via the Suez Canal to India and the Far East radiating out from British ports. On the Continent a high proportion of the main international rail routes fanned out from Ostend and Calais, serving destinations long favoured by Britons on business or holiday. Without their custom there would have been no Golden Arrow or Night Ferry, Blue Train or Bombay Express, Rome Express or Sud Express, possibly not even the Orient Express. And British patronage had brought into fashion the near-home resorts of Le Touquet, Deauville, Dinard and, further afield, had added to the cosmopolitan glitter of Paris, Rome, the Côte d'Azur, Venice, the Italian lakes and rivieras and the leading ski resorts of Switzerland.

The Britons who travelled by the old sea and new air routes to govern, manage, defend or trade in their country's worldwide possessions expected to be away from home for long spells. On return, with several months' paid leave in hand, in pursuit of their greens or perhaps of a bride, they brought welcome cash into the tills of London's hotels, restaurants and nightclubs and a touch of hesitant virility to tennis and cricket clubs in the lush, green countryside for which they pined during their years of exile.

These men, officers, lawyers, colonial officials, importers, tea planters, with their wives if they were of senior rank, permeated their spheres of influence abroad with the ethics, condescension and jolly civility inculcated in them at their public schools. They took in their stride the pomp and ceremony, the formalized social life, the spacious houses and the plentiful servants associated with their calling. They believed in the Empire as a force for good and, with self-satisfaction, saw themselves, its rulers, as a race apart.

The Navy's role was to protect the sinews of Empire, its shipping lanes and outposts – in effect, to police the trade routes of the world. There were British owned or leased dockyards or replenishment depots, formerly coaling stations, at intervals of two or three days' steaming along the main imperial sea route – Gibraltar, Malta, Suez, Aden, Bombay, Trincomalee, Singapore, then Perth or Hong Kong; and at other faraway strategic points such as Nova Scotia, Bermuda, Simonstown. British merchant ships, including many of the giant liners, often flew the blue ensign denoting that the master was a member of the Royal Naval Reserve. Throughout the seven seas a British presence, represented by a white, blue or red ensign afloat or a union jack ashore, was never far away.

More to the point, the semi-independent navies of India, Australia, New Zealand, Canada and South Africa flew the white ensign, wore British uniforms, operated interchangeable warships, received common training and were liable at any time to sail under Admiralty orders. It has often been said that Britain stood 'alone' against Hitler and Mussolini from the fall of France in the summer of 1940 to Pearl Harbor at the end of 1941. In truth these kindred navies were among the land, sea and air forces from commonwealth countries that were to rally so valiantly and indispensably to the British cause in that dark period; and it is time for due tribute to be paid.

* * *

After Malta the overseas base that mattered most and was most enjoyed by Royal Navy personnel was Hong Kong. It was a long way from home but on a crisp, sunny, autumn morning after a leisurely five weeks at sea along the imperial route Hong Kong looked very inviting. The scene had an effervescence that any newcomer found exhilarating. There was the harbour, a vast blue stretch of water ringed by mountain ranges, alive with every kind of commerce from sampan and junk to tramp steamer and ocean liner, a bustle that never ceases. There were the deft, chattering coolies on the quayside; and beyond the harbour precinct, in the shadow of its Peak, that huge rock on the fringe of the mysterious Chinese continent, no mere colonial post but a vibrant, jostling cosmopolitan city: beautiful, exciting, energetic, awe-inspiring, yet oddly serene and relaxed in that benignly reassuring way of British possessions the world over.

In the late 1930s Hong Kong, a hub of Far Eastern trade routes, played host to glamorous cruise ships bearing the rich and rare from distant lands. There were 'white' Russian families, refugees from the Bolshevik revolution, who had settled there, many of them to work in the hotel and restaurant business, introducing aristocratic tastes and, not least, an international cuisine. There were nightlife entrepreneurs promoting cabaret acts by alluring girls from Balkan countries as well as traders, fortune hunters, *taipans* on leave from mainland China, tycoons on business from neighbouring countries.

Here, also, was a destination for several shipping lines from Europe, notably the fortnightly P&O liner service from England, newly augmented by a weekly air service by Imperial Airways. With the passage by sea from western Europe needing a month or so, or by trans-Siberian railway and thence by coastal steamer a fortnight or more, or by the flying boat about a week, the feeling of remoteness was real enough.

Real, too, was the British presence, focus of the colony's establishment, begetter of its social life and, although little more than a red, white and blue beacon in a swirling yellow ocean, the source of patronage and power. The union jack flew on buildings ashore and in its corner of the ensigns of most of the war and merchant vessels afloat. The military barracks were hardly unobtrusive – the lumpy, confident gait of Britons was to be seen in every downtown street and in the gardens of the villas in the foothills of the Peak. Occupying or bordering the few green open spaces in the centre of this Manhattan-style metropolis, close by the skyscraper of the Hong Kong and Shanghai Bank, were the palatial and exclusive British club and, symbol of symbols, the colony's cricket ground.

A naval officer arriving in Hong Kong to join his ship would not be travelling light. His baggage would include a hefty wooden chest, a large metal case, a trunk, a couple of suitcases, a hold-all, a helmet box, a golf bag to carry clubs, sword and walking sticks. Among the contents would be epaulettes, frock-coat, sword-belt and gold striped trousers for ceremonial occasions; blue uniform suits for cool weather and white ones for hot; shoulder-strapped shirts and white shorts for day wear in the tropics; short uniform jackets, blue and white, for evening wear on the job; a tailsuit, dinner jacket and white tuxedo for smart civilian evenings; stiff and soft white shirts, butterfly collars, black and white bow ties; plain clothes and sports attire for all weathers; a cocked hat, uniform caps, civilian hats and the blessed sun helmet; an accompanying variety of footwear; books, underwear, pyjamas, first-aid kit and a telescope. Without this array of accoutrements even a sub-lieutenant could hardly be expected to do his bit for King and Empire.

On his voyage out the young officer would have been struck how British subjects or dependants of every hue seemed to abound all the way from Gibraltar eastward. Holding sway over so many people would give a sense not only of power but of responsibility – even, in many cases, of humility. And this might apply most strikingly in Hong Kong where the Briton would be more than usually conscious of his privileged position. The Chinese seemed tremendously anxious to please and happy to be employed or do business for a pittance. And to give credit, a boon being the chit system – an officer had no need to carry cash, apart from a few coins to pay the rickshaw driver for he merely signed a chit for the price of whatever he bought or ate or drank and at the end of the month the traders having sent the bits of paper around the ships and barracks, the items would turn up on his mess bill.

As the newcomer would soon learn, unmarried and grass-widowed officers on shore leave had three pursuits at their disposal. One, the standard 'run ashore', indulged usually by four or five officers together, involved some boisterous drinking at the club, dinner at a restaurant, a strip show if in ribald mood or otherwise a cinema, more drinks. . . . Those with promotion on their minds preferred a strenuous evening of sport after which these hearties would drink and eat lightly, return on board early and talk naval shop over a glass of beer until bunktime. For the third category there existed a rigidly structured social life, shaped by the fact that for every white nubile lady of the right class there was a waiting list of approximately thirty politely eager officers. The acknowledged hunting grounds for this protected species were parent-sponsored cocktail parties, the best way to get invited being to corner and charm an amenable daughter at one of the great social parades – a full-dress ball, an at home or a garden party in one of the high-up milieus.

To this end on arrival in the colony each officer took an early opportunity, dressed carefully in his best attire, to call at the official residences of the governor, the naval commander-in-chief and the general officer commanding; and if his captain was a married man with wife in company, at their shoreside apartment, too. The ritual involved either signing a book or leaving a visiting card, an investment yielding in due course an ornate invitation card which, although 'requesting the pleasure . . . ', was, of course, a command as strict as any other in the course of duty.

For the resident the higher up The Peak he lived the more important he was assumed to be. Besides invitations to Government House the other status symbols were an overdraft at the Hong Kong and Shangai Bank, membership of the Hong Kong club, a place in the governor's box at the Happy Valley racecourse and a pew near the altar at St John's Cathedral. But only the governor himself had first call on the front seat of the Peak Tram (funicular).

The ethos of Kiplingesque superiority remained strong between the wars and in Hong Kong the only contact most European residents had with Chinese people was in the form of domestic staff. There was virtually no Chinese middle class with whom the British could work on equal terms, while the few rich Chinese kept very much to themselves. The Chinese visible on the streets were mainly of the coolie class.

According to Paul Gillingham[2] it was commonly believed that European men outnumbered women in Hong Kong by ten to one even though many single girls came out from England in the hope of catching an eligible bachelor from one of the big firms or, better still, the services. For those without families locally accommodation was available at the Helena May Institute in Garden Road, the so-called 'virgins' retreat', where a strict maternal code was enforced. Lady Clementi, a governor's wife, was said to read all new books bought for the Helena May library and 'any reference to a kiss or a cuddle and the book was removed'.

Because of the poor ratio of men to women the world's oldest profession flourished in Hong Kong. Legalized brothels regularly had the services of a health inspector until a change of heart caused the government to close them down in 1932. Some held Lady Clementi responsible, while others blamed pressure from the League of Nations and the British Parliament. After the closure of legalized brothels, venereal disease spread so widely among the troops that the colony reputedly had the highest incidence of any British station overseas.

The issue created a wave of public indignation. The Revd Sandbach of the Methodist Church, which ran the Soldiers' and Sailors' Home in Wanchai, was so alarmed that he wrote to the governor requesting the reopening of the brothels. 'Homo' wrote to the *Hong Kong Telegraph* to say that 'Hong Kong's greatest peril today lies in the fact that there is a chronic shortage of the female sex. The female is ridiculously overvalued out here. . . .' In 1938 the very first page of the Navy's China Station Fleet Orders was warning that 75% of Hong Kong's prostitutes were infected. But sexual appetites were not to be quashed and not least because the Chinese girls in Wanchai were really lovely. They paraded up and down outside the Soldiers' and Sailors' Home and the China Fleet Club in their cheongsams, split up to the thigh, with their hair done in European fashion. And in 1938 they were available for only 9*d* for half-an-hour or 1*s* 3*d* for all night.

These girls were often the only source of female company for British servicemen stationed in Hong Kong. A gunner with the Royal Artillery in 1938 recalls the great gulf which existed between the British Tommy and the European women. 'There was no point in trying to ask out English girls as they wouldn't even look at you. We soldiers and the Chinese prostitutes had a lot in common. They were outcasts from their society and we were outcasts from ours.'

For naval officers unwilling to await their occasional turn in respectable female company there was one brothel which, although unofficial, was regarded as officers' perks. They could sign a chit there, just as they would for dinner at the Gripps (the Hong Kong hotel), the Repulse Bay or the Peninsula restaurants. At the end of each month the old Chinese madame, with huge red umbrella on high, sailed around the fleet in a sampan, handing in her clients' chits, the item appearing on their mess bills as 'Extras: $3'. This monthly ritual was watched closely by all the sailors who, naturally, liked to feel up to date about things phallic, not least about which of their officers were still apparently capable of making it.

One young naval officer, a submariner, Michael St John, who evidently had a special way with him, recalls:

> As a lieutenant on about £450 per annum naval pay I was a member of 25 clubs, owned a Ford V8 roadster in Hong Kong, and when there regularly took a girl friend to dinner and dance (to Al Philippino Jazz) at one of the big hotel restaurants once or twice a week. There were endless bathing picnics, shooting of pigeon in the New Territories and snipe at Wei-Hai-Wei, golf and tennis everywhere we went.

After social visits (by submarine) in 1938–9 to Penang, Port Swettenham (for Kuala Lumpur), Surabaya (in Dutch Java), Bali, Jesselton (in North Borneo), Manila, Amoy, Tsingtao and Ching-Wang-Tao (for Tientsin and Peking), back in Hong Kong 'the whole Peak was like a vast wild garden dotted with the best examples of Victorian/Edwardian colonial architecture', and beautiful open country was always nearby, both on Hong Kong island and Kowloon.[3]

Although cultural pursuits were not high on Hong Kong's agenda a determined supporter or contributor could find a ready response among the more active *cognoscenti*. The author, who was in Hong Kong on several occasions in the two years from autumn 1937, found the *Sunday Herald* receptive to short stories, the *South China Morning Post* to poetry, the *St John's Review* to articles, the ZBW radio station to short plays and the Peace Pledge Union to debate; and he soon became involved in the production of a revue which ran for three nights at the China Fleet Club's admirable theatre and in the promotion of concerts featuring a professional soprano of international repute, the wife of a commander then serving in the China Fleet. For a young officer off duty flexing his half-formed intellectual muscles, Hong Kong was a most stimulating resort.

* * *

If life was less fulfilling for the other ranks, from their point of view Hong Kong had come a fair way in thirty years. The *China Mail* of 31 December 1904 reported at length an annual highlight for sailors under church and Missions to Seamen auspices, this being a tea and meeting with the Lord Bishop in the chair and a menu of refreshments ranging from 'the more solid beef and mutton through chicken and ham to mince pies, plum puddings and dainty little cakes'. The proceedings having opened with a hymn, a prayer and a long address by the bishop 'the Hon Mr Gershom Stewart in a racy speech, which won the closest attention of the audience and was punctuated by frequent bursts of applause, spoke of the value to the British Empire of both the Naval and Mercantile marine, maintaining that they are indissolubly joined together and the very being of our Empire depended upon the well-being of these services.' Other speakers having emphasized the virtues of sobriety and of 'hope, love and faith for all who wished to make their lives happy and useful', the party continued with solos sung by Mrs Brown and Mrs Chapman and a selection of Christmas Carols, until brought to a close by votes of thanks by two spokesmen for the sailors.

In 1905 when the British China fleet comprised, among other vessels, 3 battleships, 7 cruisers, 6 sloops, 10 gunboats and 12 destroyers, reclamation works leading to the creation of a new 39 acre dockyard were well in hand. A few years later the old accommodation hulk, HMS *Tamar*, was moved from the middle of the harbour to a more comfortable berth alongside a dockyard wall. The year 1905 also saw the creation of a local volunteer naval reserve and, belatedly, the opening of a new Seamen's Institute in central Hong Kong to meet the requirements of sailors who were ashore on forty-eight hours leave, sleeping accommodation being otherwise very limited. In an opening speech the presiding clergyman hoped for a better supply of literature and a good billiard table as well as provision for the sailors' spiritual and moral needs bringing him 'a little nearer the realisation of perfect manhood'. In an approving reply the governor, having remarked that the sailors' work being done at sea 'where we do not see them, it is not then to be wondered at that some unpleasant forms of recreation – such as nuisance with insobriety and frequenting low houses – should come before our eyes in Hong Kong, which tend to lower the prestige of the white man before the Chinese'.

Poor long-suffering sailor – his every move was being scrutinized, even on a visit later that year to Tokyo whence the *China Mail* correspondent was able to report, 'It is with pride that I write that both from personal observation and from all available reports Jack behaved himself splendidly. He is a boisterous individual but he never permitted his jollification to exceed the bounds of decency and the impression left upon the minds of the people here is that the British tar is a good fellow. . . . '

By the late 1930s the pressure on overnight facilities for naval personnel on leave in Hong Kong had lessened partly because of more abundant accommodation, coupled with more congenial amenities, notably in the new China Fleet Club in Wanchai, partly because the fleet was now both smaller and, in terms of being away on duty, busier. From 1937 the two largest ships on the China station were an aircraft carrier and a depot ship to service the submarine flotilla, besides which the fleet comprised only a handful of cruisers, destroyers, sloops and gunboats.[4]

Frederick Wigby was a member of the crew of HMS *Westcott*, the destroyer attached to the submarine flotilla and recalls Hong Kong at this time:

> We tied up alongside the dockyard wall. One could smell the place from there. In time we all grew accustomed to it. That night Clarkson and I went ashore to explore. We visited the China Fleet Club, then made our way to the pictures, surprised to find that all the pictures showing were the latest American ones, also that the cinemas were kept very clean and tidy. After the pictures we decided to have our first rickshaw ride – back to the dockyard.
>
> The following day we moved from the dockyard to a buoy in the harbour and the next day we went on exercises with submarines. Usually they fired torpedoes at targets and we would tear around and pick them up. On returning to harbour each night the torpedoes would be returned to the submarine parent ship.
>
> Leave was given nightly. Clarkson and I would go ashore together. Usually it was a trip to the Fleet Club for big eats, a couple of pints and a game of Tombola. Sometimes we would take a walk down Wan Chai. This was where all the girls plied their trade. It amazed me how happy they always were. I found that most Chinese were very good natured and put up with quite a lot from the white people. At night the Chinese played a game called Majong. All one could hear was the 'click, click' of the ivory and bamboo pieces being played. This, with the smell of joss-sticks and cooking-pots upon charcoal fires all inter-mingled, was the real Hong Kong.
>
> Sometimes we would catch the Peak Railway so that we could admire the view from the top of the Peak. Other times we would go to see the football matches or horse-racing at Happy Valley. What always distressed me was the poverty of the people. This was especially disturbing in the mornings when I returned to the ship after spending all night ashore. One would see hundreds of Chinese – of all ages –

lying out in the streets. I soon found out that life was very cheap in China. Most of the Chinese believed in reincarnation, so that what they didn't have this time on earth they believed they would have the next time.

When the ship was lying out in the harbour a sampan was used to ferry liberty men to and fro. It was usually paddled along by a girl, waggling one oar, balanced over the stern on a single pin. During the dog watches tradesmen and dobey girls were allowed aboard. If one wanted a pair of boots made all one had to do was to put one's foot upon a piece of paper. The bootmaker would simply draw a line around one's foot. The following night he would return with a lovely pair of hand-sewn boots: these always fitted perfectly. All our washing was done by the dobey girls.

An elderly lady was allowed on the messdecks so that she could mend and darn our clothes. She was known as 'Sew-Sew' a grand old character who spoke sailor's lingo like a native. She was very popular; one could always borrow a couple of dollars from her till pay day. Never did I see her write anything down, but she always remembered who had borrowed from her when pay day came round. The tailor's name was Jelly-Belly. He, too, was a great character and could make one a suit in a very few hours. He made me a civvy suit that lasted me for years.

Hong Kong fascinated me. There was always plenty to explore. There were shops where one could see young and old carving intricate designs on ivory with the most primitive of tools. Little boys would also be carving designs on cedar wood chests. These were beautifully executed. I thought the boys ought to have been at school. Perhaps I was wrong as they had to work to survive. Poverty and starvation were very rife indeed, especially amongst the sampan dwellers. Sometimes you would see them dredging around the ship's gash-chutes trying to find pieces of waste food that had been thrown down the chutes. It was all pitiful to watch.

In May 1937 we took part in the Military Parade held ashore for the Coronation of King George VI. With the festivities over we sailed for Wei-Hai-Wei. After arriving there we soon found out it wasn't much of a place to be in. Ashore there was only a Canteen built from palm fronds. At the same time there was plenty of food to be had. One could buy a chicken already roasted – these chickens were called Wei Hai runners by the matelots and were reputed to live on wastepaper and cigarette ends – anyway they tasted good with a pint of beer to help them down. Trips ashore mostly consisted of a cricket or football match, big eats and a game or two of bowling in the Canteen alley, followed by a sing-song in the Canteen itself.[5]

Being more often than not on detached duties, and fully stretched, the more so as the advancing Japanese forces in mainland China became more menacing to western interests, the British warships stationed in the Far East at this time were seldom all together except, briefly, around Christmas in Hong Kong and in high summer in Wei-Hai-Wei. Although the palmy days of Shanghai, the Navy's most sought-after port of call (now under constant threat from Japanese soldiers and airmen) and of Peking (now in a Japanese-occupied zone) were over, life went on at its usual highly-charged pace.

But the great event in any Briton's life was to be homeward bound, a process that was becoming easier by the year. In 1928 local aviation history had been made when four flying boats flew into Hong Kong from Singapore, and eight years later, the flight from Penang to Hong Kong having been inaugurated, Hong Kong was linked to London by air. In that same year Pan America started a Manila-Hong Kong service linking Hong Kong with San Francisco, 6½ flying days away. But even though the prices were beginning to fall by 1938, the cost of air travel remained prohibitive for most people, a return to London being priced at £288 compared to £70 second-class and £105 first-class by sea, or even less by the trans-Siberian railway route.

However, until the advent of the jet age, the usual mode of return to Britain continued to be by steamship. Paul Gillingham recalls:

> As home leave was a rare occurrence, those leaving by ship were given a tremendous send-off from Kowloon Wharf. Farewelling was a major social occasion – one saw off friends, colleagues and acquaintances or just went along for the party. P&O ships sailed from Hong Kong on alternate Saturdays and, amid the streamers, brass bands, waving crowds and sweating coolies, there were usually a few shroffs' agents trying to secure payment for chits which departing passengers had forgotten to honour. For shop-keepers and hoteliers it was often the last chance to secure payment in a society in which credit was automatic; but once the propeller turned, all debts were automatically cancelled.[6]

In those pre-war years, of course, most homegoers were expected to return – it was inconceivable that the long, sunlit days of British supremacy in the Far East might be approaching the beginning of their end.

* * *

The Singaporeans in their damp, stifling equatorial climate were equally impervious to what the fates held in store for them. In February 1938, after years of false starts and indecisions, a great, purpose-built naval base was opened with due ceremony, marking the transition of Singapore from primarily a trading community to potentially a world-class fortress, a Gibraltar of the orient, and lynch pin of the British imperial system of far eastern defence. But the officers and men of the ships sent down from Hong Kong for the opening celebration were not amused.

On the north side of Singapore island, 14 miles from the bright city lights, shore leave was uninviting. The new dockyard was in effect a self-contained town with garden-suburb housing for officers and officials and their families. It would offer cinemas, canteens, churches and sports facilities including seventeen football pitches, but since it was surrounded by high walls and dominated by the accoutrements of a vast naval establishment, the ambience for visitors was neither cosy nor stimulating. The graving dock, almost as large as Southampton's; the floating dock, able to lift a battleship; the heavy-duty cranes, oil tanks, warehouses and workshops – all these were impressive, as was the awareness that in bomb-proof shelters underground lay enough stocks of food and ammunition to sustain a siege of several weeks while awaiting the arrival of a rescuing battle fleet from Europe. But this was hardly fun and it certainly was not sexy; and Singapore city besides having less to offer sailors than Hong Kong was a good deal more expensive.

Besides, the mood of Singapore was staider, more nose-in-the-air, less cosmopolitan, less raffish, more provincial, perhaps rather in the style of Liverpool in its shipowning and cotton-broking heyday. In Singapore the men at the top traded internationally, notably in shipping and in lucrative local produce like rubber. They made much money and were not the kind to let their hair down. When not doing deals behind the cooling blinds of their down-town clubs or in their punkah-louvred offices, however, they might be observed with their ladies at sundown, chotah-pegs in hand, on the verandas of the Raffles Hotel or the Tanglin Sporting Club if not of their own well-manicured mansions.

The hotel, named after the colony's founder, was and survives amid today's skyscrapers, if now largely for the tourists' benefit, as Singapore's pre-eminent meeting place. Here on its spacious covered, open-sided veranda in a garden setting, but in a position commanding the hotel's main entrance, everyone who wished to see and be seen would congregate convivially over iced drinks at the crowded, waiter-served tables to greet old friends, show off, perform the social graces – a scene that Somerset Maugham in his quiet sardonic way must certainly have relished.

Of course Singapore's new £20 million naval base was hardly there for pleasure, but, most unfortunately, it was not to be much good either in its main purpose, for exactly four years later it would fall in ignominious defeat to Japanese arms. The 1920s, the decade of the Singapore base's conception, had been a period of erratic decision-making for Britain in general and the Navy in particular, with the Americans trying tentatively, and without much love for Britain, to take a lead in international affairs. There was also a growing belief in Japanese ruling circles that the pontificating, pacifism-inclined western democracies were becoming, in war-making terms, little more than paper tigers. The opening of the base in Singapore on the southern flank of what they were coming to regard as, rightfully, their own sphere of influence was, to the Japanese, a last straw, a pointed provocation, something sooner or later to be avenged. And as the Whitehall warriors, and not least the naval establishment, peered eastward through their telescopes and rather liked what they saw, the Japanese were laughing quietly behind their hands.

As they saw it, Singapore, with its reliance on fixed 15 in guns pointing seaward and on battleships rather than aircraft re-enforcement, was indefensible. The British had assumed that a combination of land-based and seaborne heavy guns would be enough, the dense Malayan jungle, just across the narrow Johore Straits from the new base, being considered a reliable safeguard against any military advance from the north. When Singapore fell in early 1942 it was, inevitably, to Japanese air power preparing the way for Japanese troops, the latter having advanced almost unopposed through the 'impenetrable' Malayan jungle.[7]

* * *

As we sail westward from Singapore along the old trail of British naval stopovers we may draw a veil across Trincomalee, an anchorage rather than a base, a kind of tropical Scapa Flow. We may also prepare to waste little time on the arid, sun-baked replenishment depot at Aden. For a warship homeward bound from the Far East which had not found time to replace its Chinese messmen with Maltese or British equivalents, Aden might provide a last chance for the Chinaman to show his mettle.

It was the early spring of 1940. The destroyer was racing homeward to help defend Britain against the Germans.

For eleven years on the China station the inscrutable Ah Fong had given faithful service as officers' messman. But his own country was already in the grip of war with Japan and Ah Fong had no stomach for the foreign devils' quarrel in Europe.

Ah Fong lay thinking in his billet on the lee side of a gun deck off which he expected to float if the ship were torpedoed. In the morning they would call at Aden. Ah Fong had done this trip before, in peacetime, and it was said he struck a better bargain in the market than any other ship's steward. And Mahomet's fruitstall on the Aden waterfront was one of the pillars of his reputation.

Next day at noon the ship was ready to weigh anchor when two sail-propelled shoreboats drew alongside. Out of one stepped the British petty officer in charge of the ship's canteen, out of the other Ah Fong, each with his own separate load of fruit, vegetables, and candy. Warily, with a polite smile, Ah Fong compared notes. Oranges, for example, 'A dozen of the juiciest for threepence', the British petty officer was saying.

The ship's postman, just back from the shore, laughed. 'Ah Fong paid threepence ha'penny', he said. 'I was at Mahomet's and heard the price.' There was a squeal of anger from Ah Fong and a shout from the duty officer, 'Come back', he yelled, 'the ship is sailing!' But it was too late. Ah Fong with his basket of oranges was already halfway to the shore.

The anchor came up and the destroyer turned seaward. 'I'll give him three minutes', growled the captain, and stopped the ship by the breakwater. Two of the minutes sped by. Then, 'Here he comes', cried a lookout.

A large motor boat with gesticulating crew was racing wildly shipwards across the calm waters of the harbour. 'That fancy speedboat must be costing him a packet', grinned the captain. But Ah Fong was smiling broadly. For held firmly on his arm as he jumped for the destroyer's moving deck was a basket of the finest, fattest oranges you ever saw. At tuppence ha'penny the dozen.[8]

* * *

After Aden we leap-frog to the far end of the Mediterranean, the Navy's intermediate bases, principally Alexandria and Malta, being featured in other chapters of this book. There at the threshold of the Atlantic, shaped like a watchful lion guarding the narrow straits separating Africa from Europe, in its day the most potent and, perhaps, most famous symbol of British sea-based imperial power, stands that great, fortified mass, the rock of Gibraltar. From its airport on reclaimed land close to the Spanish frontier we walk along Gibraltar's gregarious main street, past the eager shopkeepers with their tourist-orientated wares, past the church, past the sentries guarding the governor's palace and, after a short climb, we gain the terrace of the Rock Hotel; and facing westward over the town's port and roof tops, savour one of the great panoramas of the world.

To the left across the straits are the distant mountains of north Africa; ahead, beyond Algeciras on the far side of the bay, the rugged coastline of southern Spain; to the right, behind the coastal belt and its fertile, increasingly residential hinterland, the foothills of the towering, snow-capped Sierras. And each of these vistas, besides its distinctive setting and topography, seems to have its own climate – cumulus cloud over Africa, perhaps, giving way to bright blue skies over the Spanish littoral, and inland, towards the Sierras, clusters of dark clouds heralding rain squalls and thunder storms. While sunshine predominates, the Gibraltar weather is variable, often windy, sometimes wet, one effect of all this meteorological diversity being sunsets which at their most vivid and dramatic have few rivals anywhere.

In the foreground of the view from the hotel are the extensive breakwaters that guard the port, at one time a substantial naval dockyard but nowadays, increasingly, a haven for commerce and leisure. Elasticity must have been Gibraltar's watchword in pre-war days. After quiet spells for days or weeks on end, interrupted by a liner's call to land and embark passengers or by a warship's visit for recuperation or repairs, the Navy would arrive in strength for a period of drills and practices. The highlight every spring was the visit for a fortnight or so of the two great fleets, the Mediterranean and the Home, following their protracted annual combined exercises in the Atlantic. With the dockyard berths fully occupied by every type of warship, from battleships to destroyers, many vessels would be anchored in orderly lines in the bay, the whole offering a unique display of concentrated naval power, bettered only by one of those relatively rare ceremonial reviews at Spithead.

With several thousand sailors suddenly in their midst, Gibraltar's main street and entertainment districts must have burst at their seams but for the readiness of shop and restaurant keepers to expand their activities into backyards, next door or the upper floors of their own premises. For in off-duty hours the main street would play host to a continuous mass of uniformed visitors, all in high spirits, happy in the company of seldom-met friends, in pursuit of beer, souvenirs, food, floor shows and, if possible, a bit of female company.

Through the open windows of the cabarets, with names like the Trocadero and the Universal, would have come the sound of castanets and tap-dance shoes as Spanish flamenco artistes performed to the 'ole's' and 'bravos' of seamen awash with cheap 'English' beer and Malaga wine, and with hostesses to cater for their every need, bar one. For there were no brothels in Gibraltar, the nearest prostitutes being in La Linea the Spanish settlement just across the border.

In the hour before expiry of leave the naval provost marshal's patrols would take over the streets, moving the jostling, singing, half-sozzled libertymen towards the dockyard gates and taking into safe custody those who were too far gone to walk. By midnight all would be quiet, the traders dozing over their bulging tills, the sailors dead to the world in the fug of their ship-board messes.

Gibraltar, like Malta, was for many centuries a cause and a focus of conflict. So long as the Moors were in occupation of most of Spain, Gibraltar was a key strategic fulcrum of their empire. When Spain got rid of the invader in the fifteenth century it naturally wanted Gibraltar, a promontory of the Iberian peninsula, for its own. But others, for their own imperialistic reasons, also coveted Gibraltar – Britain from the seventeenth century and then, with Spanish power on the wane, France. At this point Britain, the former enemy, the victor at Trafalgar and already too long in occupation of Gibraltar for Spanish taste became friend enough to join with Spain in ousting the French from Iberia. After this British relations with the Spaniards remained cordial for a time, long enough to form local economic ties and, symbolically, to share sponsorship of the Spanish Calpe hunt.

But the cancer in the relationship remained, this being the clause in the Treaty of Utrecht of 1713, following Rooke's decisive feat of arms whereby 'The Catholic King does hereby for Himself, his Heirs and Successors yield to the Crown of Great Britain the full and entire propriety of the Town and Castle of Gibraltar', in Spanish eyes now an imposition, riddled with loopholes, that rankles to this day.

By the 1920s with the British firmly in occupation and the naval dockyard well established, the creation of a new city council gave the Gibraltarians a high degree of internal self-government. Since then the greater the extent of local democracy the more definite the periodical vote in favour of remaining under British rather than Spanish protection.

The Calpe hunt, a barometer of local feeling, was often in the news, most notably in the early 1930s. After he had kept the show on the road at great personal expense through many difficult periods over forty years, its aristocratic master, Pablo Larios, Marquis of Marzales, was so insulted by Governor Godley's view that the jointly-sponsored hunt was suffering from its master's advancing years, that he resigned, taking most of its best hunting land with him. George V, as joint royal patron, having admonished Godley for interfering, promptly instructed the next governor,

Harington, to put matters right. And this he did by offering the services of his wife, Lady Harington, an accomplished horsewoman, as joint master, an arrangement that so pleased the old Spaniard that he promptly re-entered the fold with his land, Pablo remaining actively in the saddle until his death in 1937.

By this time more serious days had come to Gibraltar as a British local base for the Italo-Abyssinian and Spanish Civil wars, soon to be followed by its role as a critical advance base for British and later for allied forces in the Second World War – events that were to bring Gibraltar more fully into its own than ever before.[9]

* * *

To the west of Gibraltar the only base of significance under direct Admiralty control and, after Hong Kong, the most popular overseas station in the interwar years with British naval personnel seeking a break from big-fleet rituals and red tape, was Bermuda, headquarters of the America and West Indies Squadron. This force typically comprised four or five light cruisers and a couple of sloops, and for at least two-thirds of every year they were on detached service individually, on a round of social or diplomatic visits to ports in the West Indies and on both coasts of north and south America from Alaska and Newfoundland to Tierra del Fuego. This was a fairly strenuous life involving long-distance steaming, 50,000 miles during a 2½-year commission being not out of the way, and the need when in harbour for the ships to be at their smartest and most alert, their companies on their best behaviour and ever-ready to socialize. Zealous officers anxious about their promotion prospects missed the chance to shine on warlike drills and duties in a more competitive professional milieu under the watchful gaze of hard-driving admirals.

In Bermuda the Admiralty maintained a dockyard, including a floating dock, manned and equipped to keep the squadron in operational shape, including readiness to deal with civil disorder, earthquakes, ships in distress and any other incident at which the presence of one of HM ships might be appropriate. By these means and the constant round of high-profile visits to some of the largest and most sophisticated cities and resorts in the Americas, as well as to some of the remoter outposts of trade and colonial rule, the squadron, with its gift for showmanship and hospitality, kept the flag flying for Britain in a way unmatched by any other power. A Royal Marine band beating retreat on some foreign quayside on a once-a-year visit, prelude to cocktail parties on gleaming, beflagged quarterdecks and dances ashore attended by handsome young officers in their mess kit, worked wonders for British commerce and prestige in a region of the world where showing the flag Royal Navy-style was a unique stimulus to investment and goodwill. And cheap at the price considering that the officers paid for most of the onboard hospitality out of their own pockets – admittedly at duty free prices, but, even so, to a higher tune than they could afford without abstaining at other times.

The 100 islets that comprise Bermuda, with their pretty flower-drenched houses and smart waterside hotels set in the bright blue Atlantic, tended to be hit by gale-swept rainstorms and the low-level roads and inter-islet bridges swamped by waves rather more often than the tourist postcards implied. With bicycles and boats the only authorized modes of transport, guests attending parties, particularly ladies in long evening gowns, could not rely on arriving dry-shod but otherwise officers and men were happy in this easy going and, outside the five-star establishments, basically simple paradise.

For the expensive hotels the main trade from the early prohibition days had been weekending Americans. One of two British luxury liners, the *Monarch of Bermuda* and the *Queen of Bermuda*, left New York at midnight each Thursday, opening the bars as it cleared the harbour, to close them again after the return voyage as the liner neared New York the following Tuesday morning, its passengers having staggered round their hotel golf course over the weekend when not sleeping off their man-size hangovers. Out of this lucrative if limited business much of today's more variegated, and less alcoholic, Bermudan tourist trade has grown; and while the Navy provided few customers, the prices in the hotels being beyond the means of officers and men, the presence of HM ships in port was part of the attraction. For that was the age when glamour was highly rated and the role of Britain's America and West Indies Squadron at that time was indeed to peddle in a still susceptible New World that very commodity – glamour.[10]

* * *

When it claims for Portsmouth the title Britain's Premier Naval Port the city's tourist literature has got it right. In deference, presumably, to the Navy's reputation as the 'Silent Service', however, this proud flag seems to be flown with decorum rather than with fanfare; and more's the pity. For here in the heart of a still operational Royal Navy dockyard with in-commission warships berthed conspicuously on jetties beside the signal tower, is an exceptional array of exhibits recalling highlights of the Navy's history – in the shape of HM ships *Mary Rose, Victory* and *Warrior* in their restored grandeur and in the increasingly comprehensive Royal Naval Museum.

This immaculately presented collection lies beside the river within yards of Portsmouth rail and bus termini and is open daily to the public; and if the ambience tends to be rather severe or, in modern jargon, not visitor friendly, with the feeling of a press-gang waiting around the next corner, this plus the entry charges must be considered by the trustees as fair price for us to pay for what Their Lordships no doubt regard as a rare bestowal of privilege. But in competition with other heritage and leisure attractions in Portsmouth – the D-Day, Southsea Castle, Royal Marines and Sea Life and, in Gosport, the Submarine museums – they could be wrong.

For reminders of the Navy's greater days may be seen in many other places around Britain. It is acknowledged that the Portsmouth area, besides its historic artifacts, can boast the lion's share of naval barracks and technical schools and of

21. & 22.) A group of Edwardian admirals awaits events in Portsmouth (above) and a Royal Marine guard greets French president Poincaré with the Prince of Wales in attendance(below).

23.) A generation later, a more homely show – a naval guard of young seamen under training heads a Warship Week procession during the Second World War.

offices concerned with personnel administration, many of these in elderly buildings of distinction. However, the visitor must go to London to appraise the old Admiralty headquarters, with its frontage on Whitehall and the Horse Guards Parade; the magnificent RN College at Greenwich, incorporating the National Maritime Museum; the naval relics in the Imperial War Museum; and afloat near Tower Bridge, the Second World War cruiser, HMS *Belfast*.

Also redolent of those sunnier days are Plymouth Hoe and the important dockyard and naval establishments of adjoining Devonport; the RN College at Dartmouth; the great artificial harbour of Portland, formerly headquarters of the school of anti-submarine warfare; Chatham, until recently, with Sheerness to handle the larger ships, a principal dockyard port, and now an extensive heritage exhibition based largely on its own history; the spacious roadsteads in the Firth of Forth, backed by the former dockyard at Rosyth, and in the Moray Firth at the approaches to Invergordon. All of these were augmented in one or other of the two world wars by bases of varying importance at Dover, Harwich, Londonderry, Greenock, Liverpool, Milford Haven and, most notably, scarring the memories of all who served there, the bleak, grim, windswept, far-from-home anchorage of

Scapa Flow. Guided cruise-ship voyages around the British Isles to visit castles, gardens and wildlife might well be extended to embrace the naval theme, many of these extra ports of call, besides their historic interest, being in locations of great and, for those with long memories, poignant beauty.

During the centuries since Henry VIII built Portsmouth's first naval dock, the shape and character of that great city has been determined as much by geography and the recurring threat of war as by the evolving technical and maintenance resources needs of the Navy. While Portsmouth today spreads further afield, for most of this period it has been confined to the island of Portsea, in effect a moated citadel with only a heavily guarded southern flank open to the sea. Thus, in accommodating a growing population to provide a growing range of services, the urban area became eventually an unusually dense concentration of cheek-by-jowl housing, commerce and fortifications, with the expanding naval dockyard and back-up facilities as the focus, paymaster and *raison d'être*.

Among the other geographical features that determined Henry VIII's choice was Spithead, with its outlying anchorage; a deep-water channel close inshore at the approach to the harbour's narrow, readily defended entrance; and the safe, wide tidal lake inside the entrance with its obvious potential for development as a great naval base and dockyard.

At the turn of the century, before the pressure on space at Portsea had become too intense, the officer and middle classes had staked their claim on the salubrious seaside suburb of Southsea, with its rail link with Fratton junction, its branch of the city's tramway system and, on Palmerston road, its own relatively genteel shopping centre. Here, as Dr Riley recalls, was a fashionable meeting place 'for the élite and the cultured society of Southsea', the adjacent tree-lined streets being flanked by the houses and villas of the 'nobility and officers as well as persons of wealth', a district 'much improved in appearance in recent years'.[11]

The great feature of Southsea was, and still is, the extensive open common separating the beach from the built-up area. This was a relic of the days when, as part of the defences of Portsmouth against a possible, usually French, invader, this large flat space was left uncluttered to provide an unobstructed field of fire for the gun batteries in their emplacements in Southsea Castle and by the main harbour entrance. Besides its role as a promenade for Southsea's smart set, the common became inevitably the focus of a new resort as Southsea awoke to its potential as a holiday destination in what the railways were not slow to promote as part of the sunshine belt of southern England.

With war rather than peace on its agenda, a highlight of Portsmouth's history was the construction in its dockyard in 1906 of John Fisher's revolutionary battleship, HMS *Dreadnought*, to be followed in subsequent years by a flow of capital ships of similar ilk. This era saw the erection in the shadow of the city's impressive new guildhall of a modern naval barracks and at various nearby locations of a range of specialist schools reflecting the growing influence of twentieth-century naval science and technology, the demand for sites being such that the all-important gunnery school had to make what it could of Whale Island, an artificial hump up-harbour on reclaimed land.

The First World War saw further important innovations in naval affairs. In Portsmouth, according to Joy Harwood, where there was an acute shortage of labour, 'for the first time women stepped in to fill the gaps, acting as postwomen, van drivers and munitions workers. . . . They deputised for tram drivers and conductors . . . and were in the Police Force. There were even women working in the Dockyard; at the start of the war there had been only fifty in all, but by 1918 this figure had increased to more than 1700.'[12] According to the Royal Naval Benevolent Trust:

> A new era commenced when, in February 1916, Lord Jellicoe caused a signal to be hoisted ordering a Lower Deck representative of each ship under his command to appear on board the flagship. Subsequently he organised the *Grand Fleet Fund*, entrusting its administration to a committee of Officers, Petty Officers and Men, which, during the succeeding six years, afforded relief in the form of *18,000 grants* totalling over *£70,000.*
>
> After the Armistice the Admiralty, building on the work and methods of the Grand Fleet Fund, instituted the R.N.B.T. thereby creating one central benevolent organisations for C.P.O.'s, P.O.'s, N.C.O.'s and Men of R.N. and R.M. and their Dependants. It was arranged that the Trust should receive the Naval share of the profits from the Navy and Army Canteen Board which became N.A.A.F.I. in later years.
>
> Thus the Trust's main source of income is derived from the *INDIRECT* support of the serving men through the contribution, made by all ships and establishments, of a portion of the rebate paid by the N.A.A.F.I, and the R.N.B.T. HAVE NEVER YET MADE AN APPEAL TO THE PUBLIC FOR FUNDS.
>
> The aims of the trust continue to include: to provide relief in cases of necessity or distress to those who have served or are serving (on the lower deck); and to make contributions either directly or through other benevolent or educational institutions to the care, training, maintenance and welfare of the families and dependants of such persons in cases of necessity or distress.

These developments together with the establishment by the Navy of a female uniformed branch of non-combatant duties ashore, precursor of the WRNS, were among the early cracks in a hitherto all-masculine and officer-led edifice.

But it needed the Invergordon Mutiny of 1931 to bring home to the public how hard times had been for the lower-paid naval families between the wars. In naval ports like Portsmouth, when the fleet was in for home leave and repairs, these towns would swell and burst into life, their main *raison d'être* restored to them. But when the ships departed, it was like the onset of a slump. The sailors' wives and families now began a sentence of loneliness, the worse for being short of cash and, before air mails became widely available, for the slow transit of letters. And feeling the pinch, too, were the civilian populations of the ports – shopkeepers, suppliers of services and many workers dependent on the Navy for their livelihoods.

Not that local needs beyond the affluent enclaves like Southsea were all that high. Arthur Arnold gives us this glimpse of life on Portsea in the 1930s:

> It would have been strange if a mighty naval port such as Portsmouth had not developed close to the Main Gate of the Dockyard, an area full of that local colour which provided such rich material for writers such as Kingsley, Marryat, Dickens and others. Off Queen Street which led from the dockyard gate to the naval barracks, the side streets, alleys and courts certainly had some sinister looking spots, especially at night when the street gas lamps only partially pierced the murkiness. The period of which I write was one of 'hard times' – people went shabbily dressed and often poorly fed and housed. Even so, the area's many shops were varied to provide most local wants, whether civilian or naval. As a newcomer to Portsmouth, I was interested to see for the first time, such things as 'TIDDLY UP THE LINE' suits and cholera belts advertised in the shops of naval tailors. I recall too, seeing for the first time tobacco done up on spools wrapped in rope, on display in many tobacconists' windows.
>
> Just inside Queen Street on the left from the Royal Naval Barracks, was the Queen's Cinema, which, in a modest way, brightened up the place especially at night. Close to the cinema was a photographer's and in the window were two coloured prints of blue jackets with pretty girls in hammocks. They were in their underclothes only – these saucy females – quite 'risky' for those days but so well covered that I doubt if they would have felt all that cold had they walked outside on a winter's day! Across the street from the cinema was a Maltese café called 'The Live and Let Live'. Jose, the proprietor, was a quiet little man and kept the place open till about three a.m. One night when his customers got out of hand and the crocks started to fly in all directions, he ran out to fetch the beat policeman who was one of the 'old school' and just the chap to handle such a situation. It took only a matter of minutes to set matters straight.
>
> A little further along on the opposite side was another Maltese café. This did not keep open during the night and customers could see the food as it was being kept sizzling on huge trays in the window. These were heated by gas and two of them were always filled with fried onions with a vast quantity of well browned sausages. On cold winter days the smell which wafted on to the street as the door opened now and again was not liked by some but to others it must have been truly ambrosial in those difficult times of high unemployment and little relief. Food shops were plentiful and there was a jeweller's shop which seemed to flourish despite its position. Close to this was one of Portsmouth's bric-a-brac-cum-second-hand shops which sold a lot of the Navy's surplus odds and ends such as cutlery. For a few pence it was possible to buy there items of pewter, china

and glass which are now eagerly sought by collectors. A shop which sold birth control appliances down towards the end of Queen Street always seemed to have the same books on display in its window. These were *The Awful Disclosures of Maria Monk* and *The History of the Rod*. On the other side of the road was a shop the owner of which had an arrangement with the beat policeman to awaken him in time to provide the casual needs of Dockyard workers by way of tobacco etc, going to work with the first in-muster.

The religious life of the area seemed well catered for, as church, chapel, synagogue, and the Salvation Army Hostel were all available. A common lodging house in St George's Square gave shelter to 'needies' and the naval personnel had their own premises to go to or the Salvation Army Home. Besides many small businesses, there were also a brewery, bakery, printing works, even a knacker's yard, mineral water firm, and a plentiful supply of pubs. A good many of the pubs displayed notices requesting 'Ladies' not to stay longer than ten minutes! This was directed at the oldest business of all – prostitution! There was a good sprinkling of prostitutes. Most of these women kept their houses neat and clean despite the slummy little houses' poor external appearance. Some of them engaged in such perversion as flagellation, got drunk at times but generally, by playing the cat and mouse tactics whilst importuning on the streets, managed to avoid trouble.

This scene would be incomplete without reference to some of the 'characters' who helped to give it local colour. One such was little Madame Legalle who never passed a policeman without saying 'God bless the boys in blue!'. I believe she said it to matelots as well. There were still a couple of barrel organs and the two chaps who tried to make a crust in those times by their use must have had a pretty thin time of it. The 'mudlarks' by the Harbour Station, the gamblers playing for coins under the station on Sunday afternoons, the two or three turbaned gentlemen from India who were pedlars of silks, a solitary black man with a small attache case who I think sold 'cures' of some kind, French onion men, another Eastern chap who turned towards Mecca and fell on his face in prayer on the footpath wherever he happened to be at the appropriate time. By night there was always someone moving about, usually sailors who did not require sleep it seemed and the rats and alley cats grew fat and sleek on the many bits of fish and chips which they threw away on the way back to their ships![13]

For geographical as well as historical reasons, interdependence between naval and civilian communities was perhaps closer in Portsmouth than anywhere else. An unnamed man interviewed in Portsmouth by the WEA Local History Group has happy memories of his days as a delivery boy:

Where I lived was close to Whale Island and we used to get lots of 'Bluejackets' walking up our street. I began to think, 'That's the life for me' also, my father was in the navy as a cook so perhaps that added a bit of incentive. When I was

> a youngster there was a great feeling for the Empire and for the forces – the best dressed people you ever saw were in uniform. We had our big Empire and at school we kept Empire Day and marched past a picture of King George V and saluted. There was a patriotic feeling and that was one of the things that made me want to join the Navy. So, I went to the recruiting office in Edinburgh Road and signed on for 12 years when I was 15¼.

An unnamed woman, also interviewed by the WEA Local History Group recalls her early married days in the same period:

> Bob (my husband) joined the Navy in the supply branch; as he was well educated, clever and hardworking, he soon became a Petty Officer and got a Commission at 28, ending up his days as a Lieutenant Commander.
>
> My dad bought us a house in Chelmsford Road, as a wedding present. When the greatest drain on the finances were rent and food for most people, we did not have that worry as the house was ours; and as Bob was at sea, I did part time work in my dad's office, for which he paid me ten shillings a week, and I had my lunches at home. With the ten shillings I got from dad, I paid my rates, electricity and gas, and usually I had sufficient left over, to buy myself a dress at the Guinea Shop in Commercial Road. When I had the money to spare, I bought my clothes at Knight and Lee in Palmerston Road, and even there a decent coat cost only £5.
>
> After the 1938 crisis, the Government gave all married personnel marriage allowance and my allotment went up to two pounds a week. When war began, and I joined the Wrens (1940), I let the house, stored the furniture and, as Bob was already at sea in the Nelson, I lived at home with Mum and Dad. I cannot recall what I was paid as a Wren and Leading Wren, but I do remember that as a Petty Officer Wren I got about £3 a week. Militant feminists and equal opportunists today would not accept the fact that women be paid only two-thirds of men's rates but that is what we received. I don't recall ever being angered by this. It was just part of the system, and I must say that six of the best years of my life were spent in the Services.[14]

In 1942, on standing down from the post of Commander-in-Chief Portsmouth, a stint that had embraced the 1940–1 winter when Portsmouth was one of the three or four most savagely blitzed cities in Britain, Admiral Sir William James was bidden to lunch by the lord mayor. During the air raids, besides hits on the dockyard, the naval barracks and other ships and installations, the central area of the city had been so devastated that for a while street patterns were obliterated by the debris of the once-orderly rows of close-packed terraced houses. The news of these raids on their radios caused much anxiety to men serving at sea whose homes and families were in Portsmouth. In his farewell speech, James used this factor to illustrate his theme of unity and common purpose:

> Portsmouth and the Royal Navy had been linked together ever since the first king's ship took the water. The Royal Dockyard has hammered into shape a thousand vessels to carry the White Ensign to the four corners of the globe. This war, which has heralded a new era of greatly intensified air attack, has inevitably strengthened the bonds. A unity of purpose stayed us all during the long-drawn attack from the air. If ever there was a dividing wall between the city and the Royal Navy it was blown away on a certain 10th of January and is now in the rubble heap.[15]

Today the Royal Navy may not be quite what it was but in the eyes of those in the know it is still the best. If it is less conspicuous this is not only because it is smaller but because its personnel off duty no longer wear uniform. In the early evenings The Hard no longer swarms with bell-bottomed bluejackets newly released on leave. A major warship entering or leaving harbour may still attract the crowds but, with a diversified economy and less dependence on the Navy, the Portsmuthian has other concerns. It may be said, however, that if the environment is an important influence on aptitude and character, over the centuries the people of Portsmouth have a great deal to answer for the high esteem in which the Navy has long been held.

AGAINST THE ODDS, 1931–45

CHAPTER SIX

Uneasy Peace

When an unusual illness threatens it is important to call in the right doctor. After the Invergordon sickness of 1931 there were those at the Admiralty who felt tempted to smile kindly and prescribe a period of rest and recuperation. Fortunately for all concerned Their Lordships had more sense. They sent for Joe Kelly.

Admiral Sir John Kelly was a heavily-built sailor with a craggy face, thick eyebrows, large chin and a bluff outspoken manner. A strict disciplinarian, he masked a humane nature with a salty, sometimes scathing wit. Those who did not know the man, and the few who had seriously crossed his path, stood in awe of him but almost everyone who had served with Joe Kelly thought the world of him.

All the crews in the offending warships and, for that matter, in the entire Home Fleet now knew what to expect – a prolonged, intensified term of competitive drills and exercises, of what the Navy called strafe. With a masochistic shiver, everyone expecting this treatment welcomed it; and with it the fresh and vigorous leadership that would create in each ship's company a renewed sense of purpose.

The formula was simple and, as the well-honed product of Joe Kelly's nimble and practical brain, well within the intellectual grasp of every rank – rise early, clean up, rush about, clean up, put it all away, clean up, yawn, subside in exhaustion. If at the end of the day the ship was spotless, its boats smart and the sailors properly dressed, all was well. Taut discipline but, as Kelly insisted, 'a joke a day keeps the willies away'.

Summoned from the sinecure post of admiral commanding the reserves and on the eve of retirement, Joe Kelly, on his own admission, was passing his best. No longer an innovative admiral, not even up to date in modern tactics and technology, Kelly was uncertain whether he could produce the mental and physical effort the post demanded. But the call to come to the aid of the service he adored was irresistible.

His first task was to go on board every ship and present himself. To the assembled sailors he would say, 'In Whitehall, they looked around for a really good admiral to come here and sort out the mess. But they couldn't find one good enough, so they sent me. That's all that lot deserve, they reckoned. So here we are, and we must show them. There's a job to do and together we'll do it. I've not come here today to make a speech but just so you can recognize me. I don't want any of you seeing me out of uniform ashore to scratch your head and say, who's that funny-looking bugger over there? We've got important work to do and together, with all our faults, but with certainty of success, we'll do it.'

Monday, every Monday morning, appropriately, was the great shake-up day. The larger drills ranged from collision stations through striking down the topmast to laying out the kedge anchor. On a smaller scale there were many time-honoured romps from away lifeboat's crew to rig the quarterdeck for church. On this occasion Kelly made his mark, even in the history books, with a signal to all the assembled ships, 'Send poached egg to flagship.' Having chosen a moment when the ships' boats were all happily occupied on some distant errand, the order required each ship to recall one of its boats post-haste to embark a competing egg and convey it flat out to the flagship. For the first time in living memory the officers' cooks were the key men in a naval evolution, the creator of the winning egg becoming the hero of the day. Frolics of this kind made Kelly's hard-played games worthwhile.

Behind the scenes Joe Kelly concerned himself deeply with the welfare of officers and men. He reported regularly to the Admiralty, for whose clumsy performance during the prelude to mutiny he had a barely concealed contempt, on the progress of the fleet's rehabilitation. He took soundings at every level. Among his chief sources of information was a naval chaplain, Reggie Churchill who, with his ear well to the ground, provided an extra bridge between the c-in-c and the lower deck to the extent that Kelly's official reports 'no doubt echoed many of Reggie's impressions of the sailor's views.'[1] And Kelly never hesitated to interest himself in individual cases, sometimes with oral comment or advice, sometimes by personal letter, occasionally by digging into his own pocket to help alleviate a hardship. Some officers who had served with him many years before were amazed, on gaining a hard-won promotion, to receive a congratulatory note from old Joe. Geoffrey Brooke, a naval officer, recalls:

> I was only thirteen at the time but I remember well when Joe Kelly came to lunch where I was staying for Christmas 1933. He was then Commander-in-Chief at Portsmouth having recently finished his work as the post-Invergordon C-in-C Home Fleet. I was awaiting, without much confidence, the result of the Dartmouth entry exams. The result arrived eventually to be followed by a parcel containing a 'purser's dirk' (seaman's knife) and a nice letter in Admiral Kelly's own hand, congratulating me and delivering a little homily on the Navy being the most wonderful organisation in the world.
>
> There are many stories about Kelly but the one I like best originated during his command of the Home Fleet and was still told in the flagship when I came to join her. An AB, supposed to be washing the quarterdeck screen, was leaning against it surveying some distant vista. The Admiral came up behind him and,

taking up an identical posture, said as sweetly as his gravelly voice allowed, 'It's all right mate. Father's got the weight.'

I believe Joe Kelly had no great brain but it is easy to see why he was beloved of officers and men alike.[2]

Joe's younger brother Admiral Sir Howard Kelly, although equally outspoken, no less irascible and with an even more commanding presence, was in style and range of interests the more urbane, a difference that irked Joe whose more down-to-earth and better-natured methods were usually more effective. The two brothers quarrelled frequently, often in public, sometimes afloat. After a particularly tense exchange, during which Howard told Joe 'to mind his own bloody business', the two brothers met by chance in Bond Street. Joe would have walked on but Howard touched his arm and said smilingly, 'Haven't we met somewhere?'

'Have we?' asked Joe coldly.

'Well', said Howard, 'I think your mother knew my father.'[3]

When Joe died, worn out, soon after handing over the Portsmouth command, Howard donned his ceremonial uniform for the funeral and in genuine sorrow and remorse, and in full splendour, led the mourners.

* * *

Joe Kelly having put the show back on the road, it fell to Chatfield to equip it, produce it, rehearse it and, against many odds, ready it for its greatest ever challenge. The obstacles ranged from external factors, such as public apathy, political constraints and a chronic shortage of resources to in-house controversies and disputes over fundamental issues such as the role and protection of battleships, the role and deployment of cruisers, and the role, composition and control of the Navy's air arm in any future conflict.

Alfred Ernle Chatfield, Beatty's flag captain in the First World War, a key figure at the Washington disarmament conference in the early 1920s, and Commander-in-Chief successively of the Atlantic (Home) and Mediterranean fleets, was First Sea Lord from 1933 to 1938:

> For once, the system could not be faulted for, as time was to show, Chatfield was the right man in the right job, and no one else could have matched him. . . . Reconstructor rather than creator, Chatfield was unusually versatile: as competent ashore as afloat; consistently successful as staff officer, ship's captain, organiser, fleet supremo and sea lord: cheerful, patient, persistent, predictable.[4]

When Chatfield took over at the Admiralty, only fourteen years had elapsed since the end of the First World War, the war to end all wars. Many of those who had fought in that war, particularly the survivors of the slaughter in the trenches, and who still suffered with shell shock, nightmares and old wounds, wanted no more of it. For different reasons pacifist ideas were gaining ground among the intelligentsia, including articulate writers and undergraduates – if you lay down in front of the advancing tanks the enemy, shamefaced, losing heart, would turn around and make for home.

In any case the country was so poor, so weighed down with war debts, so decimated by slump and unemployment that to advocate heavy expenditure on reconstructed armed forces when the prospect of a new major war seemed inconceivable, was hardly the route to popular acclaim.[5] If the mood among home-grown politicians and their electorates was not exactly helpful to Chatfield's plans, that of some fellow-professionals was for different reasons hostile. In the world at large, with disarmament conferences and naval-limitation treaties still in spate, there were forces at work, not least strong anti-colonial sentiments in a newly-ambitious yet increasingly isolationist United States of America, that were inimical to British naval aspirations.

Among the unhelpful fellow-professionals at home were those barnacled and vociferous old tarpots to whom expenditure on such new-fangled toys as aeroplanes and submarines posed an unacceptable threat to the supremacy of the battleship. 'Most admirals cherished the battlefleet with a religious fervour . . . a battleship having long been to an Admiral what a cathedral is to a bishop', wrote Liddell Hart.[6] While Chatfield, a former gunnery specialist who had served much of his time in battleships, was not unsympathetic, the balanced view now required of him called for polite resistance even to his former and once-progressive mentor, David Beatty, who, as late as November 1935, with short shrift to air and submarine power, was writing:

> A Navy comprises three elements: the battle fleet, the cruiser squadron, and the small-craft flotilla. Our battle fleet consists of 12 battle-ships and three battle-cruisers, to which, of course, will be added in the event of war such smaller cruisers, flotilla element *and aircraft carriers* as may be necessary. . . . *First of all* the battle fleet needs to be strengthened for it is the foundation of the whole structure of naval strategy.[7]

But the most seriously antagonistic fellow-professionals were to be found in the senior ranks of the Royal Air Force, that glamorous new service with its accomplished public relations lobby and its natural appeal to some of the more gung-ho and socially well-connected elements of British society. After the First World War, for political reasons, the successful naval air service was taken under the fledgling RAF wing, partly to help the RAF acquire an all-round identity, partly because it seemed logical for the procurement and operations of all non-civil flying machines and dirigibles to be under the same management.

With scarce resources it was inevitable that the RAF would come to prefer the development of bomber and fighter types and of support services that suited its own strategic and, for that matter, political ambitions rather than of those which would be regarded as subservient to naval requirements. After all, this was still the age when the pundits foresaw naval strategy centred in a future war on Jutland-style actions between battleships, each with a secondary gun armament able to provide defence against air attack, in which even an enemy aircraft carrier would be sunk by gunfire rather than by aircraft, the primary use of the latter being for reconnaissance and for spotting the big guns' fall of shot; and if or when naval aircraft were to go seriously on the offensive, they would be armed with torpedoes rather than bombs.

However, attitudes were changing and by 1936 Chatfield, still struggling for the Navy to wrest control of naval aviation from the air ministry, was insisting that 'the air side is an integral part of our naval operation . . . and the presence of the air weapon will make the whole difference to the nature of the fighting of the Fleet.' At last, in July 1937, following a government enquiry, the Fleet Air Arm returned to the Navy.

This was in the nick of time – in 1939, although well endowed with aircraft carriers, the Royal Navy deployed only 230 aircraft, as against over 600 each by the US and Japanese navies, the British flying relatively inefficient multi-purpose types, making it 'particularly difficult for its naval aviation to make that quantum jump from being a supportive, ancillary weapon of the Fleet to being a dominant and even decisive one'. It was not until 1941 that the Navy, in the throes of its desperate war against the U-boats, gained *operational* control from the RAF of the latter's land-based coastal command, now being equipped, at last, with suitably armed long-range aircraft capable of supporting the Navy's mid-Atlantic convoy-defence tactics.[8]

One boon for Chatfield was the lifting of the Ten-Year Rule in 1933 whereby, according to the government, it could be assumed on any given date that there would be no major war for at least ten years. While this had discouraged expenditure on weaponry that might never be used, it had also sapped that sense of urgency without which the armed forces could hardly be kept up-to-date and viable for come what may. The dangerous fatuity of this irresponsible rule soon became evident – ten years after abandoning the rule, Britain was in the thick of the Second World War, the first round of which, against Germany, had begun four years previously.

It needed time as well as money to build a major warship and, being short of both as well as limited by the international disarmament agreements, Chatfield was obliged to modernize existing battleships rather than produce new ones, with the result that, in terms of heavy ships, the Navy that went to war in 1939 was largely a navy of First World War vintage. New battleships, aircraft carriers and cruisers were on the stocks to augment in due course an operational strength which in 1939 comprised 15 battleships and battlecruisers, 6 aircraft carriers, 63 cruisers and, among other men-of-war, 168 destroyers and 69 submarines.

Two years previously Chatfield had confided to Dudley Pound, who would himself soon take up the First Sea Lord reins, 'I am very well though tired . . . and anxious to get away from the Admiralty. . . . I have done my task. I have got over the Naval Conference, the Cruiser Question, the Battleship Enquiry and the Fleet Air Arm, with one or two wars thrown in at the same time.' A year later, as Chatfield left office, Pound wrote to congratulate him on having been 'the finest First Sea Lord within the memory of any living Naval officer'. Wars, international negotiations and battles with the RAF apart, as both First Sea Lord *and* Chairman of the Chief of Staffs Committee Chatfield had held his ground not only against the Treasury accountants but in the face of a succession of vacillating politicians. During his tenure there had been three prime ministers and three First Lords of the Admiralty, two changes of foreign secretary and one of chancellor of the exchequer and, among the chiefs of staff, two changes of army and three changes of RAF professional heads.[9]

No mean feat, indeed, for this dedicated sailor to have got the Navy on top line for war in such a fickle and often adverse climate.

* * *

The year 1935 was the year of George V's silver jubilee. There were also a number of events that, despite rude gestures from Germany and Japan, seemed to herald better times ahead – and one of the sunniest summers on record.

Although unemployment in Britain was still high, it was falling and by the end of the year it would be below two million. The government's rearmament programme, a stimulus to industry, was under way, and the slump almost over. With the international danger signals only at amber, rearmament was seen as precaution, not prelude. It was a good year for celebration. Most people in Britain were comfortably off, the middle classes the most so. As never before and, as it would turn out, as never again, the mid-1930s would prove to be the heyday of the middle classes, the British predominantly, but also, emerging fast into the limelight, the American.

Rich, cigar-smoking Americans, guide and etiquette books in hand, film stars, writers, crooners were among the ambassadors of a new and freer lifestyle, the dissipations and glamour of which appealed to the British younger set. When the whoopee-makers could afford to and wanted to be smart they met in cocktail bars to drink Manhattans, Bronxes, White Ladies, Dry Martinis. Sports cars, jazz, sexy women, cigarette holders, wisecracks, smart restaurants, sleazy night clubs were the new totems. The bright young things danced to the latest melodies from New York – in 1935, tunes such as 'Smoke Gets in Your Eyes', 'Red Sails in the Sunset', 'Anything Goes'. On hotel bookstalls were *Time* and *Life* magazines, novels by Scott Fitzgerald and Ernest Hemingway; Hollywood stars such as Garbo, Gable, Astaire, Rogers and the Marx Brothers dominated the cinema billboards.

The silver jubilee procession through London of 6 May was a momentous event, as this excerpt from the diary of a witness suggests:

> It was a brilliant summer's day with temperatures in the seventies. I had left the family home in Kent at six-thirty wearing my midshipman's uniform, the early start being on orders of the police, who wanted everyone off the streets before nine. I emerged from Charing Cross station soon after seven-thirty into a dense throng of sightseers. Most were bound on foot for vantage points beside the lavishly

24. & 25.) In the years preceding the First World War, the launches of HMS Neptune *(above) and HMS* Queen Elizabeth *(below) draw the Portsmouth crowds.*

26.) *A religious service marks the opening of a graving dock at Rosyth.*

27.) *Between the wars, a warship returning from foreign service is welcomed home.*

decorated route: already, on some pavements, they stood six or seven deep beneath the flags and garlands. People were in jovial mood. One could move only at a shuffle, and it took more than half-an-hour to find a suitable perch in Trafalgar Square. We had a long wait but time passed quickly and, eventually, I spotted the mounted police at the head of the procession appear through Admiralty Arch. They were preceded by the sound of music from the military band and of cheering from the special grandstands in The Mall. As intended, the leaves on the lines of trees were half open, giving a fresh green effect without obscuring the onlookers' views, a detail of foresight by the organisers that impressed me very much.

The fighting services of the imperial territories were represented by immaculately drilled and colourfully uniformed contingents marching to the nearest music, there being several bands spread through the procession. An important and picturesque part of the show was the carriages or open cars conveying top dignitaries in ceremonial garb from all the British dominions and colonies. Then in crescendo came our own British VIPs, the heads of the armed forces, the royal princes and finally, in regal splendour, in their ornately gilded coach, George and Mary. All the way to St Paul's the almost continuous roar of enthusiasm reached its climax at the approach of the royal coach. Besides their cheering, people were smiling and waving flags or clapping their hands or holding small children up to see the view. The excitement was intense. That this was a genuinely popular occasion had become clear earlier on as I looked from the window of my train down the beflagged streets of London's poorest and slummiest inner suburbs. Festooned tables were being prepared for open-air parties. There was an air of festival everywhere, the more touching in those back streets for being locally inspired and improvised. It was impossible not to feel emotional.[10]

* * *

Midshipmen were required to keep a daily journal, which was part of their sea training and inspected by the ship's captain.[11] The following much-shortened extracts from one of these 'logs' provide impressions of two great events of 1935 – the naval review at Spithead on 16 July, part of the George V Silver Jubilee celebrations; and the rush to the Mediterranean less than two months later to meet the threat posed by Mussolini's adventures in Abyssinia. The matter-of-fact prose does not hide the sense of excitement that was felt on both these occasions:

Friday, July 12. The Home and Mediterranean Fleets left Sandown Bay at 0430 and proceeded slowly up Spithead. Shortly before 0800 the Fleets prepared to anchor. In the battleship *Barham*, on letting go our second anchor, the new quarter deck awning was spread and all power boats hoisted out. The weather was calm and hot with an oppressive sun shining through a dry mist.

Berengeria's passengers honoured us with a cheer as their ship passed close down the port side in the forenoon.

Saturday. I ran the morning officers' trip in the 2nd P.B. [picket boat], the entrance to Portsmouth harbour being most alarming, for as I negotiated the 'bottle-neck' I was confronted with a horde of large paddle boats, steamers, drifters, and launches crammed full with libertymen, which leaving shore at 0700 together were carrying all before them down the harbour leaving a large pall of black smoke over the dockyard. At 1100 RA2 [the squadron admiral] walked round the messdecks. In a complimentary signal afterwards, he expressed satisfaction with the state of the ship.

Sunday. The finest and hottest day of the weekend made a perfect setting for the Fleets which was entirely appreciated by the streams of passenger vessels and yachts which began the rounds of the ships while we were still at church on the Q.D. Trips were being run from London and all parts of the Southern coast.

Monday. At 0900, the Reserve Fleet moored ship. The assembly of ships for the Review was now complete, the Dominions being represented by Australia and India, a total of 157 Naval ships. Anchorages were allotted also to ships of the Merchant Navy, Fishing Fleets and Yacht Clubs, bringing the complete total to over 500 ships, stretching along a length of water of 10 miles and a width of up to 5 miles. In the afternoon Admiral of the Fleet H.M. the King arrived on board the *Victoria and Albert* after a state drive through Portsmouth. Being ashore at the time I witnessed the procession from the roof of a tramcar, which due to the concentration of the crowds along the route was held up in a very convenient position for my purpose. RA2 and wardroom officers gave a dance to friends which was held on the quarterdeck. Press reporters came off in the 2300 boat. The fine evening promised well for the morrow.

Tuesday. The morning was hot and airless. All ships dressed overall as the anchorage filled up with the last arrivals. I ran the 2nd picket boat bringing off two loads of guests. The scene was most exciting; every ship gleaming, the grey paint of the men-of-war being relieved by the brighter colours of the liners, yachts and pleasure craft. At 1300 a hush fell across the waters and a fair breeze from the Westward arose to lift the flags. Officers and guests having lunched well now stood about in expectant groups.

After a long wait, a quiet murmur heralded the appearance of *Victoria and Albert*. Very slowly she came, preceded by *Patricia* and succeeded by *Enchantress*. As she approached her moorings the Fleet broke the spell with a 21-gun Royal salute. All the ships' bands then played the National Anthem. RA2 joined the flag officers of the Fleets and selected masters of the mercantile marine and fishing fleets onboard the Royal Yacht, to be presented to his Majesty. At 1600 the *Victoria and Albert* entered the lines, the King visible on the fore bridge. Just before 1700 we manned ship and waited until at last our turn came. The band played the National Anthem and the ship gave three cheers as the yacht passed slowly by. It is difficult to express one's emotions at a moment like this without shuddering with embarrassment but I will quote from *The Times*, 'The sight of a Sailor King steaming not only through his Fleet but through lines of yachts, merchant vessels, and fishing craft must have caused a thrill to some hundreds of thousands of those who witnessed it.' Finally the Fleet Air Arm flew past, dipping in salute to the King, streams and streams of aircraft in one continuous roar.

Guests began to disembark at 1730. I was sent in the 2nd picket boat to patrol round the *Victoria and Albert*, our duty being to prevent any vessels from approaching within 200 yards of the Royal Yacht. At 1800 the firing of a gun was the signal for every steamer, yacht and boat in the World to make at full speed for the Yacht and circle slowly round, cheering and acclaiming the King who stood on deck. After 15 minutes we were hemmed in to 50 yards of the Royal Yacht. By 1930 the pressure had eased off and until 2000 when we were relieved, the situation was more or less in hand. At 2300 the ships illuminated themselves, followed by a searchlight display, bouquets of rockets and illuminations by flares, and we could hear the cheers of the crowds ashore who in their thousands thronged the coast from every vantage point. At midnight I was glad to turn in and dream of flags, guns and coloured lights. . . .

The next day, 'under ominous clouds and in choppy seas', the King led his entire fleet to sea for war exercises, these comprising for the most part gunnery firing against surface and airborne targets, the latter including a real, radio-controlled aircraft. This 'despite its slow speed and closing range had ample time to carry out its attack before collapsing in the sea after being winged, at last, by a shot from one of the battleships,' the midshipman commenting ironically, 'I thought this an excellent recruiting campaign for the Fleet Air Arm.'

The exercises finished, the Home and Mediterranean Fleets formed up in two long parallel divisions with the Reserve ships on the flanks, and the *Victoria and Albert* turned about and steamed back between the lines to be cheered once again by every man in every ship. The Royal Yacht at last disappeared astern, the signal 'Splice the Main Brace' fluttering at her halyards.

With a hint of war in the air, HMS *Barham* was despatched to Plymouth to give leave and, with a new crew, make haste to the Mediterranean. International efforts to thwart Mussolini's designs on Abyssinia were putting the League of Nations at sixes and sevens. The idea now, prompted by Britain, was to apply economic sanctions against Italy but the front against Mussolini was weakened by American isolationism and French indecision. If it came to armed intervention, the ultimate sanction, it seemed likely that the brunt of military action would fall on Britain; and with the Mediterranean as the expected theatre of war, this meant primarily a job for the Royal Navy. Clearly *Barham* was in Plymouth dockyard, not for rest and relaxation, but to prepare for action. The types of stores, ammunition and new equipment, the special training of key personnel and the fitting out of an operations room, all bore witness.

A few weeks later, as these further extracts from the journal show, HMS *Barham* was ready to leave for the Mediterranean:

Tuesday, September 3rd. At 0830 we slipped from Devonport, No 5 jetty. Once clear of the breakwater, hands were exercised at actions stations, which dissolved into gundrill and control parties lasting all day. Our speed of 16 knots was increased to 18 before the evening, and surprised liners, cargo steamers and tramps were startled at the unusual spectacle of a battleship churning past at a speed rarely witnessed.

Wednesday. Our speed was further increased to 20 knots. No chance was wasted to work up in gunnery proficiency, all armaments being exercised. At 2030 the hands went to night action stations, and then each watch in turn to defence stations.

Thursday. Thick fog in the middle and morning watches. Searchlights, starshell, torpedo and more gunnery exercises were carried out all day.

Friday. At 0700 to the Eastward of Gibraltar we fired 15" and 6" sub-calibre at a target towed by a tug, after which, at 0915 we entered harbour, and took in 1000 tons of oil. At 1400 we slipped and proceeded to anchor in the bay where director tests were carried out.

Saturday. H.A. control parties carried out height finding exercises on our aircraft. At 1315 we proceeded to sea to carry out 15" full-calibre and 6" full-calibre firings at a battle practice target. We returned to the shelter of Gibraltar Bay to recover the aircraft and then, at 1900, proceeded towards Malta at 18 knots.

Sunday. The ship's company went to divisions and after prayers were addressed by the Captain who outlined the political situation and announced that after a 36-hour stay at Malta we were to proceed to Alexandria and join the Fleet which was concentrated there as a pointed hint to Mussolini.

Monday. 4" and 15" guns went to drill in the forenoon, the afternoon being given up to rigging derricks and providing gear for ammunitioning. The ship stopped at 1600 and after the seaboats had gone away the hands were piped to battle. Zig zagging was then exercised and searchlights after dark.

Tuesday. An extensive programme of 15", 6" and 4" sub-calibre runs at a target from Malta began at 0600. At 0800 we entered Grand Harbour. Just before dinner (lunch) we commenced ammunitioning and continued with all hands in sun helmets until supper time when one watch was given leave; the duty watch continuing until 2230. I worked the crane most of the day alternating between the after and midship lighters.

Wednesday. We embarked the rest of our ammunition before breakfast. During the forenoon, we took in water while the crane and the foremost screen derricks hoisted in stores and provisions. We slipped from the buoys shortly after 1400. Once clear of the breakwater hands went to action stations and a 6" full-calibre shoot was immediately performed. Then we fired a 4 round per gun 15" full-calibre run. At 1800 we went in to Calafrana to collect our floatplane; then off to Alexandria at 18 knots.

Thursday. Pompons and machine guns were exercised AM, a make and mend clothes being given in the afternoon. At evening quarters part of watch drills were carried out.

Friday. The ship was cleaned up in the forenoon. At 1500 we arrived off Alexandria and carried out 15" and 6" sub-calibre runs at a target towed by a destroyer and 4" full-calibre at a sleeve target towed by one of the F.A.A. aircraft. At 1630 we entered Alexandria harbour.

Saturday. The forenoon was occupied disembarking stores for the Fleet and oiling from Plumleaf. At 1030 we fell in by divisions and VA (the admiral commanding the battleships) came on board to inspect and address the ship's company. He welcomed the ship to the Station and expressed a hope that the extra work entailed in working up our efficiency in so short a time would be taken in good part as we especially, being now the most powerful battleship in the Mediterranean, should be prepared for any duty which may be detailed for us.

We had read in the press news of a speech by Sir Samuel Hoare at Geneva outlining the British policy which is to stand by the League of Nations, the general attitude being that unless Mussolini withdraws his aggressive measures, he may find himself at war with the League of Nations, with Britain and France at its head. Having gone so far, I think Mussolini is almost bound to go on. At 1300 we slipped, weighed and proceeded out of harbour where the same gunnery exercises as yesterday were carried out.

Sunday. At 0545 we stopped of Port Said, embarked a pilot, and proceeded up the first stage of the Suez Canal. Abreast the inner end of the breakwater we let go an anchor and our stern was pulled round by a tug so that we lay facing and at 90° to the canal with our stern at buoys in a large basin. Divisions at 1015 were followed by Church. At 1300, the ship was finally secured and the hands piped down.

From this berth at Port Said the four forward 15 in guns, their muzzles open, commanded every passing vessel. This threatening stance had the desired effect on the crowded Italian troopships which daily entered the canal. The cheering and shouting soldiers lining the decks as their ships approached became silent minutes before protocol obliged them to stand in salute in the presence of a major warship; and when they resumed their cheering after passing under the guns it was on a markedly subdued note. Even so, their propaganda-induced hysteria, sometimes kept up noisily right through the night as their troopships lay off Port Said awaiting the canal pilot, was irritating and, observing the quality of most of the troops, unconvincing.

The more we saw of our potential enemy, the more certain we became that, in a fight, we would rout them. We believed our commander-in-chief, W.W. Fisher, was urging Whitehall to let the Navy have a go. We were ready and so was British public opinion. We had only to bottle up the Mediterranean with naval patrols in the Straits of Gibraltar and at the approaches to Suez and Port Said to cut Italy off from its now numerous armies in Abyssinia. The Italians would then have either to call off their war or send their navy to fight it out with ours. However, while the outcome of the latter was not in doubt, the cost in world-wide effect might well prove too high. Wars sooner or later with Japan as well as Germany were now on the cards and the loss of only two or three Royal Navy battleships as the price of victory in the Mediterranean could make enough dent to invite further aggression.

But the Navy's hands were tied by the half-hearted pronouncements at the League of Nations. Britain would act only with the consent of the international community and, for war measures, this was not forthcoming. Even France, anxious not to offend the Italians, backed away. Appeasement is a word associated usually with the Munich crisis of 1938 but it was the leading powers' weak-kneed response to Mussolini's self-glorifying adventures in 1935 that continued the rot begun with the Japanese invasion of Manchuria in 1931. From 1935 on, passing one signpost after another, Rhineland, China, Austria, Czechoslovakia, Albania, it was to be downhill all the way until, eventually, Poland in 1939 and Pearl Harbor in 1941 cried halt.

To those of us who were in Port Said in the sunny autumn of 1935, however, only the immediate future counted. The anglo-french community in its tree-lined quarter of the town was friendly and hospitable. There were sporting, swimming and social facilities for all ranks. The night life, soigné or vulgar as one wished, was inexpensive. Passing trade from the non-stop flow of passenger and freight ships through the canal brought vitality and prosperity to the natives. Port Said was a cheerful and well-appointed community and one could wish for no more agreeable billet.

As time went by, the odds of war with Italy began to lengthen. On duty we remained on the qui vive but, apart from its presence in the harbour, the chief show of naval force was the weekly ceremonial march of our sailors round the town. Headed by the Royal Marine band, informed by a modest degree of nautical swagger, this was always a popular event, chalking up one more success for British gunboat diplomacy. Then, in early December, having passed examinations held at Alexandria and being due for promotion, half-a-dozen of us set sail for England in the P and O liner *Viceroy of India*. We were home in time for Christmas.

* * *

The man of the moment at that time of crisis was Admiral Sir William Wordsworth Fisher, Commander-in-Chief of the Mediterranean Fleet, who, according to Sir Charles Madden, was an imposing figure and a classical scholar 'with flowing white hair, rather unusually long for an Admiral. He was a great lover of Malta and in the afternoons walked all over the island making friends with the peasants and all he met', the villagers of Mgarr, whose priest he befriended, gaining a good deal from the admiral's munificence. One day, wearing old grey flannels, he landed from his barge at the Customs House where a party of American tourists were shepherded aside to let him through. 'One lady said "Who on earth is that?", to which her friend replied "Looks like an out of work actor to me." W.W. Fisher bowed to her and said "An actor if you will, Madam, but so far never unemployed." He then swept majestically on.'[12]

When Fisher took over the Mediterranean Fleet in July 1932, he was known not only for his commanding presence and wide-ranging interests but for a style and an intellect that might have taken him to the top of any profession. In the Navy, he had come to notice as a junior officer for his scientific approach to developments in gunnery; after commanding a battleship at Jutland, for his leading eleventh-hour part at the Admiralty devising means for the final defeat of the U-boat; and in 1928–30, as a senior member of the naval staff, for his ability to reconcile political and strategic issues as a prelude to policy formation. As a visible figure afloat, an exuberant manner masked on the one hand a gentle way with young or vulnerable people and on the other a tough, quick-thinking tactical mind, the latter attribute showing itself in his pioneering approach to night engagements between darkened fleets. So skilled became his fleet in this technique, that in the combined exercises in the spring of 1934 it took the Home Fleet by surprise and, in an 'action' in appalling weather off Portugal, surrounded and 'defeated' the 'enemy', Fisher being then 'hailed by the press as the greatest naval genius of modern times', one correspondent describing his 'victory' as 'spectacular beyond the dreams of the most ambitious Hollywood producer'.[13]

During the first three years of his appointment Fisher worked hard, with ceaseless zest and determination, to bring the Mediterranean Fleet to the highest possible pitch of efficiency. As Mussolini's warlike ambitions, notably his designs on Abyssinia, became apparent, morale was at its peak. After the naval review in July 1935, his squadrons augmented rapidly by units borrowed from the Navy's other fleets, Fisher soon found himself at the head of a powerful armada of war-ready men-of-war distributed between Gibraltar, Malta, Alexandria, Port Said, Haifa and Aden. With Malta too close for comfort to Italian air fields, to distance himself from the possibility of a reckless or provocative act by the volatile dictator and to be nearer to the likely scene of further operations, he set up his main base in Alexandria.

This great cosmopolitan trading post with its enclosing breakwaters and, by advance-base standards, its potentially adequate repair and supply facilities, and with its mixture of French, Levantine and Arabic influences and historic artifacts, offered beguiling prospects to the newcomer. But Alexandria, even when British-style recreational facilities were made available, was never all that popular with Royal Navy

28.) A squadron of twentieth-century battleships was a formidable sight. Before, during and for a decade or so after the First World War, a nation's strength and importance tended to be measured by the number of battleships (and their more lightly armoured and thus faster sisters, the battle-cruisers) it could deploy, and by this criterion, at least, Britain was for many years regarded as the world's greatest power.

29.) Before the Fisher revolution, a typical man-of-war in the battleship category was HMS Bulwark.

30., 31. & 32.) In contrast with HMS Bulwark was HMS Barham *(top), one of the daughters of Fisher's famous Dreadnought prototype. The scale of this class of warships is well demonstrated in this view of HMS* Warspite *in Malta's Grand Harbour (centre). In the inter-war years, this usually crowded port was a regular haven and headquarters for the battleships and other heavy units of Britain's Mediterranean fleet.*

libertymen. The locals were considered grasping and devious, ever ready to rip off the unwary or the gullible, and there was much yearning for Malta. For the affluent who felt at home in a sophisticated international ambiance, however, Alexandria had a good deal to offer; in modern terms, from the opulent yacht club overlooking the harbour across town to the smart restaurants and night clubs on the *corniche*; while the European-style centre with its fine public buildings, shops, clubs and gardened villas was an oasis in a swarming desert of bazaars, crowds, noise and poverty. A hard city, a harsh city, a city without a soul were among the epithets, yet no one can deny that Alexandria then, and later, offered much to Britain and its forces to be grateful for.

Fisher had a far from easy ride in putting and keeping his ships on a war footing. Despite the strenuous efforts made by the Navy's depots and dockyards, there were shortages of supplies and equipment. Perhaps the most dire of the shortages was that of certain classes of ammunition – at one time, it was said, some of the warships could be spared barely enough anti-aircraft shells for a fifteen-minute engagement. Another blow was the sudden withdrawal by the cold-footed French of their offer to the British fleet of backup repair facilities at France's Mediterranean naval ports. In the long run, however, the human factor was bound to provide the main cause for concern, the more so when, towards the end of the year, the threat of an immediate, single-handed war seemed to recede following the agreement by some supporters of the League of Nations to impose economic sanctions against Italy. By early 1936, with resources and personnel still at full stretch, a growing number of ships and their crews, having been overseas continuously long past their appointed time, were becoming seriously overdue for home leave and refits.

Under Fisher's firm leadership there was no faltering, no falling off of drive and efficiency; the Navy had come a long way since Invergordon. But it was with some relief when, around Easter, the logic of events led to the view that it might be best to leave the bombastic but much-discredited Italian dictator to stew in his own *fait accompli* in Abyssinia. The ships on loan from other stations could be returned whence they came, allowing the Mediterranean Fleet to resume its customary peacetime rituals and Fisher, after his extended tenure, to hand over the command to his successor, Sir Dudley Pound.

W.W. Fisher was no mean showman and perhaps his most spectacular achievement in the Mediterranean was the demonstration staged by his fleet off Alexandria on 21 November 1935 for the benefit of the Egyptian prince, Mohamed Ali, a group of cabinet ministers and other VIPs from Cairo. Embarked in a British cruiser, these guests found themselves stationed close behind the target at the receiving end of full-calibre bombardments by a concentration of naval might including five battleships, a squadron of cruisers and numerous destroyers. From their grandstand, almost within splashing distance of the fall of shot, the visitors witnessed the awe-inspiring power of broadsides of 15 in shells, the menace of close-range salvoes from the cruisers and the fury of massed torpedo attacks by destroyers tearing at speed through smoke screens, with dummy bombing raids by waves of Fleet Air Arm aircraft aimed on the visitors' cruiser as a hair-raising finale. Not only were any local doubts resolved that day about which was the better side to be on and the Italians reminded of the fragility of their lines of communication with Abyssinia, but the world at large was given a telling glimpse of the British lion in angry mood in Mussolini's forecourt.

While this was Royal Navy panache at its most eloquent, its value as a tool of diplomacy depended, of course, on whatever political will lay behind it. A caustic observer of Fisher's demonstration might well have asked – well, it's one thing to shoot at a slow-moving, inanimate target, but might it not have been another story if the victim had been able to fire back? While the confident naval crews would have had no doubt about their answer, their masters in London, attuned to reactions in Berlin and Tokyo, might well have felt less sanguine.

In the summer of 1936, tired by his exertions in the Mediterranean, W.W. Fisher took up the post of Commander-in-Chief at Portsmouth. A year later, busy with preparations for the coronation of George VI, of which another naval review was to be a feature, the Admiral collapsed at a parade on Southsea common and on 24 June 1937, aged only sixty-two, he died. Thus was the Navy deprived of the one man who many felt would have been the ideal candidate, following Chatfield, to lead it into the Second World War.

* * *

The fleet's resumption of peacetime routines had been short-lived. The Spanish Civil War, breaking out in July 1936, had called for much activity by the Navy in support of endangered neutral merchant ships, whether on the high seas or in the offing of Spanish ports, and in the provision of succour to refugees, including the evacuation of British subjects from besieged areas. During the following two years, with German troops posing threats in central Europe, and even Italy daring to invade Albania, and with the precautionary moves by British forces engendered by the Munich crisis, came the additional burden of coping with the fall-out from Japanese aggression in the Far East.

On the face of all this, however, every effort was made to induce a business-as-usual mood on Royal Navy stations, with customary emphasis on drill, training, protocol and the quest for efficiency. In this spirit, the attention to minute detail that was a hallmark of the naval method was well illustrated in a book by Commander Rory O'Conor, executive officer of HM battle-cruiser *Hood* from 1933 to 1936, outlining the principles of naval discipline in a major British warship. Under the title *Running a Big Ship on Ten Commandments*, O'Conor decreed:

1. *The Service* – The Customs of the Service are to be observed at all times.
2. *The Ship* – The good appearance of the ship is the concern of everyone in *Hood*, and all share the responsibility for this.

3. *The Individual* – Every man is constantly required to bring credit to the ship by his individual bearing, dress and general conduct on board and ashore.
4. *Courtesy to Officers* – The courtesy of making a gangway and standing to one side to attention when an officer passes, is to be shown by every man.
5. *Execution of Orders* – All orders, including those passed by Bugle and Pipe, are to be obeyed at the run.
6. *Punctual attendance at place of duty* – Every man is personally responsible, on all occasions, for his own punctual attendance at his place of duty.
7. *Permission to leave work* – A man is always to ask permission before leaving his work.
8. *Reporting on completion of work* – Any man on finishing the work for which he has been told off, is to report to his immediate superior. Parties of men are to be fallen-in and reported.
9. *Card playing and gambling* – While card playing is allowed at mess tables and on the upper deck, any form of gambling is strictly prohibited. Gambling includes all games of chance for money stakes.
10. *Requests* – Any man wishing to see the Commander is to put in a request to his Officer of Division. In urgent cases, his request is to pass through the MAA and the OOW.

After discussing each 'commandment' in detail, O'Conor averred that, 'if the Commander has a framed copy of the Standing Orders (the ten commandments) always placed before him on his Defaulters' Table, he will find that he can, without difficulty, connect 99 per cent of the offences directly to one of the "commandments"'.[14]

Gieves, the ubiquitous and versatile naval outfitters who published the O'Conor testament, and whose representatives were liable to turn up wherever a British fleet was stationed, however temporarily, sometimes knew sooner than its own crew where a ship was bound; and if they had a duty to perform for one of their clients, however trivial, would adopt whatever means best served their purpose, an initiative well illustrated by Geoffrey Brooke:

> At the start of a cruise HMS *Nelson* was casting off from South Railway Jetty. Her stern was being pulled out by a tug, the sea around a miniature maelstrom, when the telephone from the quarterdeck rang on the bridge. I was midshipman of the Watch and heard the communication number report to the Captain that there was a man in a rowing boat waving a parcel and trying to come along side. This was hardly the moment, of course, for such an evolution, but the engines were stopped while a line was thrown down for an obviously important item. When the boat was clear and the Home Fleet flagship recommenced her interrupted progress, the Captain asked what the hell the parcel was. When the reply came I could willingly have died – 'From Gieves, Sir, for Midshipman

Brooke'. The skipper looked long and hard in my direction but I had just had time to take the precaution of being out of sight. The offending package proved to contain no more than the visiting cards the many-sided tailor had promised to deliver before the ship sailed.[15]

Pranks were, of course, the order of the day and as a means of inculcating an awareness of the minutiae of shipboard life, were at once a facet of education, self-discipline and *esprit de corps*. In the mid-1930s, Frederick Wigby, a newly-fledged stoker on a destroyer's messdeck, after there had been an accident with some of the messtraps:

I found out that my (hammock) lashing had been threaded through the handles of all the broken cups, thereafter it led through the spout of the tea kettle where the end of it had been tied into a monkey's fist. My lashing had been soaking in cold tea all night. It was impossible to undo it at all. I had to cut the darned thing and buy a new lashing and replace the broken cups. It was all in good fun. Shortly after this – one Sunday morning – it was young Mackenzie's turn to be cook of the mess. He was ordered to make a straight rush, potatoes and runner beans, and to put some macaroni up the galley for afters. This macaroni was in long stalks and as Mac was breaking it up, Melton said to him, 'I expect the Caterer will want the macaroni stuffed'.

'Stuffed?' said Mac, looking very surprised. 'Stuff it with what?'

'Jam, of course,' replied Melton in a flash, without turning a hair.

'How do you get it in the hole?' asked Mac again, not knowing exactly what to make of Melton.

'It's quite easy really,' said Melton. 'Just fill your mouth with jam and blow it slowly into the little hole in the end.'

Mac filled his mouth with jam, picked up a stalk of macaroni and commenced to blow. The jam flew out of Mac's mouth all over the messdeck and also all over our No. 1 suits. Everybody roared with laughter. Mac got his own back eventually. When we returned from Church Parade, ready to enjoy our usual Sunday dinner, everyone wanted to know where the runner beans were. Mac, instead of slicing them, had taken all the beans out of the husks and all he had left was a cup full of beans. The husks were in the gash bin. Whether or not Mac had done this on purpose, I never did find out.[16]

At the end of the gunnery course at Whale Island, Portsmouth, the sub-lieutenants often staged some boyish form of demonstration. One April Fool's Day,

the officer on the Footbridge saw an elephant with mounted mahout dressed as a Sub-Lieutenant, escorted by four more Sub-Lieutenants, approaching across the narrow bridge from Portsmouth. This he reported by telephone to the

Lieutenant of the Island who, having been made an April fool once that morning, dismissed the hoax and replied 'Let it pass'.

Concealed behind the drill shed during the march past the elephantine procession, wheeling out to join it behind the last class, was spotted by the Captain at the saluting base. Determined not to return the salute of a masquerading mahout on an elephant, he said, 'Remove that elephant, commander'. 'Remove that elephant', said the Commander to the Commander (G), who passed it on to the Parade Training officer, who passed it on to the Chief gunner's mate, who deflected it in the nick of time to a side road. While the Admiralty made a Trunk call to the Captain and the whole Navy loved the joke, I fancy the Sub-Lieutenants' leave was stopped for some days for making a mockery of the parade.[17]

Pranks apart, the rigmarole that went into many commonplace evolutions seemed laughable. Every time the duty picket boat was called away on board a major warship, the midshipman in charge, buckling on his dirk, hastened aft, saluted the quarterdeck, saluted the officer of the watch, received his orders, saluted the officer again and, from the gangway's upper platform, prepared to wave his picket boat alongside. During this time, the crew members would have manned the boat over the lower boom and down the jacob's ladder, raised steam, laid out the cabin cushions, squared off the boat's gear, tidied their own uniforms and, under the petty officer coxswain's orders, brought their craft to lie off its parent ship. If the captain was to be embarked, departure would be from the starboard gangway, while for other errands it would be from the port; in either case the seamen, standing smartly facing forward at the bow and stern of the picket boat, would flourish and work their boat-hooks in unison before neatly holding their picket boat in position at the gangway's lower platform. The midshipman having taken over the wheel from the coxswain, both standing together behind the spray shield on the mini-bridge abaft the tall brass-topped funnel, was now ready to proceed.

If the captain was their passenger and he was bound in uniform for an official meeting at a headquarters ashore, he would be piped and saluted over the side of his ship, to be received by the boat's midshipman standing at the salute; and, having been waved forward by the officer of the watch, the picket boat would be on its way. In the stern cockpit the captain would acknowledge the mark of respect paid by all hands standing to attention on the upper decks on his own ship and, as the picket boat passed by, of those of the other warships in company. Similarly, the midshipmen or coxswains of other ships' boats, if aware that a ship's captain was embarked, would salute the passing potentate and, at the landing stage, if on an errand of less importance, make way for the arriving captain. On a ceremonial occasion, in his best uniform and with his pennant flying in the bows of his picket boat, similar deference would be paid but in a stepped-up form – bugle calls to invite attention, other ships' captains at the salute, passing ships' boats with their engines stopped and so on. The midshipmen used an informal warning code – four fingers of one hand held aloft to denote a four-stripe captain in the cabin, with a small reversible disc on the funnel, one side indicating that salutes were acceptable, the other that, the great man being off duty, salutes were not required.

With every ship's smartness and efficiency advertised by the conduct and appearance of its boats, the midshipmen on duty afloat were under constant surveillance. In a keenly competitive atmosphere, every lapse or transgression was liable to be reported. Yet the rules, multitudinous and pernickety though they were, allowed much scope to the midshipmen in charge of boats to use their seamanship and command skills in coping with unusual challenges or mishaps; and if any of the latter were serious (but not lethal) and the midshipman, having done his best, was clearly shaken, the only comments would be benign and there would be no reprimand. Examples of such situations might include accidents resulting from an unexpected effect of tides, currents, winds or storms on local navigation, passenger falling overboard, a collision with another boat, damage, perhaps costly, to the boat by an obstruction at the landing stage; while every manoeuvre to bring his single-screw boat alongside a ship's gangway in an exposed anchorage or a shore-side jetty in a crowded harbour, in ever varying circumstances, was an opportunity to demonstrate dash, style and competence, with no prouder participant or onlooker than his own crew whenever the midshipman pulled off a really smart manoeuvre.

It was in this realm that the peacetime Navy excelled, in this hard-driven combination of initiative and conformity, of alertness and careful attention to detail, of colour and showmanship in a basically mundane routine. Here at an impressionable age was the proving ground for executive authority and, in particular, for command in the Navy of that era, for one day standing calmly and stoically on a windswept warship's bridge on the *qui vive* for every eventuality, for then being hopefully the first to spot a distant puff of smoke or a nearby periscope and sound the call to action stations; and, imbued with the offensive spirit, to be ever ready in the Nelsonic tradition 'to engage the enemy more closely'. . . .

In this energetic milieu was expressed the Navy's great attribute – the readiness of its personnel to make the most of their lot, of each officer and man to make his own ship (or boat) the best of the bunch, to keep open the safety valve of grousing while enjoying the everyday good humour and jokiness, even the pranks, that underlay the tense if lightly worn professionalism. For the officer, his midshipman's time and, above all, the opportunity offered while still in his teens by the command of a ship's boat of winning the respect and often the affection of his own lowerdeck crew, was a unique form of indoctrination fashioned by the Royal Navy to a finer art than that achieved by any of its peers. The results would be for all to see in the forthcoming Second World War.

In the development in this and other ways of the potential all-round leader, however, the formula had, most regrettably, one very serious fault – apart from the study of navigation, *it lacked any intellectual content.*

* * *

In the view of historian Martin Brice, it may be said that 'the Second World War began in the Far East on the night of July 7th/8th 1937' when some Japanese soldiers outside Peking were fired on, supposedly by Chinese police.[18] Whether one goes along with this premise, the fact was that the invasion and occupation by the Japanese of large areas of China at this time was having a disturbing effect on western interests, including those in Peking and in the principal trading rivers and seaports, with British and American warships, in their guardian role, on occasion in the firing line.

Even the Royal Navy's summer base in Wei-Hai-Wei was not immune from the Japanese intrusion. On lease from the Chinese government this tranquil anchorage in north China, undefended during most of the year, now had in the new conquerors an unwelcome and interfering landlord, the Japanese insisting on dominating the entrance to the anchorage with a menacing heavy cruiser and on deploying officious armed patrols in the areas used for recreation by the British visitors.

But as the Japanese, having taken Shanghai, marched on Nanking, the transient Chinese capital, and Hankow, the River Yangtze became for several months a major battlefield, western forces, notably the patrolling gunboats, being caught in the crossfire. The American gunboat *Panay* was sunk and some British gunboats were damaged by Japanese bombs, these attacks and frequent hostile incidents flying in the face of numerous safeguards, ranging from the Nine-Power Treaty of 1922, whereby foreign navies were accepted in Chinese waters to help protect the international settlements and, in particular, their trading infrastructures and shipping, to repeated assurances at every diplomatic level that the Japanese in their new war with China intended to respect the established rights of all the neutral states.

But the Japanese hostility to western interests had been evident since the Tanaka doctrine of 1929, declaring Japan's determination, for economic as well as political reasons, to advance westward into and beyond China, a first step being a declaration in 1934 that maintenance of peace in the Far East would in future be a Japanese responsibility. Chinese acquiescence was to be secured by an 'Asia for the Asiatics' policy whereby, western infiltration and communist influences having been banished, Japanese efficiency and technology would become the engine of Far East development, with China as a principal beneficiary.

But the Chinese had other ideas and the Japanese, aggrieved and frustrated, decided at last to seize by military conquest what they most urgently wanted. As their operations in China expanded and their impatience with all impediments, and not least with western diplomacy, grew, incidents involving British warships multiplied. Some of these were accidents but most seemed to be deliberate aggressions or provocations in defiance of agreed procedures and, with casualties sometimes at stake, much of the time of senior naval officers was spent calling personally on their Japanese counterparts to register their protests. Although the official responses were generally conciliatory, both governments wanting to avoid any build-up towards war, it was known that some of the more fanatical local Japanese commanders hoped their actions might, indeed, lead to conflagration;

and so strained was the reaction in London that, following the partial mobilization at the time of the Munich crisis in the autumn of 1938, the despatch of a battleship squadron to Singapore was for a time seriously on the cards.

With most of its ships in turn on a semi-war footing in the danger zones, and with the possibility of a really big bang at any moment, the China fleet was keyed up and busy but not so stretched that it could not meet its show-the-flag commitments at the extremities of its bailiwick and play its part in the deliberately life-goes-on social and sporting whirl at its bases in Hong Kong, Wei-Hai-Wei and Singapore.

By the summer of 1939, however, with the news from Europe worsening and the Japanese army now close to the borders of Hong Kong, the high jinks were becoming edged with anxiety, the bursts of laughter separated by silences, optimism blurred by the darkening clouds. But no one in his worst nightmares could imagine that a year hence much of the British army would be in full retreat from a vanquished Continent, with bombs on London and the threat of a German invasion on the immediate agenda, or foresee the ferocity of the Japanese advances throughout south-east Asia and the savagery of their occupying forces in the former European colonies.

Anyone leaning on the sea wall at Wei-Hai-Wei that August to watch the departing British warships as they sped south in readiness for war might well have wondered – is this the end of the road? Is Britain as a world power under threat? Will we ever again, here or elsewhere, see the likes of this unique, ubiquitous navy, of this benignly dogged, not-to-be-trifled-with instrument of the great *pax britannica*?

The Second World War broke out on different dates for different countries. For Britain and its overseas possessions the date was 3 September 1939. In one sense, however, Brice had the right idea but, as we have seen, the seeds were sown earlier in that decade in the face of events in Europe and east Africa as well as in the Far East. The seeds were sown in appeasement. For Britain, impoverished and weakened by the earlier war, partially disarmed, uncertainly led by good-natured politicians, unsupported at moments of crisis by the League of Nations, there may have been no choice. But the price to be paid for appeasement was very heavy. The onlooker at Wei-Hai-Wei would, indeed, have waited in vain.

CHAPTER SEVEN

Battle Royal

Of all the reverses suffered by the Royal Navy during the six long years of the Second World War the hardest to bear was the loss of the battleship HMS *Prince of Wales* and its consort the battle cruiser HMS *Repulse* to Japanese air attack off the coast of Malaya on 10 December 1941. This was not only a humiliating defeat in naval terms but worse, a severe shock to the national morale already fraying after eighteen months of Britain's struggle, virtually alone, against Germany and Italy.

> It was upon the public at home, where the outlook was already grim, that the blow appears to have fallen hardest. Many people have said that the loss of the *Prince of Wales* and *Repulse* was the worst news of the whole war, and Mr Churchill's personal anguish . . . is easily appreciated.[1]

Indeed, Winston Churchill, on whose dogged perseverance everything depended, was badly shaken. Having underestimated the threat posed by Japan, Churchill had insisted on the despatch of these two valuable warships to be the nucleus of an intended Singapore-based capital ship deterrent and to act as a warning to the Japanese to lay off British interests in the Far East. In one blow this bluff had been called and, with the Japanese army already ashore in Malaya, Britain's capacity to fight off the new enemy had been fatally undermined. Singapore, Hong Kong, Malaya, Burma, the Dutch East Indies – by the summer of 1942, all would succumb, and even India and Australia were to be at risk.

Meanwhile, caught unawares by the devastating Japanese air attacks on its naval base at Pearl Harbor on 7 December 1941, the United States was at last in the war. But, the Americans having their own wounds to lick and their own priorities, their advent was small consolation to the survivors of the *Prince of Wales* and *Repulse* who could look only to newly-vulnerable Singapore for succour.

Rescued from their sinking ships, or from the sea by the escort destroyers, there were several hundred survivors, including the captain of *Repulse*; the admiral commanding the force and the captain of the *Prince of Wales* being among the 840 officers and men who were lost. This tragedy is blamed usually on the absence of air cover, but the power and disciplined ferocity of the Japanese bomb and torpedo attacks were such that an attendant aircraft carrier, though its fighters would have driven off or destroyed some of the bombers, might well have provided a third victim.

As it was, the ordeal suffered by the crews of the two defeated ships could not have been more harrowing. By all accounts these men fought in their battered, broken and sinking ships to the end; and when at last they were ordered to quit, those who chose to seek passage in a rescuing destroyer, rather than take to the water and hope to be picked up later, waited their turn in orderly, sometimes jokey, queues before shinning down one of the ropes to safety.

> I found several patient queues formed at the upper deck guard rail. . . . There were hundreds of men gathered along the side in both directions. Some were already jumping off forward. A dozen lines down to the destroyer were thick with wriggling figures. There was no untoward noise of any sort, all concerned were simply going about the business of saving themselves with proper determination. . . . At last there was no one in front of me. I gave my precursor a few feet and went too. . . . As the battleship heeled increasingly away, the men at the other end of the rope had to pay it out, nullifying most of one's efforts. . . . In one exhilarating heave [with the help of eager hands] I was over the destroyer's rail. . . . I saw the man after me come safely over and then 'Slip!' roared the destroyer captain. . . . The ropes swung down, heavy with men, to crash sickeningly against the battleship's side . . . and, as the engine room telegraph clanged, the grey wall opposite began to swing inexorably away. . . . The destroyer stood off a cable or so and in silence . . . we watched aghast [as] the great battleship began to roll slowly away.[2]

Another survivor recalled:

> As the ship heeled further over I found myself on its side. Climbing over the bilge keel, I found myself standing on the ship's bottom close to a huge torpedo hole. As the ship's propellers began to submerge, I began to swim away but found that I was being sucked down, and had almost given up when I could see that it was light in front of my eyes. I then struck out for the surface and a few moments after saw the bows, forward guns, and fore part of the bridge of the POW as she stood upright and whilst swimming away watched her disappear. I had previously inflated my lifebelt, and after swimming around for a while, a messmate called to me and I found a few survivors standing on a water logged boat floating just below the surface. Joining them we saw many bodies in the water, and after a while some of our aircraft flew over us. Then a destroyer appeared, lowered a boat, and started to pick up survivors. We kept calling out

to the boat as each time it turned towards the destroyer we thought it had missed us, but it finally picked us up.[3]

An officer on the admiral's staff left this record:

At the time of all these happenings I was standing on the Admiral's Bridge. We saw the first torpedo coming towards us and felt a nasty jar but very little noise in the midst of all our own anti-air-craft. This gave us a list to port. Later on, when the second main torpedo attack was made on us, after *Repulse* had disappeared, I saw about four tracks of torpedoes coming towards us. One of them hit dead under where we were standing, throwing up a huge spray of water right in front of us; at the same time the sky seemed full of these yellow bellies and another torpedo hit us on the other side. There were of course several misses but the Japs had done their work.

About half an hour later, nine bombers came along at a fair height in a perfect formation of line abreast, they did not seem to mind all the A.A. Barrage which we put up against them. They came along like a solid steel rod straight for us and dropped their bombs. The one bomb that hit us was a big one possibly 1000 lb, the engines stopped and there we were quite useless waiting for the next attack which thank God never came! It was not necessary. The ship had righted herself to a certain extent as a result of being hit on both sides but now we started to accentuate the list to port. All the men from down below who could be got up were on the upper deck.

I was still watching proceedings from our bridge when the order came to abandon ship. To get down to the upper deck would have meant going down no fewer than six ladders. By the time I was half way down the first ladder, the ship was beginning to list really badly and my anxiety was not to hurt myself before getting in the water and thereby spoil my swimming. After the first ladder I was on the 'flag deck' which by that time was about 12 ft instead of 50 ft above the water on one side and quite ungettatable on the other side. I decided to jump on the low side. Before doing so, I jerked my binoculars, cap and shoes off; this could not possibly have taken more than two seconds but when I looked at the water again the 12 ft drop had gone and I just stepped in, as one would go into a swimming bath by the shallow end. I swam like hell. I did not get very far away however when I was closely pursued by the ship's mast which hit me on the head and pushed me down under water for what seemed an eternity. However, I disentangled myself from the rigging and shot up like a piece of cork, as a result of my lifebelt being blown up. I just had time to get my breath when a nest of guns from the other side of the ship came tumbling down and took me down in the depths again. This time I thought I was done for. But Providence was on my side. I bobbed up again, looked round to see if anything else was coming up to hit me and saw the old ship upside down and bottom up. My next thought was the danger of being sucked down when

> the ship finally disappeared, so I started swimming like hell again toward the most beautiful biscuit tin that I have ever seen floating about. I think I reached that tin not a minute too soon! It kept me afloat and gave me time to recover my breath. After a time, I started to swim again with my biscuit box until I eventually reached a carley float with about six men in it. When I got to my float three men hauled me onboard and I was saved.[4]

Most people, when they consider leadership, fighting spirit and *esprit de corps* in naval warfare picture Nelson standing bemedalled on the deck of HMS *Victory*, the sharpshooters' bullets flying around him; Jellicoe or Beatty on the exposed bridges of their flagships as they calmly signal their squadrons into a broadside-firing position; A.B. Cunningham on his flagship's bridge urging his ships into closer, more lethal combat; young, tin-hatted captains of cruisers, frigates and destroyers on their open, shrapnel-pitted bridges exemplifying the dash and daring that they expect, and receive from, their highly-trained, danger-scorning crews.

The other side of the coin of naval professionalism is less often seen or envisaged – the coin of steadiness under prolonged fire against odds, the measured reaction to damage, confusion and the sight of wounded comrades, the individual initiatives and improvisations within an overall framework of organized response to disaster, the grimly cheerful resilience of men exposed to dangers almost beyond endurance. These backs-to-the-wall attributes, this capacity for endurance, evident many times over throughout the ordeal and aftermath of the *Prince of Wales-Repulse* fiasco, are what has long given the Royal Navy an edge over its competitors.

This spirit is well depicted in a scene in Singapore recorded by Geoffrey Brooke, having himself survived the sinking of the *Prince of Wales*:

> Next morning our sagging spirits received a terrific boost from the sight of our Royal Marines parading; they were fully armed and in brand new uniforms, drawn overnight. The two ships' companies were mustered for a roll call so that accurate lists could be constructed of the missing. It took time and we sat around in groups swapping experiences.[5]

Many servicemen who were at a loose end in Singapore at this time, aware of the growing risk of entrapment by the advancing Japanese army and denied orthodox means of evacuation, were ready to consider almost any scheme that offered a sporting chance of escape. Among those who won through was an MRNVR sub-lieutenant and former RN telegraphist, V.B. Ash, who has recorded:

> After destroying my wireless station off Penang I, together with my ratings, was ordered to pack a small suit case and proceed to the jetty to await a transport to evacuate us to Singapore. It was the wait here in the rain and wind that must have brought on a fearful cold and I cracked up on the ship in one of the

Officer's cabins with pneumonia. On arrival at Singapore I was taken by car to Alexandra Hospital. I was on the danger list for some time but later recuperated in five different convalescent houses but was bombed out of each one. I finished up back in hospital – a nervous wreck. Day after day we were bombed.

One morning a bomb landed on the hospital and afterwards all walking patients were ordered to assemble outside. When the senior doctor came to me he said I would be better at Combined Headquarters and to wait there for a car. Alongside the jetty was a large motor launch which I understood was waiting to evacuate the Admiral. They gave me a blanket as I sat in the sternsheets. When the Admiral arrived, after supervising the destruction of all cars and lorries on the jetty, he turned to a Commander and said 'I think Ash will be far more comfortable in a gunboat. Take him out to the *Dragonfly*.' That was the last I saw of the Admiral. He saved my life but he must have suffered a terrible death.

We sailed from Singapore at dark dodging the capitulation by a few hours; and I heard much later that all the doctors, nurses and patients were slaughtered in the Alexandra hospital. Next morning, soon after daybreak, I was rudely awakened by loud hooters and the pipe 'Action Stations'. The First lieutenant had given me his cabin. It was below the upper deck, and just outside there was an ammunition hatch where several ratings had assembled, it being their Action Station. One of the ratings went up on deck to 'have a look-see'. When he returned, I heard him say to the others 'Well lads we've had it. There are nine bastards coming from the left, nine bastards coming from the right and nine from aft.'

Knowing he was referring to planes I immediately took two blankets off the bunk and wrapped them round me in case of shrapnel etc. Shortly afterwards there were two big bangs, out went the lights signifying we had been hit. This was confirmed a minute later by the pipe 'Abandon ship'. The ratings outside my cabin were up the ladder like a shot and I followed them. On reaching the upper deck I saw it was nearly awash and that we were sinking fast. I also noticed they had lowered one whaler which was a few yards from the ship. I was so weak I knew I would not have been able to have stayed afloat long in the water, so I jumped in and managed to swim the short distance to the whaler. Shortly afterwards nine Jap planes swooped down on top of us and machine-gunned us at point-blank range. Many in that boat were killed outright and several others badly wounded. The whaler was beginning to fill up with water due to holes made by the bullets, so I ordered the men with tin helmets to bale, and also ordered the dead to be thrown overboard. Twice more the planes swooped down mopping up all of us in the boat, and also those in the water hanging on to rafts or any woodwork floating. I remember well praying hard with my eyes shut that He would protect me, and He did. To this day I know it was a miraculous escape.

As dusk set in I noticed some land in the distance and slowly we made for what turned out to be an uninhabited island. At high tide there was only about three yards of dry sand, and then just dense jungle which we found too thick to penetrate.

> . . . There were twenty-two of us. Two of our survivors were Malay ratings who were able to climb a palm tree and throw down some coconuts, otherwise we would have starved. After some time we decided to patch the holes up in the whaler with mud and made west for Sumatra. At Padang we were put onboard the British Destroyer *Stormcloud* laying alongside. She took us out to sea, and later transferred us to the Australian cruiser *Hobart*. She, in turn, took us safely to Colombo.[6]

After an almost incredible series of high-risk adventures Geoffrey Brooke, having got clear of Singapore and survived the long, hard trek to Padang, made it the hard way, across the dangerous seas, to Ceylon. In his case, in early February 1942, after nearly two months in Singapore as a survivor of HMS *Prince of Wales*, in an atmosphere of growing confusion, during which he had been recruited into rearguard operations against the approaching enemy and on consolidation prior to evacuation of naval stores and personnel, and then without further particular responsibilities, Brooke was ready to go.

The Japanese army was by now on the island, and the daily bombings and artillery fire were assuming an almost intolerable intensity, when Brooke left the RN headquarters ship, HMS *Laburnum*, to take up an allotted billet on board the *Kung Wo*, an elderly, unarmed River Yangtze steamer of 5,000 tons with a single thin, tall funnel, commandeered by the Navy. This vessel, already damaged and its lifeboats holed by bomb splinters, was to be the temporary refuge of 140 mainly naval passengers; and with earlier shiploads of civilians and service personnel lost at sea to enemy action, the omens were hardly reassuring.

Sure enough on Friday 13 February, having quit Singapore the previous evening, the *Kung Wo* was spotted and soon afterwards attacked and sunk by Japanese aircraft. Taking to the leaking boats, the survivors eventually gained the almost foodless island of Pohm Pohm, 80 miles from Singapore, where they were joined by two launch-loads of refugees, the combined party, including wounded, now comprising women as well as a sprinkling of Brooke's former *Prince of Wales* shipmates.

By 15 February, the day of Singapore's surrender, the launches having taken the majority to Sumatra, Brooke remained in charge of sixty naval volunteers, subsisting on a small supply of tinned food. Benku, wild, humid and uninhabited, visited daily by Japanese reconnaissance aircraft, was as poorly endowed with edible produce as it was generously supplied with mosquitoes and hermit crabs which, at night, took their toll on the waning stamina of the visitors as they sought rest in the sand on the fringes of the beach.

On the seventh day, a scarlet pimpernel in the form of Lieutenant Cunyngham-Brown MRNVR appeared in a canoe with news of junks that he had organized for the rescue of castaways. He was able to divert one of these to Benku and this took Brooke and his party to the relatively civilized island of Sinkep, still if precariously in Dutch hands, where they joined a larger body of migrating refugees. Thence they proceeded by stages along a surprisingly well organized but very arduous and often dangerous rescue route across water, up rivers and overland, through Rengat, Basrha and the Sawahlunto railhead, to the outwardly prosperous and serene Dutch-administered port of Padang. Here on 8 March a Royal Marine Colonel, A.G. Warren, in calm and selfless control of the exodus, with Japanese forces only 60 miles away and the port effectively blockaded, gathered Brooke and seven other officers together. He told them he had bought a prauw by which to make his own escape but had decided he must stay put and see his job through. He went on, 'There is room for you in this boat. You have been selected as the most useful to the war effort in other theatres, and I am ordering you to go. You will sail tonight. It is a very long way [to Ceylon] and there is considerable risk.'

Embarkation some way up the coast having been achieved, the prauw set sail and headed westward. The ensuing escape lasted almost forty days on board this 45-ft long, two-masted, shallow-draft, usually coastal sailing vessel, open-decked apart from the small shelter amidships, the gear in poor shape, with eighteen men on board on short rations. The journey included a 1,000-mile sea leg, a machine-gun attack by Japanese aircraft and spells of appalling weather. This extraordinary feat, culminating in rescue by a freighter in sight of the coast of Ceylon, must rank high among the sagas of against-the-odds ocean voyages. Brooke, allowing for his usual modesty, tells the story well in his book, *Alarm Starboard*.

And the abandoned prauw? The freighter's Captain decided that the empty vessel, afloat, was a danger to shipping and must be despatched by gunfire. As Brooke recalls, his was 'a silent group that watched from the stern rail. . . . The ship's officers kept away, realising it was not their moment'. As the sinking prauw receded out of sight 'I saw in my mind's eye the little red letters under her counter, *Sederhana Djohanis, Sarak*, surrender with Malayan grace to an otherwise cheated sea.'[7]

* * *

In the early months of 1942, apart from a hastily-assembled and rather dated British fleet based on Colombo, there was nothing to stop a Japanese sweep across the Indian Ocean into the Persian Gulf and Red Sea, there to link up with German forces advancing through Russia and across North Africa.

To be rid of the opposition the Japanese sent an aircraft carrier force supported by battleships and cruisers into the Bay of Bengal, intent upon a repeat of their attack on Pearl Harbor, with Colombo as their new target. But the British naval Commander-in-Chief, Admiral Somerville, appreciating the threat, had taken most of his fleet to sea, thus saving it to fight another day.

A lone submarine, HMS *Trusty*, was replenishing with torpedoes when 'out of a low, black thundercloud hummed a swarm of hornet-like fighter dive-bombers. The Japs had ganged up to strike at a large fleet. They found the birds flown.' The remnants, a depot ship, an elderly destroyer, a merchant ship and *Trusty* bore the brunt of the onslaught. 'I wondered if the overhead procession was ever going to end.

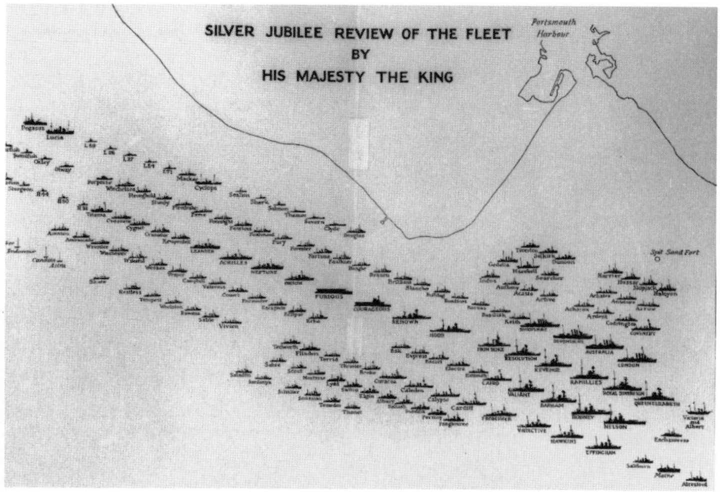

33., 34. & 35.) A large and immaculate British armada gathered off Portsmouth in 1935, to be reviewed by George V in his yacht Victoria and Albert *(centre), as part of the silver jubilee celebrations. Although dominated by traditional styles and technologies, the assembly included two aircraft carriers, portent of a slowly dawning air age. Yet even in the Second World War, when this relatively novel type of warship and its varied flights of aircraft became increasingly decisive factors in naval operations. British hearts were still more deeply stirred by the triumph or the loss of a battleship.*

36. & 37.) Throughout the Navy's twentieth-century heyday, while submarine crews would earn the highest possible marks for gallantry and perseverance, the most versatile and hardest-worked type of warship was undoubtedly the destroyer. The submarine interior is from a painting by Stephen Bone.

Squadron after squadron zoomed low over the breakwater, their bombs plunging with sickening violence into the sea beside us.' *Trusty*, miraculously unscathed, was soon back on station. Its Captain, William King, was to reflect later that his ship's ordeal in Colombo's vacated port could claim to be one of the events at the high watermark of the German-Japanese victory which, thereafter, 'ebbed to defeat'.[8]

The high water, hardly discernible at the time, had been a long while coming, Britain's war (with Germany) having already lasted 2½ years; and, with over three years to go before the Japanese surrender, the ebb still had a very long way to flow. For the Royal Navy there had been many setbacks and there were more to come – the hard-fought evacuations of the army from northern Europe, from Norway through Dunkirk to western France, in the face of the advancing German forces in 1940; the retreats from Greece and Crete and into Egypt in 1941; the loss of *Prince of Wales* and *Repulse*, and then of Singapore; and the agonizing, protracted destruction of ships on the high seas, in and out of convoy, notably in the north Atlantic and the Arctic and on the Malta run.

On the credit side, however, there was much to celebrate – the sinking of *Graf Spee* and, at a high cost, *Bismarck*; the brilliant sea and air battles against the Italian navy; the allied landings in north Africa and southern Italy; the sense that every arrival in Malta, Murmansk, the Clyde and Liverpool was a kind of victory; in the last day of 1942 the far-reaching rout of a superior German naval force by convoy escorts in the Barents Sea and, later, the crippling of *Tirpitz* and the end of *Scharnhorst*; and the triumphant allied invasion of Normandy in 1944.

* * *

The Navy had been hard at it from before the outset. Across the world, on the eve of war, British warships, including those of the Reserve Fleet, were being readied and gathered for action. The Home Fleet, based once again at Scapa, was sweeping down the North Sea on the alert for German prey; ships were in place to protect the troops as they crossed the Channel to join their allies in France; cruisers in northern waters and submarines in the offing of German ports were on patrol to report and impede enemy movements, part of a new maritime blockade of Germany; steps were in hand to protect seaborne trade in English coastal waters and, backed by naval forces based at Portland and Plymouth, to initiate and escort convoys of merchant shipping in the western approaches to Britain, while thwarting U-boat movements through the English Channel; and networks of offensive and defensive minefields were already taking shape.

At the sea the shooting war began at once. On 3 September 1939 the British liner *Athenia* was torpedoed and sunk y a U-boat, with considerable loss of life; two weeks later the aircraft carrier *Courageous* was despatched by the same means off Land's End where its aircraft were on anti-U-boat duty; a month after that the battleship *Royal Oak* succumbed in the Scapa anchorage to another U-boat; and meanwhile, the toll of shipping to U-boats on the high seas having already begun to cause concern, havoc had been played off the Thames estuary by magnetic mines laid by aircraft as well as by U-boats. On the other hand, bombing raids on British naval bases sank no warships during 1939.

Retaliation was swift. In the early weeks of the war, the losses of U-boats to British attack, following the first such loss on 16 September, soon reached double figures, the victims of British submarines having already by mid-September included two cruisers damaged and a destroyer sunk; and before Christmas the German battleship *Graf Spee*, on a raiding mission in the Atlantic, was to be scuttled off Montevideo after being driven into that port by a small force of British cruisers. In all weathers, around the British Isles, into the Atlantic and across the North Sea the presence of Royal Navy ships, continued to ensure for their country, while denying to the enemy, command of the sea, the absence of which would prove the Achilles heel of Germany once again.

While the Navy was at full stretch the lack-lustre government of Neville Chamberlain, the British people at large, the army awaiting events in the lee of the Maginot Line and, to an extent, the Royal Air Force were sitting on their hands hoping that the war on land would, somehow, go away without ever having seriously to fight it. Alas after a few months of 'phoney' war, of indecision about strategy, of being at odds with the French high command about objectives, there was to be a very rude awakening.

By way of rehearsal, and, for those who were alert enough, of warning, enter right, in the spring of 1940, the sadly mismanaged Norwegian campaign. For some weeks, an expedition to support Finland in its grim fight against Soviet aggression had been on the cards but, as the allied politicians and their advisers wavered and the Finnish defence crumbled, the Germans struck northward. By seizing Denmark and Norway, control of the part-sheltered shipping route through territorial waters on Norway's western littoral could ensure a flow of vital seaborne imports, including Swedish iron ore shipped through the port of Narvik, while providing advance bases for Atlantic-bound U-boats. The British and French, long aware of the strategic importance of the Norwegian route, were about to queer the enemy pitch, in the first place with minefields, when the Germans pre-empted them. By calling in aid what was left of the force that had been prepared for the relief of Finland, the allied response was rapid, though the role, instead of being offensive, had to be defensive after all.

At first the Navy, indulging in good old-fashioned point-blank warfare, had a field day. Dodging the dive-bombers, and not without losses, British men-of-war stormed up the fjords, creating mayhem among trapped German warships, between-whiles escorting allied troops to their chosen landing points. The performance of the army and air force high commands, lethargic following years of insulation from the realities of combat, was disappointing – front-line guns supplied with the wrong ammunition, aircraft parked on frozen lakes lost as the ice gave way under enemy fire. But, with Churchill as its First Lord, and following several years of hard training on active service, some of it in or near a firing line, the Navy responded with vigour and enthusiasm to the challenge.

The opposition in the form of U-boats, surface warships and bombing aircraft was tough and determined. The army, having been driven from its footholds in southern Norway, had to be rescued by sea and, regrouped, transferred further north with an Anglo-French assault on German-held Narvik as the objective. Due to a shortage of resources, tenuous and vulnerable supply routes and hesitant inter-service staffwork this proved to be a hazardous and lengthy process and by the time Narvik fell to the allies on 28 May 1940 the evacuations of the British army from France had already begun.

For the Navy much was learned in the Norwegian campaign about the uses of air power. The Fleet Air Arm, with its relatively slow all-purpose Skua aircraft, was at a disadvantage compared with what the German air forces could deploy. While a Skua dive-bombing raid on an enemy cruiser in Bergen harbour marked the first time a major warship had been sunk by aircraft, the British plane in its fighter role left much to be desired, with a speed slower than that of a Heinkel bomber in level flight. Naval aviator Donald Gibson has recorded how, as a Fleet Air Arm pilot in the early summer of 1940, he served in 803 Squadron based in HMS *Ark Royal* and took part in the Norwegian campaign. His squadron was equipped with the Blackburn Skua in the fighter-dive-bomber role. 'It was one of the poorest fighter aircraft in history. . . . Most of our targets were protected by (superior) fighters; unless surprise was achieved casualties were certain to be high.' Eight out of fifteen Skuas were lost during an attack on German warships anchored at Trondheim. 'My section followed me in the dive and I believe we got our near miss. . . . On releasing our bomb I went straight on down into the streets. I always say that I left Trondheim by road at about two hundred and fifty miles an hour. I do remember that on the outskirts I saw a horse above us – it was grazing on a bank. . . . We were the last of the survivors to land on [the carrier].'[9]

No branch of Britain's fighting forces in the Second World War had a more nerve-racking, perilous and, at the time, ill-publicized role than that of the Navy's submarines, the lonely nature of their work above and below the sea's surface, the exceptional strain on the crews and the high rate of casualties being largely unappreciated. The individual exploits that were allowed to hit the headlines tended to be overshadowed in the public eye by the more prominent and photogenic achievements of the surface fleet.

Furthermore, as submarine captain William King observed early in the war:

> We have got used in submarines to going to sea to fight with old ships, old-fashioned guns, twenty-year-old torpedoes that fail to explode and the lack of an air tube which might often save us rising to a certain death when batteries had to be recharged – fiascos in material we regard as the hall-mark of a Treasury which feared spending a million pounds to save ten million.[10]

Some of the surface ships serving in the Norwegian campaign were not well equipped for their job either, though, in the prevailing mood, the crews made light of their difficulties.

In HM destroyer *Westcott*, our venerable asdic [sonar] submarine detector could offer only gurgles and false echoes. One other model of similar vintage remained in the world and that one, we knew, reposed at the anti-submarine museum in England. At length, as we set off for Norway, exasperated by the failure of the authorities to provide us with an up-to-date version, we made a signal to the museum, copied to all and sundry, requesting an exchange. We suggested that our specimen, having seen service in World War Two, would be of enhanced value to the museum while, we hoped, the one in their tender care would be in better shape than our battered and over-worked piece. Our signal did the trick: an immediate reply assured us that a more modern model, now in store at Plymouth, would be ours next time we passed that way.

In the fjords, U-boats or other lurking German warships were only part of our problem. The chief danger was from dive bombers zooming at a steep angle down the sides of the cliffs. These fast, ferocious aircraft, diving like angry wasps to just above mast-head height, the faces of their pilots clearly visible, sought to drop their bombs down the funnels of their prey: if successful, with devastating effect. Our defensive tactic, if caught under way, was to zigzag boldly at high speed along the fjord or lie doggo, close inshore, in the shadow of a vertical cliff.

Against this enemy, our guns were virtually useless. The slow-firing main armament, designed to bring the Kaiser's navy to its knees, could not be elevated above thirty degrees and it needed a lot of luck to score a lethal hit with one of the portable tripod-mounted Lewis machine guns. Besides these types of gun, the ship sported only a single-barrelled two-pounder pom-pom mounted on a platform amidships, another much-loved relic in pre-mourning for its old friend, our soon-to-be-buried sonar. From long experience, we knew that our pom-pom could manage only four or five continuous rounds before choking itself into a lengthy silence. To provide encouragement and employment, its crew had been supplied with a drum, a set of drum sticks and a hand-held signalling lamp covered in flame-coloured paper, these to be thumped and flashed respectively and in unison, partly to cheer us all up but also, we hoped, to mislead the enemy into thinking that the moribund pom-pom was alive and kicking. Despite this deterrent, a near-miss soon awarded our first, fortunately modest battle scar: holes in the funnels and the sides of the bridge. . . .

At Scapa, having taken part in the evacuation of British troops from Andalsnes, we hoped for some respite but, topped up with fuel, stores and ammunition, we returned at once to Norway. Our mail, four or five days out of date, showed no awareness of what we had just been up to in and around Andalsnes, and it was not until a week or so later that we learned how news of our exploits had percolated through to some members of the public, courtesy of Lord Haw Haw. The bulletins on German radio by this renegade broadcaster had an awesome reputation for accuracy, even when it came to local news and gossip from England: if the clock on your town hall had stopped, he might well be the first to tell you. On the day after the operation, in a spiel about how our ships had been foiled in their attempt to rescue our defeated army from Andalsnes, he described how German bombers had driven off a British naval force after inflicting damage and casualties and, in particular, that the destroyer *Westcott* had been set on fire and sunk. It must have been awful for any relatives who may have picked up the German broadcast, as it was two days before the BBC was able to announce that all our ships had returned safely. But the *good* news from Haw Haw: one German bomber, returning to base, had been shot down in the fjord by naval AA gunfire. One up to the old pom-pom, after all, or so we liked to think.

Later, while an Anglo-French army prepared its assault on Narvik, *Westcott*'s job was to patrol Rombaksfjord, a short narrow stretch of water separating the combatants. On the Narvik side of this fjord, along a shelf, hugging the cliff, ran the slowly ascending railway into Sweden.

At intervals, cutting the corners, there were short tunnels; and in some of these, mounted on railway trucks, there were pieces of German artillery. Before advancing, the allied military wanted these guns flushed out and, if possible, destroyed. *Westcott*'s job was to steam tantalisingly up and down the fjord, hoping to tempt the guns into the open: our own guns, supported by allied artillery, could then blast away at the enemy's weapons. For nearly three days we meandered slowly up and down Rombaksfjord and, with a bare four hours of darkness each night, these were long days. At the outer end of the fjord we could turn freely and escape, but at the inner end, to reverse our course, we had to back and fill, a vulnerable moment. However, the more off-guard and unhurried we seemed the greater the chance of achieving our object. We had ample time to work out and, surreptitiously, practise a plan of action.

At last, we spotted the long muzzle of a gun emerging from the nearest tunnel. The German weapon, with a bore of six or eight inches, trundling out of the tunnel on its man-hauled railway track, had about twenty soldiers in attendance. As we watched, we saw the muzzle swing towards us but, before the enemy could fire, our own four-inch gun spoke. Its first shell struck the tunnel aperture, causing it to collapse in a heap of debris and so block the Germans' retreat. The second shell hit the gun's breech, while the third exploded on the cliff above the gun, causing a minor avalanche of rocks and stones. By this time, we were racing down the fjord towards more open water, all our guns banging away at the enemy positions. According to the military, our fourth or fifth salvo, igniting the enemy's ammunition, blew up the whole kaboosh: gun, truck, tunnel: the lot. Even our pom-pom, in good form once more, had been having a go. Most satisfactory.[11]

The Royal Navy ships assembled at various stages for the Norwegian campaign included two battleships, a battlecruiser, three aircraft carriers, a depot/headquarters ship, troop transports and a number of cruisers and destroyers and submarines; the prototype, unwittingly, of the kind of balanced, multi-purpose task force that was to become a key feature of naval operations later in the war. Besides its versatility at sea this force provided both an amphibious capability, albeit somewhat improvised, and in the concluding battle for Narvik close support of an advancing Allied army. Unfortunately the lessons of this campaign, overtaken as it was by the greater and more urgent events in northern France, did not receive the attention they deserved.

Although the morale of Royal Navy personnel, newly bloodied in war, could not have been higher, the Norwegian campaign, in terms of failure to achieve its objectives, was a notable defeat. The losses afloat were considerable – for the British, besides merchant shipping, the aircraft carrier *Glorious*, 3 cruisers, 7 destroyers, 4 submarines, compared with the Germans' 3 cruisers, 10 destroyers and 6 submarines. The Fleet Air Arm losses included the aircraft trapped below decks in *Glorious*, sunk by the gunfire of German heavy ships. If that carrier's aircraft had been flying at that time, instead of lying idle in the ship's hangar, the enemy would have been deterred if not routed, perhaps damaged if not sunk, and a valuable aircraft carrier saved. As it was it needed later battles for the value of naval aircraft to be proven beyond doubt.

But Norway in the long run was not all gain for Germany. In the view of the French historian, François Kersaudy, 'Hitler remained firmly convinced that Winston Churchill would attack him in Norway; as a result, he had the whole country turned into a fortress, defended by . . . half a million men and the greater part of the Germany navy.'[12] And in England, besides ensuring a higher priority for the construction of aircraft carriers and of better planes for the Fleet Air Arm, the debacle led directly to the replacement of Neville Chamberlain by Winston Churchill as prime minister, thereby giving Britain its most potent weapon in its darkening hour.

* * *

By 10 June 1940, having taken Narvik and then abandoned it, the last of a series of withdrawals by the allied forces marked the end of the Norwegian campaign. Meanwhile on 10 May the Germans had begun their offensive to the west of the Maginot Line; on 15 May the Dutch and on 28 May the Belgians had surrendered; and in France, where the invaders were sweeping all before them, on 24 May Boulogne and on 26 May Calais had been evacuated. On 28 May, encircled by the enemy, and, as ever, under fire, the allied armies had begun their famous evacuation from Dunkirk. Codenamed Dynamo, by 4 June a largely ad hoc armada of 848 warships, civilian vessels, harbour craft and yachts had lifted nearly 340,000 mainly British soldiers to England.

Evacuations from France continued to the end, a further 190,000 troops being saved, with a final retreat from the ports of north-west France around 17 June; and on 22 June the German-French armistice was signed. With Italy now also in the war, Britain, with the support of contingents from around the Empire, home to the exiled governments of occupied countries, its resources stretched right across the world, now stood alone. On 2 July Hitler, flushed with victories beyond his dreams, jumping at the opportunity, ordered preparations to be made for the last thrust – a German assault on England.

By the end of that summer a handful of Britain's mostly older and more expendable destroyers, having borne the brunt of the evacuations from northern Europe, had become the world's leading if somewhat weary and battle-stained experts in snatching exhausted soldiers from the jaws of a victorious enemy and, braving bombs, shells and torpedoes, as well as the elements, bringing them over the water to safer haven. In the Dunkirk operation alone, of the 41 destroyers engaged, 6 were sunk and 19 seriously damaged and, at one stage, only 9 remained operational. On 3 June a plea was made to the Admiralty for fresh replacement forces in case the evacuation had to be prolonged. Admiral Ramsay, the officer in command of Dynamo, referred to 'nine days of operations of a nature unprecedented in naval warfare' in which officers and men 'had faced heavy loss and responded to every call made to them', insisting firmly that if further demands were to be made on them, these might well prove 'beyond the limit of human endurance'.

Enough said here, millions of words having already been published about this historic operation, but a tail piece by Sam Lombard-Hobson, second-in-command of the participating destroyer *Whitshed*, demonstrates well the spirit of that era. Towards the end of their ordeal 'the physical and emotional strain felt by everyone . . . over the past week became apparent. Men drifted aimlessly about on deck, as though in a dream; and none of us wanted to eat. . . . All we wanted to do was to lie down and sleep.' At Dover one evening:

> I was to make the mistake of allowing a relaxation in discipline. It was the custom for officers to wear mess kit at dinner whenever the ship was in harbour. Against my better judgement I told the officers not to bother to change, because we were all tired and wanted to turn in early. At nine o'clock, the duty petty officer reported to me for night rounds. As I was signing the book on completion, I noticed him eyeing me. Very respectfully he whispered in my ear, 'What's come over the officers tonight, Sir?' I knew exactly what he meant – we had not changed for dinner. The news would be round the ship in a flash that the officers could not take it.

Shortly afterwards, unexpectedly, a message was received from the admirals – '*Whitshed* proceed with all despatch to Dunkirk,' the explanation being that the destroyer detailed to bring off the rear-guard party had had an accident and *Whitshed* was to take its place.

> In a very short while I was able to report the ship ready for sea. I noticed that the Captain had put on a clean shirt and bow tie – the old devil! He was not going to let the ship's company think that he was tired. Not to be out-done by this bit of oneupmanship, I too donned a bow tie and stiff collar. Captain and second-in-command thus set off to war, dressed as for dinner; and, for good measure, as soon as we had passed the breakwater, I told the wardroom wine steward to take up a bandmaster's (extra large) glass of port to the Captain on the bridge. The humour occasioned by this charade was not lost on the bridge staff. Word quickly went round the ship that the officers were on the ball; there was nothing to be feared.
>
> At the approaches to Dunkirk we were met by a launch, with the rear-guard party of two or three senior army officers and staff who had been directing the closing operations, and a demolition squad of sappers. In less than five minutes we were racing back to England. The officer in charge of the party asked if he might be allowed on the bridge, to thank the Captain. Imagine his delight on being welcomed, not by a weary old destroyer skipper in oilskins and tin hat, but by someone in evening dress. Nothing, he said, could have been staged more perfectly, to assure them that they were now safe, and that all was well back home.

At Dover, in the early hours of the morning, the admiral was waiting on the jetty to receive the returning destroyer. The final rescue effort had taken less than five hours to complete. That forenoon, technical officers from the admiral's staff inspected the ship. They declared that *Whitshed* was unfit for sea, and must go into dock. Later that summer, after further action, the ship became too badly damaged to be repaired and was paid off. Of *Whitshed*'s original wartime company, 42.3 per cent had been killed or seriously wounded.[13]

* * *

The last of the great evacuations by Royal Navy ships of British troops in retreat in Europe was from Greece and Crete in 1941. In a forlorn attempt to stem the southward tide of the Axis armies, soldiers who could ill be spared from the north African campaign had been shipped hastily into these territories only to be ordered back to Egypt in the face of superior forces. The ultimate survivors, lifted out of Crete in May, suffered a savage onslaught under skies dominated by waves of German Stuka dive-bombers. The naval losses in this evacuation were grievous; including ships that had to leave the station for major repairs – they comprised 2 battleships, an aircraft carrier, 5 cruisers and 8 destroyers. When, in later operations, 3 battleships, an aircraft carrier and several cruisers were sunk or severely damaged by enemy action, the Mediterranean Fleet based on Alexandria could boast no major warships more powerful than the handful of surviving, sorely tried cruisers.

Among the ships sunk off Crete by air attack was the destroyer *Kelly*, an event described in a private letter to his sister by its Captain, Louis Mountbatten:

> That evening on 22nd May I was ordered to proceed into Canea Bay to bombard Maleme airstrip which the Germans had just captured. Having lost the *Jersey*, I only had three ships of my own division instead of four, and they were the *Kelly*, *Kashmir*, and *Kipling*. As we entered Canea Bay a large caique was sighted loaded with German troops steering towards Crete. We opened fire and sank her very quickly, the wretched Germans jumping into the water in full marching order. After having completed our bombardment we withdrew at high speed and came across another caique carrying ammunition. Shortly after we started firing at her she blew up in a very spectacular way. Dawn broke as we rounded the North-Eastern Cape and we steamed at thirty knots down the Kithera Channel.
>
> It was a lovely Mediterranean day. Just about 8 am we suddenly saw twenty-four ominous black objects. Their distinctive shape soon revealed them as the dreaded Stukas, the Ju. 87s. They had a reputation for diving almost vertically on ships and only releasing their bombs when they were so low that they couldn't miss. They were hard to distinguish against the rising sun. The first party made for the *Kashmir* and they started diving in waves of three. I could see the bombs dropping round her and all her guns were firing. Then a wave of three peeled off from our lot and started to dive. I put the telegraphs at 'full ahead'. I gave the order 'hard-a'starboard' to bring the ship under the dive-bomber to force it to dive ever steeper in the hopes they would finally be pushed beyond the vertical and lose control. This happened and the bomber hit the sea close by sending up an enormous splash. The next dive-bomber was also forced to dive steeper and steeper and this one we actually shot down into the sea. But now to my horror I saw that the third or fourth wave had hit the *Kashmir* somewhere amidships and she was finished.
>
> I think it was about the fourth wave of the three where one of the Stukas suddenly came lower than the others and although I had the wheel over to 'hard-a-starboard', and we were turning at over thirty knots under full helm the bomb was released so close to the ship that it couldn't miss. It hit square on 'X' gun-deck and killed the crew of the twin 4.7-inch gun mounting. The next wave of Stukas had started their dive towards us and I remember shouting out, 'Keep all guns firing', an unnecessary order, for all guns continued to fire until the guns crews were actually washed away from their guns. I realised the bomb must have torn a gaping hole down near 'X' magazine, as we had lost our stability and were rolling right over. I suddenly saw the water rise on our port side in a raging torrent of over thirty knots and thinking, 'Whatever happens I must stay with the ship as long as I can. I must be the last to leave her alive.' With my arms I clung round the gyro compass pedestal. And then the sea came in a roaring maelstrom. I

saw officers and men struggling to get out of the bridge and then I took an enormously deep breath as the water closed over my head. Somehow I managed to flounder and work my way across the upside-down bridge until I got to the bullet-proof bridge screens. Here I had to pull myself under them and up to this moment it was horribly dark. A faint glimmer of daylight appeared on the other side of the bridge screens. I suddenly felt my lungs were going to burst. With my right hand I gripped my mouth in a vice-like grip and with my left hand I held my nostrils shut. I had to kick hard to fight my way to the surface. Slowly, infinitely slowly, the water got brighter and lighter and then suddenly with lungs bursting I broke surface. I looked round. I could only see one Carley raft, which someone must have had time to release before the ship turned over. I saw men all round me in the water and yelled out, 'Everybody swim to the raft.' At that moment, suddenly and unexpectedly, a row of splashes appeared between us and the Carley raft, then with a roar one of the Stukas shot overhead with her machine-guns firing at us. The dive-bombers came again, and again a hail of machine-gun bullets swept by, this time killing some of the men around the raft. As men died or were killed I had them gently taken out of the raft and men recently wounded put in to take their place. . . .

And then the miracle happened. The *Kipling* appeared from below the horizon at full speed coming to our rescue. She had seen the Ju. 87s diving on us and didn't think we would be able to survive. It was a gallant act of the captain, for he was obviously going to draw the attacks on himself now. As soon as I got on board I went up to the bridge. I was still in command of my flotilla and the *Kipling* was under my orders, but naturally I did not interfere with the captain who was a brave, brilliant and very competent man. I thanked him for coming to our rescue and asked him to go over and pick up the survivors of the *Kashmir*. This was a much more difficult job, for she went down far more slowly than the *Kelly* and there were no less than five Carley rafts and they had more survivors than the *Kelly*. The captain remarked, 'I only hope they don't get us before we pick up all the *Kashmir*'s.' I replied that this was my responsibility and told him to go ahead. After two hours, the *Kipling* had on board all *Kelly* survivors, more than half of the *Kashmir*'s survivors and it was becoming more and more difficult to pick up the remainder and avoid being hit by the bombers. After three hours there was only one more raft-load to be picked up and this proved particularly difficult because the attacks were getting worse. I decided we should stay to pick up all we could. I felt it would be better for us all to be sunk together than to leave any of our flotilla mates struggling helplessly in the water without any prospect of being saved. . . .

At last we were able to turn for Alexandria. The damage to the *Kipling* prevented her from doing more than half-speed. As we entered harbour everyone who could still walk crowded out on to the upper decks. There must have been between four and five hundred crowding every inch. All the ships' companies cleared lower deck and gave us a heart-warming cheer as we steamed past.[14]

With Mountbatten's ready assent the *Kelly* saga, including earlier sorties in which the destroyer was badly damaged on one occasion by a mine and on another by a torpedo, formed the basis of Noel Coward's stirring and widely popular film *In Which We Serve*, with Coward in the part of the thinly disguised captain, the story's hero. This conspicuous panegyric did nothing to curb Mountbatten's reputed penchant for self-publicity or to improve his popularity with some of the older admirals when he was promoted over their heads to become chief of combined operations and, later, Supreme Allied Commander, south-east Asia. Some latter-day journalists and historians with little feel for the ways of sailors or for the exigencies of war at sea have gone out of their way to question Mountbatten's judgement and competence as a naval officer. They may have grabbed a few headlines but they will have won few adherents among those who served and shared the dangers with him afloat and who still subscribe keenly to reunions in tribute to his memory.

Whatever may have been his foibles, not the least of these being his fascination with the genealogy of his own widespread and predominantly royal family, and his single-minded ambition, which was to rise on merit to the highest ranks of the Royal Navy, even at the cost of stepping down in status following his postwar position as Viceroy of India, Mountbatten's professionalism and versatility as a naval officer cannot seriously be faulted. He was innovator (in wireless telegraphy), inventor (a station-keeping appliance), reformer (provision of film projectors to ships of the fleet) and fearless sportsman (not least on the polo field); and he readily took his share of all the going duties. If his boyish gusto, a tendency to name-drop, his fast-lane drive and the flamboyant off-duty lifestyle he shared with his wealthy wife did not go down too well with all his shipmates, no one could doubt his good influence or morale and his qualifications for promotion.

As a leader Mountbatten was among those who preferred dash to caution; and without star-turns of this calibre, no fighting force can develop the offensive spirit and the tradition of invincibility and endurance that will raise it above its peers. In the risky business of war only the bold deserve and gain the prizes. It is, of course, one thing to be bold and another to be reckless. In the calm of hindsight it might be said that Mountbatten's decision to retain *Kipling* in the danger area until every one of his flotilla's survivors had been rescued was to gamble unduly with the lives of all those already embarked in the destroyer; and if the gamble had failed, he might well have stood accused of recklessness by public if not by service opinion. But as this determined gesture by a leader, who having himself just escaped injury and drowning by a hair's breadth no doubt felt strongly tempted to set the quickest possible course for Alexandria, paid off, all honour must be due to him, a truly brave, talented and chivalrous sailor.

* * *

Mountbatten's Commander-in-Chief in the Mediterranean at this perilous time was Britain's most outstanding Second World War admiral, A.B. Cunningham. Brisk and confident in manner, energetic and single-minded in action, Cunningham was very much, in modern parlance, a hands-on leader. During his fleet's rout of the Italians at the Battle of Matapan, Cunningham, exercising command from the bridge of his flagship, HM battleship *Warspite*, was in the thick of it. With his ships normally spread out on a variety of operations, and not least when they were storming along the north African coast in support of the army or fighting their way through to Malta with a slow-moving convoy, Cunningham was best able to exercise control from Alexandria where, although he preferred to be afloat and, visibly, on his flagship's quarterdeck than in any combined headquarters ashore, he could confer readily not only with his military and air force counterparts in Egypt, but with London, his bases from Gibraltar through Malta and the Levant to the Red Sea and, if they were free to break radio silence, his subordinate commanders wherever they might be.

Supplied in the main by ships obliged to sail the long way around the Cape and with competing demands from other theatres of war, Cunningham's fleet was invariably short of replenishments and reinforcements. In early 1942, with the Mediterranean Fleet decimated by its losses in the recent campaigns and the German army within striking distance of Egypt, the British sea-land-air position in the Middle East, including its capability to defend the Suez Canal, seemed truly precarious. But with the United States now in the war, and plans afoot for an allied landing at the western end of north Africa, to be co-ordinated with a renewed military assault from the eastern end, supplies to enable the British to pack a new punch were soon on their way.

By now Cunningham had been posted to the new heart of allied strategic planning in Washington where his impressive record of high command in the Mediterranean war and his plain-speaking diplomatic gifts helped to persuade the American naval hierarchy, still smarting under the Pearl Harbor debacle, that, for the time being, priority must be given to the war with Germany rather than Japan. A young, untried American, Dwight Eisenhower, as supreme allied commander, was charged with preparations for an eventual invasion of northern Europe and, meanwhile, of western north Africa. The stage was set for the long series of increasingly massive combined operations, first in north Africa, then in Sicily and southern Italy and finally in Normandy, that, having eliminated Italy, would lead eventually to the total defeat of Hitler's Germany.

For the Americans the allied landings in north Africa were an important test case and their success, and the ensuing mood of confidence, owed much to A.B. Cunningham who, under Eisenhower, was commander-in-chief of all the participating naval forces. As everything depended on efficient and harmonious teamwork at senior command levels, the relationship between Cunningham, the older, battle-hardened British veteran, and Eisenhower, his unbloodied and inexperienced supremo, was clearly critical. From the outset Cunningham made clear both his loyalty to and his readiness to take orders from Eisenhower while the latter did not hesitate to consult the admiral about the evolving plans and, off the record, seek guidance and advice. It says much for Cunningham's pragmatism and adaptability that he was able to turn so successfully to an avuncular role without impairing his chief's authority. A.B. Cunningham who went on to be the Royal Navy's First Sea Lord, was an exceptional leader. Sir Charles Madden, who served with him as executive officer of *Warspite* from 1940, has recorded his view of Cunningham at that time as a man who being ever ready to lead the fleet at sea himself 'with his burning desire to get at the enemy, kept the morale of all the ships at the highest pitch. . . . He was a fierce disciplinarian and was both feared and immensely respected, and brooked no inefficiency in anyone, but privately had a kind heart. . . .;' and he was undoubtedly 'our finest fighting Admiral of the War'.[15]

Meanwhile Cunningham's former Mediterranean command had been hard at it. Besides Matapan the highlights included the brilliant attack by carrier-based aircraft on important units of the Italian fleet in Taranto harbour; the Battle of Sirte in which a powerful Italian squadron in pursuit of a Malta-bound convoy was driven off by a light force of cruisers and destroyers under Admiral Vian; the continuing series of attacks by beleaguered Malta-based units, mainly destroyers and submarines, on Rommel's maritime supply lines, attacks which over time played a crucial part in clearing the way for the British army's westward advance following the Battle of El Alamein in the autumn of 1942; the repeated and usually costly attempts, menaced by enemy aircraft, submarines, mines and, on occasion, the Italian navy, to fight convoys of supplies through to Malta; and *Pedestal*, the mother of all such convoy battles by which, in its eleventh hour, Malta was saved and the first step taken towards regaining command of the southern Mediterranean sea for the Allies.

CHAPTER EIGHT

Turning Points

In June 1942 a secret decision was made by the authorities in Malta that, following the almost total defeat of recent convoys and failing a sufficient delivery of essential supplies by the end of August, the island, rather than have its people suffer slow death by starvation, would have to be surrendered. Inevitably, with so much at stake, the next convoy operation, code named *Pedestal*, would have to be planned as a major battle, a battle that at all costs must be won.

With escorts drawn from as far afield as Scapa and Freetown, the fourteen supply ships, all capable of 15 knots and with enough cargo to keep the islanders going for another four months, were to be covered by 2 battleships, 4 aircraft carriers, 3 cruisers and 19 destroyers, with a close escort of a further 4 cruisers and 11 destroyers. To supplement the 108 fighter aircraft deployed by the carriers (of which 38 were to be flown forward to join the Maltese defence forces), Malta was to provide in support nearly 200, mostly fighter, aircraft, while long-range bombers from Middle East bases would harry enemy airfields threatening the convoy; and from Alexandria, by way of feint, a sizeable mock convoy would sail part-way to Malta and, having made its point, turn round and go back to Egypt.

A vital component of the *Pedestal* convoy was the American-built but British-manned tanker *Ohio*. All but two of the other supply ships and all the escorts were British. Before dawn on 11 August this great armada stole quietly through the Straits of Gibraltar into the Mediterranean; and within hours it was under attack from enemy submarines and aircraft, one of the carriers being sunk. The next day further air attacks claimed their first supply ship. A laconic log of the next twenty-five hours, kept by Roger Hill, in command of the destroyer *Ledbury*, summarized the growing damage but gave no hint of the bedlam, carnage and casualties now being suffered by the harassed and hard-pressed but determined royal and merchant navy sailors:

12 August	1835	Carrier damaged by air attack
	2000	Cruiser sunk. Another cruiser and *Ohio* damaged by U-boat attack.
	2030	Two supply ships sunk and one damaged by air attack
	2110	Cruiser damaged by U-boat attack
13 August	0800–1125	Supply ship sunk, *Ohio* further damaged in air attacks
	1320–1515	Cruiser and 4 supply ships sunk, 1 supply ship damaged in E-boat attacks
	1900	Supply ship sunk by air attack

The fight for *Ohio*, which had become *Pedestal*'s symbol of success or failure, was far from settled. All that night, its back breaking, its engines and steering gear out of order, the tanker defied repeated attempts to be taken in tow by the escorting warships. At last, early on 14 August, now only 50 miles from Malta and under a constant fighter umbrella, *Ohio* was being moved slowly ahead. Even so:

> enemy dive bombing attacks continued to inflict damage on the stricken tanker whose decks were almost awash. At 16.00 hours, Valletta was in sight; then at 19.00 hours, as *Ohio* turned a corner off the Maltese coast to enter the narrow channel between the minefields, her tow parted. . . . It seemed only a matter of time before *Ohio* would strike a mine within hailing distance of her destination. As though she had not suffered enough, U-boats and E-boats continued to harry her. . . . The crippled tanker wallowed helplessly in the calm waters off Malta right through that desperate night, but at dawn on 15 August towing was resumed; and at 08.00 hours *Ohio* entered Grand Harbour to a resounding chorus of cheers from the assembled crowds. Malta was saved.

On the bridge of *Ledbury*, which had stuck with *Ohio*, at times lashed to the helpless tanker, during the final stages of its ordeal, Roger Hill was greatly moved:

> The great ramparts and battlements of Malta were lined and black with people. Thousands and thousands of cheering people – on the ramparts, on the foreshore, on the rooftops, the roads, paths and at every window. Everywhere bands were playing; bands of all the services and Maltese bands. The uneven thumps of the drums and crash of cymbals were echoed back from the great walls.
>
> The sense of achievement; the relief of having brought her there after so much striving; to have no casualties amongst my own people – these were some of the emotions sweeping over me. Standing on the bridge, berthing the ship in French creek, with the *Ohio* being pushed to the wharf to discharge her oil, was the most wonderful moment of my life. . . .

The day after reaching Malta, Hill was bidden to lunch with the governor, Lord Gort, who made clear that, if the convoy had not arrived, Malta was going to surrender in sixteen days' time. 'We had a vegetable omelette and the Governor rode off on a bicycle. Austere days. . . .'[1]

The battle had been won, albeit at some cost, five supply ships including *Ohio* having got through. In November, as Montgomery's victorious armies advanced westward from El Alamein and Axis airfields were overrun, enemy air power above the convoy routes diminished; and in that month a large convoy from Alexandria reached Valletta safely.

The arrival of that plentiful convoy, marking the end of Malta's long and devastating siege, brought forth another rapturous welcome. William King on submarine duty in Malta at that time has recorded: 'There could have been no more moving moment in the whole war. Bands were playing and tears poured down the cheeks of stalwart naval officers. The unbelieving eyes of the Maltese started from their sockets. They shouted and waved and danced. Merchant ships, and later cruisers and destroyers, arrived intact. Not one had been attacked on the run from Alexandria, and they were laden with food, guns, ammunition, torpedoes.'

It was many months since any convoy had reached the island unscathed and those ships which did fight their way through 'had arrived bombed and blackened with funnels and masts shot off'. Until then, it had been a case of 'incessant bombing, with submarines being repaired by half-starved Maltese workmen in inadequate shelters hand-scooped out of rock around the harbour. It was amazing that any base could function at all, much less continue delivering blows at the enemy.'

Although Malta was relieved, the war beyond its shores continued unabated. With the Allied armies advancing across north Africa, 'our submarines, manned by exhausted commanding officers, some nearly at the end of their nervous endurance, went out to sink the inevitable convoys of reinforcements to Tunisia. While an immense curtain of aircraft shadowed and chased them, they blew holes in the enemy's sea-line. But many were hunted to death, depth-bombed and crushed, deep under the water.'[2]

Among the British fighting men caught up with Malta's fortunes at this time, Hill and King were far from alone in their emotions. Sidney Hutchison a young paymaster officer in *Furious*, the aircraft carrier with *Pedestal* charged with the duty of delivering fighter aircraft to Malta, recalls that '*Pedestal* was an emotional experience. We were all aware that the failure of our convoy would entail Malta's surrender to the enemy for lack of fuel and food. We got close enough to the island to fly off our 38 fighters, and when our captain broadcast their safe arrival, there was a spontaneous outburst of cheering throughout the ship. Some of the aircraft we supplied were airborne in defence of Malta within minutes of landing. *Furious* returned safely to Gibraltar and, soon afterwards, delivered another load of Spitfires.'[3]

Other convoy successes in other theatres of war no doubt stirred similar emotions, the British sailor in an inspiring moment of hard-fought endeavour being a good deal less prosaically downbeat than legend might have us believe. Of all such moments the most moving in this author's view was the occasion in mid-Atlantic when a large, slow-moving, homeward bound convoy was overtaken by the battleship *Prince of Wales* conveying Churchill back to Britain following his historic meeting with Roosevelt off Newfoundland in August 1941. When they spotted the battleship and read its flag signal 'Good luck – Churchill',

> those seventy-two ships went mad. It was a great moment for everyone both in the convoy and the *Prince of Wales,* but for none more than for the Prime Minister. Quickly every ship was flying the 'V' flag; some tried a dot-dot-dot-dash salute on their sirens. In the nearest ships men could be seen waving, laughing and – we guessed though could not hear – cheering. On the bridge the Prime Minister was waving back to them, as was every man on our own decks, cheering with them, two fingers of his right hand making the famous V-sign.[4]

* * *

When Roger Hill had addressed his ship's company at the outset of *Pedestal*, he 'finished by saying: "You all know what happened on PQ17; as long as there is a merchant ship afloat we shall stay with it." There was gruff approval and grins all round. I felt a warm response and that we were spoiling for a fight together.'

Hill was recalling the famous occasion earlier that summer when a large Russia-bound convoy, code-named PQ17, was thrown to the wolves by a radioed order from the Admiralty, the leadership of which found itself worried about a possible threat from superior Norway-based naval forces. In the Arctic at this time of the year, with almost no cover of darkness, there could be little respite from attack; and to scatter or disperse a convoy in dangerous seas instead of concentrating it and tying it closely to its defence was contrary to the established principles and practice of convoy protection. In the event, this order created a situation in which the helpless merchantmen could be picked off one by one by U-boats and aircraft as well as by surface ships. With no convoy left to protect, it seemed sensible at the time for Admiral Hamilton, in command of the covering force, to add the close escorts to his strength before getting into position to do battle with the German marauders.

There has been much hindsight and prejudice over the years about the role of the escorting warships that day, including accusations that they withdrew from the scene to save their own skins. If the observations and feelings of the men on the spot are to count for anything, however, they could not be more eloquently expressed than in a report from Roger Hill whose ship, *Ledbury*, was one of the close-escort destroyers. According to his account, having largely survived several days of threats or attacks from enemy aircraft and submarines, PQ17 was well on its way to Russia when, in a quiet moment on 4 July, three signals arrived in close succession from the

Admiralty. The first timed 2111 read: 'Cruiser Force withdraw to westward at high speed.' This was followed by another timed 2123: 'Owing to threat from surface forces convoy is to disperse and proceed to Russian ports.' And hard on the heels came the 'Secret: Most Immediate' signal timed 2136 that set in motion the whole tragedy: 'My 2123. Convoy is to scatter.' The cumulative effect of these signals was decisive.

> We never doubted that the *Tirpitz*, *Hipper* and some large destroyers were just below the horizon (to westward), and about to open fire on the convoy. When Number One came on the bridge I told him when these destroyers which carried torpedoes went into attack we would go with them to make another target and give fire support. We would turn as if firing torpedoes.
>
> The four cruisers came streaking across the bows of the convoy. As we steamed through the convoy to join them the crews of the merchant ships cheered us and we waved back. We were steaming at twenty-five knots, heading West. Although no one had given an enemy position, we never doubted initially that we were going to attack a bigger force to save the convoy, but eventually, hours later, we realised that no surface action was going to take place after all and that we were leaving the convoy, scattered and defenceless, to be slaughtered by the U-boats and aircraft. As I later wrote in my official report: 'It was now realised we were abandoning the convoy and running away and the whole ship's company was cast into bitter despondency.'
>
> The most terrible and harrowing signals started coming through on the Merchant Navy wavelength. 'Am being bombed by large number of planes.' 'On fire in the ice.' 'Abandoning ship,' and 'Six U-boats approaching on the surface.' I discussed with the Pilot whether we should turn round and go back to look for the survivors. . . . But our orders were clear, we were miles away by then, and almost out of fuel. So, bitter, bewildered, tired, and utterly miserable, we stayed with the Admiral and the cruisers.
>
> There was no welcome for us at Scapa and everyone appeared put out by our reappearance from the dead. I cleared the lower deck, and, with regard to leaving the convoy, I simply said that I thought the Admiralty had made a complete balzup. They knew the *Tirpitz*, *Hipper* and heavy destroyers were at sea, assumed they were about to fall upon the convoy and had ordered 'Scatter'. The effect of this signal had been universal. There was no doubt in anyone's mind, from Admiral Hamilton downward, but that *Tirpitz* was below the horizon. . . . This catastrophic error of judgement was made personally by the First Sea Lord, the Head of the Navy, Admiral Sir Dudley Pound. As it was, I felt that as the merchant ships faced almost certain destruction we should have gone back and taken the same chance. We would have got some more merchant ships to Archangel, although we would probably have lost the destroyers (for lack of fuel) once the oiler was sunk. Still we would have tried.[5]

By not coming clean promptly about its own blunder the Admiralty allowed the impression to gain ground that, alerted to a possible threat from superior German naval forces, the guardians of the convoy had taken to their heels, abandoning unprotected merchant men to their fate. As such a cowardly action by British warship commanders would have been blatantly at variance with Royal Navy tradition, it is, to say the least, tragic that some naval, including merchant naval, opinion allowed itself to become party to the pointing finger, leaving the unfortunate warship captains to carry the can. For, as Roger Hill makes plain, all the instincts and inclinations of the escorts would have been to drive off any known threat to the convoy and, failing that, to stay and fight.

As we have seen, *Ledbury*, at least, more than redeemed itself the following month in *Pedestal*. At the end of that year a convoy-protection battle would take place off North Cape, illustrating most dramatically the wisdom of concentrating forces when under threat from a markedly more powerful enemy.

* * *

The conditions suffered in winter by the crews of destroyers and other convoy escorts on the Russian run were, to say the least, atrocious. As first lieutenant of HM destroyer *Offa*, William O'Brien had his first experience of an Arctic convoy in 1941. Having rounded North Cape on the return trip from Russia,

> We were hit by winds of hurricane force . . . it was impossible to move along the iron deck from forward to aft. We had fortunately anticipated this and got all the watchkeeping officers into the bridge area before any got isolated aft. We ate, such as it was possible to eat, in the Petty Officers' Mess and slept in the sickbay . . . in pairs, head to tail, in the two sickbay bunks. . . . [Even so] we were better off than the sailors under the forecastle where the weight of water had distorted the deck to allow the sea to pour in, to swill from side to side, into and out of the seat lockers where clothes were stored, while cups, plates and mugs, boots and belongings sluiced to and fro on the deck.[6]

In heavy seas, spray flying into the rigging and upper works froze on impact, adding dangerously to the ship's top hamper; and all guns, depth charges and equipment exposed to the elements had to be moved by hand every half-hour to be kept in working order. With electric power too sparse to provide more than token space heating in the living quarters, ice soon formed overhead and on vertical bulkheads, the slow thaw as the temperature crept upward turning the ice into slush and the air into a dank mist in which clothing and bedding could not be dried. Telegraphist Donald Goodbrand in HM destroyer *Obdurate*:

> The present was in . . . the roll and lurch of the ship, the tall spare figure of Jimmy the One traipsing through mess and work-place as he kept a vigilant eye on our

> material well-being; it was in bulkhead condensation, the knowledge that only an eighth of an inch of steel plating separated one from the wastes of ocean; in the chaos of the messdeck, the damp clothes and rank fug, smashed crockery, vertiginous gash-bucket, queasy figures bumping into swaying hammocks. . . . It was in the ankle-deep morass of slimy rubbish, food-fragments, vomit, damp socks, seaboots and messtraps that swirled from port to starboard . . . a floating mass of garbage. . . . It was in the stinking shambles of the ship's heads, the alarm rattlers signalling action stations, the frantic rush to close up . . . the five senses being locked in the omnipresent need for going on and off watch and touching the cold metal of the stanchions to maintain balance, for burrowing into mounds of Arctic clothing and feeling the deck move underfoot as the ship plunged into the blizzard.[7]

On the morning of 31 December 1942, Colin Watson, a signalman in *Obdurate*, one of the escorts of Russia-bound convoy JW51B, noted how,

> on the upper-deck, with every wave that broke inboard the ship was covered in ice. The wind was bitterly cold with heavy snowstorms. We had been issued with Arctic clothing but it never kept us warm and after a short time on watch we were numb with the cold. Life lines were permanently rigged on deck. Below on the messdecks the deckheads dripped with condensation and the bulkheads were covered with sheet ice. The deck was under two or three inches of water which seeped into our lockers. Our hammocks were kept slung and we slept in our clothes, ready to go back on watch when action stations sounded which was frequent.
>
> *Obdurate*'s station was on the starboard quarter of the convoy, *Obedient* being ahead of us on the port bow and *Onslow* out of sight leading the convoy. I was keeping an eye on *Obedient* for signals when a lookout reported sighting unknown ships. Through my binoculars I saw two large destroyers and a large ship emerging through the mist about two miles astern, looking like ghost-ships in the dim light. Action Stations sounded and the CO ordered me to make a first sighting signal to *Onslow*, which I sent by aldis light: 'Two unknown destroyers, one unknown cruiser, bearing and distance . . .' via *Obedient* as Captain D (in *Onslow*) was out of sight; time of origin 0830. The reply was one word 'Investigate'. The CO altered course towards the unknown ships until we were about a mile distant. I made the recognition signal. There was no reply.
>
> We kept on course when I suddenly saw a ripple of red flashes on the unknown ships. There followed a screaming noise of shells and fountains of sea-water higher than the mast rose alongside *Obdurate* as she received a near miss. We had encountered the German heavy cruiser *Hipper* and three large destroyers. We zig-zagged at full speed back to the convoy under constant heavy fire, but though we had several near misses we did not receive a direct hit.[8]

41.) Frozen-up aboard a cruiser in wintry weather.

42.) Wrens, scrubbing their harbour launch, roughing it in bare feet.

43. & 44.) As a naval aircraft comes to grief over the side of its carrier (above), a cruiser, its guns blazing, goes boldly into action (below).

At this opening stage of what became known as the Battle of the Barents Sea, Captain Sherbrooke in *Onslow* had at once turned northward, towards the enemy, signalling to *Orwell*, *Obedient* and *Obdurate* to join him. The only other escorting destroyer, *Achates*, was stationed to make a smoke screen to mask an emergency turn southward by the convoy.

The four O's now began a series of simulated torpedo attacks towards *Hipper*. While two of them added to the protective smoke screen, the other two advanced to within torpedo-firing range of the enemy and, having turned as though to fire their torpedoes, swiftly exchanged places with the smoke-laying pair. So long as the torpedoes remained unfired, this bold tactic served to persuade a cautious enemy to keep his distance, though not far enough to prevent him firing at the manoeuvring destroyers. Thus, within an hour of starting the engagement, *Onslow*, heavily damaged, with Sherbrooke severely wounded in the face, was forced to withdraw from the action, command of the escorts devolving upon *Obedient*; while *Achates*, crippled by gun fire and with many casualties, although continuing with its task, was in a sinking condition. There were now only three destroyers fit to fight.

Whenever his ship was in action, the second-in-command was fully occupied on a roving, trouble-shooting commission:

> We are enveloped in a snowstorm and enjoy a short breathing space. I walk around the ship. Men below decks, in the magazines, in the boiler rooms and the engine room, fire, repair and supply parties: they all want to know what is happening. Information filters through from the bridge but the broadcasting system is reserved for emergencies. I visit the men in the after magazine. As I go down the steep ladder to their bowel of the ship, the hatch above me is screwed down. This is to reduce the risk of a flash reaching the ammunition were the hatch to be opened from below in a dangerous moment. These imprisoned magazine crews, supplying ammunition up the mechanical hoists to the nearest guns, are the real heroes. Cut off from the outside world, they can only guess from the muffled sounds of battle what is going on. If the ship is hit and sinking and there is no one up top to let them out, they are doomed. After a few minutes' chat I hammer on the hatch and, as it opens, clamber thankfully into the open air.
>
> I go to the galley. The cook is boiling water. In a few minutes soup will be passed around in buckets. We're wondering quietly whether the enemy will be waiting for us at the other end of the snowstorm. If so, will it then be: 'Death or Glory, close the range, attack with torpedoes?' If not how long can we keep it up, this feinting and parrying? The snow clears. We run out through the smoke screen, hurtle in to within three or four miles of the cruiser, guns blazing, harassing him with our shells, then swing round and streak back to the convoy to replenish the curtain of smoke.
>
> The enemy, having turned away in case we've fired torpedoes, still slinks along at a prudent distance. Why do he and his destroyers not make a direct assault? It seems ridiculous that he should hesitate. With a battleship in the offing, so we're

told, a cruiser and half-a-dozen destroyers: what an opportunity! For what are we but a tiny force, cold and weary after more than a week of snow, ice, storms and darkness, hampered by the bulk and slow movement of our convoy? Then, two enemy destroyers detach themselves and speed towards us. They are within striking distance and then they turn away to the westward and make off. We are tempted to give chase. But it could be a trick, to lure us away from the convoy and leave it exposed to the long-delayed attack. We hold back. Our job is with the convoy, between the convoy and the enemy; and as long as any merchant ship remains afloat, there we must stay. Now, the news travels swiftly down the ship that two British cruisers are on their way. Our action has been in progress for over two hours. While they keep radio silence, to avoid detection by the enemy, we can't know where they are. . . .

A broadside of 8" shells descends. The ship is heaving and quaking with the explosions, and the air is screaming with flying metal. I see a flash by the funnel and smoke from the bridge. I hear shouts and men are running. I glance quickly around the after end of the ship. Our guns there are momentarily silent, their control instruments dead. But one telephone is working and word comes, 'the bridge had been hit'. As I move forward to investigate and rally the repair and first aid parties, a hurrying seaman stops me. 'The captain's dead, sir,' he says breathlessly. I hesitate. 'Good luck, sir,' he adds. I feel he is appraising me. If the captain has been killed, I am now in command. My great moment! But I feel no elation, only dread. I am completely in the dark about the battle orders, let alone the present state of play. While some captains make their seconds-in-command privy to the operations orders, mine takes care that no one but he has the full picture. The navigator knows the tactical plan but not what the captains agreed orally at the pre-sailing convoy conference. The doctor, who acts as cypher officer, knows what has passed in code by radio but not what has been received by other means. All this crosses my mind as I go up by the inside route, past the wheel house. Bedlam. It seems that all orders are now by voice pipe or, to the more distant points, by hand signal. With a sweep of his hand, the coxswain shows me how a horizontal spray of splinters swept through the bridge structure: just above the heads of the men in the wheel house, just below the feet of the men on the compass platform. 'Ever so neat,' he says. 'Missed us but spitchered the electrics.' I emerge on to the bridge. And, to my great relief, there he is, in his usual place beside the pelorus, white in the face but all of a piece, calm and cold as ever, quietly passing orders to the wheel house.

He catches my eye and smiles a wintry, thin-lipped smile. 'Bad luck, No. 1,' he says drily.

I turn away. I see a first-aid party removing a wounded man from the damaged gun director. I give a hand. I go to the sickbay where the doctor is cleaning and dressing other wounds. He beckons and, for a while, I act as his assistant. On deck, I see to a temporary replacement for severed guard rails.

> Our guns are quiet as we manoeuvre through the smoke: I order spent cartridges and loose gear to be ditched. Meanwhile, that grim game of hide-and-seek goes on. So, we emerge once again into the arena, and there they are! Our two cruisers have flung themselves upon the Germans on their disengaged side and caught them unawares.[9]

Before it could retaliate, *Hipper* received three hits, one of which put a boiler room out of action, reducing the enemy cruiser's speed. A few minutes later one of the German destroyers, straying across the cruiser *Sheffield*'s path, was shot out of existence at point blank range, while another German destroyer was put to flight by the cruiser *Jamaica*.

Meanwhile, according to historian P.K. Kemp, the convoy had narrowly escaped disaster, the battleship *Lutzow* having made a sudden appearance within 2 miles of the merchant ships, approaching from the unguarded south. 'The danger was extreme, with the whole convoy open to attack at point-blank range. But the *Lutzow* hesitated, and a minute or two later a providential snow squall blotted out the sight of the ships from her menacing guns: nor did she send her destroyers in to attack. By the time it cleared, the gallant *Obedient* and her sisters were there to guard against this new threat, and soon afterwards the *Lutzow* received (from *Hipper*) the German Admiral's signal to withdraw. . . . The convoy, saved by the stubborn defence of its destroyers . . . proceeded on its way,' all the 14 freighters (9 American, 4 British, 1 Panamanian) arriving safely at Murmansk, to deliver among other cargoes 202 tanks, 87 fighters, 33 bombers, over 2,000 military vehicles and 25,000 tons of oil fuel and aviation spirit. And ten days after the event news reached Sherbrooke, half-blind, propped up in bed in Murmansk, that he had been awarded the Victoria Cross.[10]

For the German leaders, however, there would be no medals. When Hitler had heard of the German battle plan, he was exultant. There was every chance he would be able to announce a famous naval victory to his New Year's Day gathering of top-rank cronies. It would be a proud moment.

But as the day wore on without clearcut news, Hitler became increasingly impatient. There had been a radio message from a London source to the effect that a German cruiser and destroyer had been severely damaged in an action off North Cape. A signal from a U-boat watching from the sidelines hinted at a great battle with many ships on fire. Hitler's reluctance to accept that his squadron must keep complete radio silence until safely back inside the fjords was aggravated by the reticent nature of the German admiral's initial report. Two rather long-winded and inconclusive amplifying reports were delayed by a communications failure, and it was evening before the gist of them reached Hitler at his headquarters. Enraged, the Führer at once decreed that all Germany's battleships, battle cruisers and heavy cruisers be put out of commission forthwith. His naval chief, Raeder, hoping that a cooling off period might bring a change of mind, delayed five days before obeying Hitler's summons to a meeting. But the ensuing altercations were such that Raeder resigned his post, to be replaced by the U-boat ace Doenitz. Although diverted resources now provided an overdue fillip to U-boat deployment, this spurt came too late to be decisive.

After an interval, Hitler's ban in part rescinded, some German capital ships reappeared in northern Norway but their threat to our continuing Russian convoys, although at times worrying, lacked conviction. The end of this saga was to be marked by the disablement and eventual destruction of the battleship *Tirpitz* at its Norwegian anchorage by midget submarines and bombers and, when the battle cruiser *Scharnhorst* ventured out to sea in December 1943, by its sinking in what proved to be the final engagement between heavy ships in European waters. U-boat and air attacks would persist but, so far as the menace from surface forces was concerned, it would be all plain sailing on the Arctic run. From that small but glittering acorn, the Battle of the Barents Sea, a mighty tree had grown.

* * *

On Monday 11 January 1943, after a week in Murmansk awaiting a homeward convoy, *Obdurate* embarked seventy wounded survivors, mostly from *Achates*, and set sail at high speed for Britain. Accompanied by another destroyer with a similar cargo of ex-*Onslow* survivors, the two ships sped through miraculously calm seas, unharried by enemy action, to arrive only four days later at Scapa. After a short interval, *Obdurate* continued alone to Newcastle. Here nineteen ratings who had missed the original sailing from Rosyth rejoined the ship, among them Victor Loosemore:

> In December 1942, the fleet destroyer, *Obdurate*, had put into Rosyth for maintenance and the crew were given home leave. As the Supply Petty Officer, I ordered provisions for delivery shortly after expiry of my leave and set off for my home in Bournemouth. On my return journey the train to London was delayed for several hours whilst a bomb on the railway line was dealt with. On reaching London I realised I had missed my connection up north. I reckoned there would still be time to arrive before the stores were delivered, but I took the precaution of reporting to the R.T.O. at Waterloo to have my delay officially recorded. Twelve hours late, I arrived at Rosyth in the evening of the 22nd December and found that *Obdurate*'s berth was empty: owing to changed orders the ship had already sailed. During the next few hours I was joined by about 18 other ratings, most with good reasons for being late.
>
> The next day I was given charge of the party and we took passage to Seidisfjord in Iceland to join our ship, but found that *Obdurate* had already sailed to join the convoy to Murmansk. We were put ashore in the bleak fjord in our light travelling clothes in mid-winter on a jetty which housed only a Naval signal office. I learned there was an American Army base near so I made off to see the Officer in charge

> and he kindly gave us a nissen hut with a stove and beds that he had spare, and it was there for nearly two weeks we lived on American Army diet. Each morning I reported to the signal office for any instructions or news of the *Obdurate*. It was not until the 11th January that I was told the *Obdurate* had been in action and was returning with wounded men, and we were to be ready to board the ship whilst refuelling. But the *Obdurate* had changed plans and was sailing straight for Scapa Flow. However, it was not long before another destroyer bound for Scapa Flow arrived and we boarded it for the return journey.
>
> Upon entering Scapa Flow we passed the *Obdurate* on her way out, sailing, we learned later, for Newcastle to effect repairs. Another period of explanations followed and eventually I was given travel documents to conduct the party to Newcastle, where we arrived on the 20th January. After 30 days in search of the ship, my record of stores needed a good deal of sorting out.[11]

For a destroyer to sail on a month-long convoy operation through the Arctic nineteen men short of complement and without having reprovisioned since the previous expedition would be considered a serious matter. In *Obdurate* the first of these impediments was alleviated by the accident that sixteen absentees from a cruiser, embarked at the last minute for passage to rejoin their own ship, stayed put all the way to Murmansk and back, their ship having not awaited them in Seidisfjord. This party happened to include a handful of Royal Marines who, having been formed into a crew for X gun, gained the distinction of becoming, possibly, the first Royal Marine gun crew to go into battle in a warship smaller than a cruiser.

The second calamity was less easily overcome. In the last-minute flap of getting *Obdurate* ready for sea ahead of schedule,

> I failed to check the provisions inventory. As Loosemore was an exceptionally reliable man, it did not occur to me that I need concern myself with this detail; and it was not until *Obdurate* had set course for Iceland that I realised that neither Loosemore nor the provisions were with us. When I reported to the captain that, unless I could conjure up a few supplies in Iceland we should be down to emergency rations within a week, he quite understandably blew his top.
>
> After fuelling from the resident tanker in Seidisfjord, the assembled escorts lay at anchor awaiting sailing orders. On this starlit, bitterly cold snow-covered Christmas Eve, I set out with my begging bowl on a round of our sister destroyers in our motor boat. My fellow seconds in command, having greeted me with appropriate derision and exaggerated shrugs of helplessness, and having extorted from me promises of free rounds of gin at our next port of call, parted cheerily with whatever they could spare from their own far from plentiful stocks: a sack of potatoes here, a haunch of mutton or a loin of pork there, some bread, butter, biscuits and vegetables, and a miscellaneous assortment of tinned foods from soup, bully beef and sardines to spam, baked beans and apricots. My return to *Obdurate*

was observed with interest by the sailors, some of whom, on appraising my haul, teasingly rubbed their stomachs and raised their eyes to heaven as though praying to be saved from starvation. In short, and fortunately for me, the best of good humour prevailed, only the captain looking sulkily the other way.[12]

In Murmansk on 4 January, the first full day in harbour since leaving Iceland, a brave if belated attempt was made in *Obdurate* to enjoy a festive Christmas lunch. Some decorations and a few boxes of crackers appeared on the messdecks and, with the help of beer from ward room stocks, a carefully hoarded menu of roast beef with potatoes and cabbage, followed by a plausible if somewhat ersatz home-made Christmas pudding, was much enjoyed by all, the meal being accompanied by an energetic concert on the broadcasting system by members of the ship's company.

There were two sorrows – owing to almost continuous air raids on Murmansk, attracting retaliatory gunfire from all the gathered warships, the lunch was held in two instalments; while one watch ate and drank, turning up the loudspeaker volumes to drown the deadly cacophony, the other watch was at action stations contributing grimly to the mayhem. And the second sorrow – after ten long days and nights of confinement to the ship's bridge, of strain, danger, snatched naps and cramped discomfort, the captain, Claude Sclater, having excused himself, stayed in his bunk, in deepest sleep, the whole day through.

* * *

Sclater was a martinet. Within the first few weeks of commissioning *Obdurate* in September 1942, he had notched up three seconds-in-command in a row.[13] Their faults were usually that their attitude to discipline was too lenient, that to him and his views they were not subservient enough. Like Queeg of the Caine Mutiny, Sclater knew the rule book inside out – in harbour off duty he was constantly dipping into the Navy's bible, *Kings Regulations and Admiralty Instructions*. On the bridge in action, however, Sclater was outstanding. Calm, cool, quick-witted, decisive, he was a superb tactician and ship handler under fire. With his closest subordinates, the navigating officer, the coxswain and the yeoman of signals, he worked harmoniously, but everyone else in his ship he took for granted. When he ordered open fire or full speed ahead, he expected his second-in-command and his engineer officer and the 250 highly-trained men over which they held sway to provide the required services promptly and efficiently. While blame when things went wrong was instant, praise when they went right, and encouragement at dark times, was seldom given.

If the captain's magnanimity was in short supply this was due as much to his exceptionally tough war record as to his temperament. As commanding officer of the destroyer *Wild Swan*, from the evacuations of troops from Boulogne in May 1940 under point-blank enemy artillery and mortar barrages through a long series of engagements with U-boats in the north Atlantic to the sinking of his ship following German bomber attacks in the Bay of Biscay in June 1942, Sclater had seldom been out of the firing line.

Telegraphist Donald Goodbrand made this note in *Obdurate* in 1943:

> The skipper was a strange mixture of fiery temper and cynical aloofness. The story of him and his ship is the story of a combination dedicated without rest to engaging the enemy on every possible occasion. . . . He was a disciplinarian of the old school, an unsmiling strategist with his roots deep in the naval tradition.
>
> The way I remember him best, it would be action stations on a freezing rough day in the North Atlantic or somewhere between Iceland and Archangel. An asdic contact has been obtained and along with another destroyer we are detached from the main convoy escort to hunt for possible U-boats. The Skipper crouches over the binnacle, bulbous and duffel-coated, an alert ear cocked for the informative echoes that 'ping' from the asdic apparatus in a corner of the bridge. The two ships exchange signals, manoeuvre, converge on a bearing. Depth-charges! The Skipper looks hopefully astern, beyond the creamy frothing triangle where the screws thresh, seeking the black surfacing hull that he has waited for so long. But there is nothing. The Skipper murmurs something inaudible. Stooping over his compass he is like a rock against the reeling background of storm, welded there, shrewd in the ways of his ship. The wind is icy wild, lashing into the sombre cloud-stippled Arctic sky. . . . He is intent on the business of killing Germans. His purpose is fixed and unalterable. This is his job and nothing will stop him doing it.
>
> I came to respect him because he brought his destroyer safely through every imaginable danger, hardship and vile condition of service afloat. I admired him because he is the type of man who is responsible, to use that well-worn phrase, for winning the war at sea. And looking back to the loneliness in which he commanded, I think he was greater than we realised.[14]

Petty Officer Bob Burns also knew Sclater well:

> As a peacetime member of the RN from November 1932, I was privileged to serve under several naval officers who distinguished themselves in the 1939–45 conflict. These included the destroyer captain CEL Sclater (HMS *Wild Swan*). Like others of his kind, he had certain definable qualities that commanded respect from their Lower Deck members, firstly in confiding to the men how important was their contribution to an efficient and successful destroyer crew. A large proportion of the lower deck were Hostilities Only ratings – often finding life at sea in war time pretty bewildering, they were proud to be classified as one of the team. He was however strict with offenders who did not comply with regulations, but these were rare occasions. Another activity he insisted upon, when conditions allowed, was morning prayers, and amidst daily death and destruction the troops' response was respectful and sincere.

At the present author's request, Bob Burns summed up his view of the qualities to be expected from a destroyer captain in the Second World War:[15]

(a) to exhibit at all times efficiency and fairness, in particular to the younger crew members;
(b) to have faith in his junior officers, many of whom lack experience;
(c) to keep the crew informed of impending actions;
(d) a close liaison with the Chief and Petty Officers, whose contact with members of the Lower Deck is invaluable;
(e) always be approachable to lower deck ratings, and never be afraid to offer praise when applicable.

If Sclater lacked some of the desirable attributes, his performance when it mattered most, on the bridge of his ship in action, was, as we have seen, beyond reproach. But a price had to be paid for the exceptional burden carried by many wartime destroyer captains, and this tended to show itself in lapses of charisma, humour, ebullience and the ability to distribute encouragement – facets of those doughty and colourful qualities of leadership which help to shape a ship's zest and personality and a crew to realize its potential. Roger Hill:

> By October 1943 I had had four years of pretty hectic war. I was tired and feeling the strain. If you are going to be taut and react instantly to every emergency on the bridge of a destroyer, you are going to pay a price. The high speeds at night with everything darkened knocked your nerves. If you started the war with a certain number of points, which represented as much as you could stand personally, these points were used up as you lived on your nerves. When something happened like dodging the bombs, or being under the fire of five enemy destroyers, the points were used up even faster. What happened when your points ran out? The courageous man who felt he was cracking went to the Senior Officer and said so; and I say courageous with reason, for it took more courage to do this than to stick to the job. In the RAF the bomber crews carried out a prescribed number of operational flights and were then rested. In this way a man finished his operational tours of duty without any disgrace. The only rest a destroyer captain received was when his ship was sunk or damaged. He then went to another command or, if the repairs were a few weeks, he got leave. Casualties were high, so the experienced captain usually stayed at sea in command.[16]

Two last words. From Bob Burns: 'Sclater typified the hard worked destroyer captains of WWII. Their loyalty and dedication was never really appreciated, and well-deserved decorations were thin on the ground.' And from Admiral Gueritz in tribute to Admiral Selby, a conspicuous member of the fraternity: 'It is doubtful whether the people of our country have ever recognised the debt we owe to such men, who grew up in the destroyer tradition, bore the brunt of those early war years, confronted the disastrous consequences of our unpreparedness . . . and endured the unutterable weariness of war on military expeditions and endless convoy battles.'[17]

And who were these men? They were the pacesetters of the younger generation of naval officers, they were the picket boat captains of yore, those keen-eyed young midshipmen, ten to twenty years on; and the last of that obsolescent species, the salt-horse professionals.

* * *

In eulogizing the destroyer captain, no disrespect is intended towards those equally heroic and dedicated commanding officers of submarines, corvettes and motor torpedo boats; and not least those valiant pilots and observers of the Fleet Air Arm. As the war went on, these men emerged less from the diminishing pool of former picket boat skippers and more from the ranks of the naval reservists who, taking their cue from the regulars, were soon to become indistinguishable from their mentors in performance and achievement over a given range of functions.

It needed a special kind of courage for a submariner to lie entombed with his crew in silent, slowly suffocating apprehension on the seabed, hoping that the next wave of depth charge attacks from the hunting destroyers would not be the end of them, and by his demeanour bring heart to his shipmates. It required exceptional grit to endure the hardship, discomfort and monotony of life in a corvette as, on the flank of yet another homeward convoy under threat from the U-boats, it pounded and cork screwed and thumped its way through the north Atlantic storms. It was a steely nerve that went with hand-to-hand fighting as the high-speed, flimsily built gun or torpedo boats fought it out in a sudden night-time skirmish with their German counterparts in the shallow North Sea waters. That same blend of dash, optimism, willpower and instant calculation formed the naval aviator as he took off into the howling wind from the bucking flight deck of a carrier on a near-impossible mission. Anyone who comes up smiling from an ordeal like this one deserves the greatest admiration:

> In April 1941, Donald Gibson's squadron was embarked on HMS *Formidable* in the Eastern Mediterranean. It was now equipped with Fulmars, a type 'which could not be described as a fighter although it had a little more speed than the Skua,' better guns, and was a good deck landing aeroplane. During an encounter with Italian bombers, 'things began coming into my cockpit, and my rev counter and other instruments disintegrated and oil covered my windshield. . . . I had been shot right through the right wrist and there was a hole through the fleshy part of my right forearm. I had also been hit in my left thigh and on the inside of the left leg near the groin. There was another hole in the lower part of my Mae West with blood and flesh on it. . . . After some time we sighted the

Fleet. We still had engine power but, being almost out of fuel, I expected it to fail at any moment.' On landing, 'we caught a wire but very fast, the hook was pulled out of the aircraft, we then struck the island (the ship's superstructure), skidded on up the deck and collided with the starboard forward gun turret. . . . We somersaulted upside down straight over the stem and into the sea and were run over by the ship. I heard the noises of the screws as we passed under the ship. . . . I had difficulty in leaving the cockpit and then a very slow ascent.

When I surfaced I looked round for Peter Ashbrook (the observer) but he was, alas, never seen again. HMS *Hereward* came in from the screen and picked me up. . . . My life has ever since been haunted by the fact that my action caused the death of a gallant officer. Lessons are learnt hard in war. . . . It was decided in HMS *Formidable* that I should be put ashore and take the next ship to Alexandria and hospital. . . .' Within a few weeks Gibson, passed fit for full flying duties, was cheerfully back at work with his squadron.[18]

Indispensable and efficacious though they were, these roles were more specialized and less dictated by the fleet's tactical requirements than that of the ubiquitous destroyer, the crew of which had to be exceptionally versatile. A fleet destroyer might be in the Arctic one week, escorting a convoy or the cruisers forming a convoy's covering force, and heading for the Mediterranean the next in support of an Allied landing in north Africa, Sicily or, having traversed the Suez Canal, one of the eastern theatres of war. With types of armament and ammunition that, with luck and good management, could stop any hostile warship, submarine or aircraft in its tracks, a very high speed and an adequate self-sufficiency in fuel, stores and the amenities of life, it could play its part as well on detached service as in fleet operations, and in rescue work as in the bombardment of installations ashore, in ferrying troops as in hunting submarines, in seeking out an adversary as in engaging him. If this called for an exceptional range of skills on the part of the captain and, indeed, of all the officers and men engaged in fighting the ship, it also demanded from the engineering department a high degree of stamina, adaptability and technical proficiency in providing not only the ship's motive power, but its various water supplies and the steam-based, electrical, mechanical and hydraulic services on which all the other functions depended.

While in general the engineering equipment in the smaller warships was appropriate and dependable, this was not always the case in the larger vessels. In the eyes of some experts, the methods of design and construction of British warships, governed over-much by conservatism, caution and parsimony, led sometimes through undesirable compromise to below-par performance.

Roderick Macdonald, on duty as the navigator of HM destroyer *Fortune* in the Indian Ocean in 1942, observed of the Eastern Fleet at that time, that

the old British R-class battleships 'with leaky valves, joints and inefficient evaporators ran short of the fresh water essential for boilers and hydraulics. Their people were tightly rationed for washing, cooking and drinking to half a gallon a day. The destroyers were better off but ran out of potatoes, and sailors loathe yams, the oriental alternative. Cockroaches in squadrons embarked with the victuals. Mail was sporadic and took a long time to arrive. Conditions in the mess decks were hot, humid, crowded and generally deplorable with deadlights (on the portholes) closed.' Referring again to the battleships, 'the disgraceful obsolescence of our ships, due to political scrimping and professional failure to keep pace with modern sea warfare, put at desperate risk the lives of those who manned them.' The day was saved by 'the quality of the Eastern Fleet's officers and men in morale, discipline and training, together with an undiminished belief in eventual victory.'[19]

Later, the British Pacific Fleet, as junior partner to the Americans in the main maritime theatre of war against Japan, was having a hard time as it strove to keep up with the Joneses. Louis Le Bailly, then a lieutenant (E) in HM modern battleship *Duke of York*:

Although chemical treatment of boiler water to prevent internal corrosion of boilers had long been adopted by the British power station industry and was used most satisfactorily in US warships, senior British officers feared side effects which would damage turbines and machinery: and secondly, boiler cleaning at intervals of only 750 hours (instead of with chemical treatment at 2,000-hour intervals) was essential to give crews a rest; and this despite the desperate shortage of operational escorts everywhere and that the boiler cleaners would, in most cases, be the most hard worked part of the ship's company anyway. However an in-service trial in HMS *Victorious* on passage to the Pacific proved conclusively that the trial boilers with chemical treatment were in better condition after 2,000 hours than untreated boilers after 750 hours. As a result, permission was given in Sydney for all British Pacific ships to use chemical treatment in evaporators and boilers.

Then there was our shortage of drinking water and the difficulties of keeping pace with the boiler water consumption due to steam leaks. Our bursts of high speed steaming in the high water temperatures of the Pacific meant that the boilers had to reach maximum forcing rate to produce enough steam for the speeds demanded. The water-contaminated oil fuel from our rickety tankers damaged our furnace brickwork. As soon as we anchored we reverted to four hours' notice for steam on our main engines. This meant we could start to take apart leaky steam pipe joints from which so much precious boiler feed water was lost and so much heat engendered, and substitute the more satisfactory US-type jointing material. Brave men in wet suits repaired fallen brickwork in boiler furnaces that were still hot. This work strained an engineering department already worn by watchkeeping in the appalling heat below. A senior Lieutenant (E) swapped duties with his opposite number, the senior watchkeeper in *Missouri*, and found it difficult to realise that the US ship was steam-driven. The US officer in *King George V*, on the other hand, claimed his time on board the British ship was the nearest thing to hell he had experienced as most of the steam seemed to be outside the pipes.

British boiler, turbine and gearing designs were so behind the US navy's that our miles-per-gallon were far worse. This meant more frequent fuelling at sea and more broken fuelling hoses because we were neither sufficiently skilled nor fitted for this evolution. As we took longer for each fuelling and ammunition replenishment, more high speed steaming was needed to keep up with the Americans. Had we not used the forbidden boiler compound British warships would have had to withdraw for unnecessary boiler cleaning and there would have been little or none of the BPF left mobile. My visits to US ships also persuaded me that USN deck officers were more technically minded than their RN equivalents and the few Engineering Duties Only (EDO) officers they carried were farsighted and sophisticated engineers. But this certainly did not apply to their enlisted men. British ships in the Pacific had achieved miracles of mobility, although far below the Americans, despite out-dated, inefficient ship and machinery design, because of the professional training and leadership of our long-service ratings and officers.[20]

* * *

In some areas of invention and technique the Royal Navy was undeniably in the forefront of developments that transformed the war at sea between 1939 and 1945. Most notable among these was radar by which it became possible to pinpoint ships, surfaced submarines, aircraft and landmarks well beyond the range of the human eye. With Britain ahead of Germany in the middle years of the war in the sophistication and use of this appliance, the Navy gained numerous tactical advantages, not least that of surprise in poor visibility, as an aid to navigation and in the capability to lock a battery of guns on to an otherwise obscure target.

Radar was also a key component in the evolution of the tactics that were to lead to the defeat of the U-boats in the convoy lanes of the north Atlantic. However, at the peak of the campaign, limitations were not so much of know-how as of availability of ships, aircraft and equipment. When, in 1943, in the nick of time, a great new circus got well and truly on the road, the rout of the packs of enemy submarines was rapid and decisive. And a 'circus' of miscellaneous, co-ordinated activity it certainly was: expanded, purpose-trained convoy escorts; improved shipborne and airborne detection and attack equipment; air cover all the way across, the lethal mid-Atlantic gap being at last filled by effective, long-range coastal command and shorter-range carrier-based aeroplanes; and fully rehearsed support groups or re-inforcement 'teams' of warships, the sole purpose of which, acting on up-to-the-minute radioed intelligence, was to hasten to the aid of a convoy threatened or under attack and, having driven off the enemy submarines, hunt them to extinction.

As a user of Britain's extensive and ever-improving intelligence-gathering and code-breaking services, including the now well-known Ultra/Enigma systems, the Navy was quick to blend the incoming information with that garnered through its own channels and turn the mishmash to its advantage. One effect of this was the ability within minutes for a headquarters to convey to a local commander on the high seas details of the composition, movements and likely intentions of a nearby but still over-the-horizon enemy force and, if need be, offer advice or instructions.

Critical though it proved to be, the flow of intelligence was not the only element in new ways of analyzing, sifting, presenting and applying a mass of information, the most picturesque form of which was, of course, the huge wall charts in the operation rooms of the Admiralty and of other headquarters such as that of the Western Approaches command at Liverpool. While some Wrens on ladders kept the displays up to date, others worked in the viewing galleries as members of the staff who, linked by telephone and teleprinter with kindred communication centres, could respond promptly to incoming and initiate outgoing signals involving widely deployed ships and other units, some of these at that very moment in the heat of battle.

By means of a frequently updated series of Fighting Instructions, another wartime innovation, commanding officers afloat were kept informed of the experiences in action of brother captains in other naval theatres. These instructions were made up of a distillation by Admiralty staff of the reports of proceedings as they came to hand together with 'lessons-learned' summaries, descriptions of intended follow-up measures and guidance on possible next-time responses. While the competence of individual commanding officers was thus enhanced, so was a sense of being all of one family in troubled times with an avuncular Admiralty as the watchful and sympathetic unifying force.

Unfortunately these benefits did not always percolate to the middle or lower ranks, some skippers choosing to play the cards so close to their chests that, as we have already observed, even their seconds-in-command were kept at arm's length. Deficient in true leadership qualities, and despite the evident advantages to the Navy of its newly developed prompt and plentiful communications, tight-lipped officers in senior positions, admirals as well as ships' captains, were often still too concerned with bolstering their egos by recourse to some of the less attractive customs of a long-caricatured 'Silent Service'.

* * *

One of the great feats of the Royal Navy in the Second World War was the way it managed its phenomenal diversity and expansion without loss of fighting efficiency, while responding to every call made on it throughout the six long years of conflict. In 1939 serving personnel amounted to 120,000 officers and men; and by 1945 this figure had grown to nearly 900,000, including volunteer and called-up reservists, recalled retired personnel and over 70,000 Wrens. Some 74,000 officers and men of the Navy and 30,300 of the merchant fleet were killed. Nearly 3,000 warships of all sizes and over 5,000 merchant ships were lost.

As the be-all and end-all of this great, far-reaching enterprise, British warships were in action in almost every quarter of the globe. The noble battleship fought gamely to the end of its days, the ungainly aircraft carrier having largely taken its place as the new capital ship; land-based as well as sea-based naval aircraft were becoming a decisive factor in the war at sea; the cruiser, destroyer and submarine were still in recognizable shape and standing but ever more powerful and versatile; while the most marked transformation lay undoubtedly in the Navy's indispensable role in large-scale allied joint-service amphibious warfare. This culminated in Europe in the mammoth Normandy invasion of 1944 and in the Far East in the mobile task force concept that underpinned the relentless trans-Pacific step-by-step onslaught on Japan in 1945.

* * *

In Britain the hubs of the great majority of naval personnel movements were the long-established and much expanded barracks of Portsmouth, Plymouth and Chatham. Into these depots came the output of the training establishments, the survivors of sunk or damaged warships and a variety of other types in transit – men newly recovered from wounds, men found to have defective colour vision, men who had just failed an officer selection board, men awaiting the start of a technical course. Out of them went organized batches of men, recently returned from leave, from complete crews to commission a new battleship in a British yard to individual replacements in warships the world over, their health checked, their kits complete, their personal records updated.

If this sounds orderly, it was not invariably so. There was frequent disruption from air raids, with particularly serious damage and casualties in the Portsmouth barracks; conditions in the overcrowded accommodation were far from congenial; and there were numerous malpractices and oversights under the unsuspecting and sometimes indifferent noses of the authorities. This episode, related by George Melly, may well be among the worst cases, but is unquestionably authentic:

> I arrived at Chatham barracks on a dank July evening. I reported to the Petty Officer on duty. He told me the barracks were full and that I was to sleep on HMS *Argus*, a superannuated aircraft carrier rusting away in the dockyard adjoining the barracks, and which was in use as an overflow base. 'Don't bother to make yourself cushy though,' he advised me with a wolfish smile. 'We'll 'ave you out East before the fuckin' week's out.' I tried to appear enthusiastic at this prospect, picked up my hammock and kitbag, and walked through the dockyard gates in the direction indicated. Twenty breathless and sweaty minutes later I found the *Argus* looming up into the darkening drizzle,

38.) Men under training go on parade in Portsmouth naval barracks while other ratings, with their hammocks and kitbags, await their draft to sea.

39.) As the flagship prepares to sail, a last-minute delivery by a zealous representative of Gieves, the officers' outfitters, for a quaking midshipman does no good at all to the captain's blood pressure.

40.) However long their service afloat, some officers and men never became wholly immune to seasickness.

and staggered up the gangway on to the quarter deck. Formalities completed, I was shown my mess deck, and later, after a revolting supper of what appeared to be camel's entrails, slung my hammock for the first time. Bearing in mind what the Petty Officer had promised, I left my kitbag unpacked. After a few days of digging about in it to find things I needed, I slowly transferred its contents to my locker. I was to remain on HMS *Argus* for over a year.

The *Argus*, as I soon discovered, was a den of skivers, misfits and lunatics, a floating, tethered thieves' kitchen. Our captain, an elderly and scrawny religious maniac risen from the ranks, seldom left his cabin and could be heard, during the night watches, loudly declaiming the more bloodthirsty passages from the Old Testament. Despite his age and length of service, he was still, and understandably, a Lieutenant. The rest of the ship's company were all involved in a conspiracy to remain exactly where they were, tucked snugly away, a cosy and corrupt community dedicated to mutual aid.[21]

The dodgers, known as barrack stanchions, were generally long-serving able seamen, their papers mislaid or in a drafting office pending tray, who had found themselves an inconspicuous and sometimes lucrative billet beyond the range of day-to-day supervision. The kingpins were those crafty few who, lodging and perhaps doing odd jobs daily outside the barracks, reported weekly in uniform to receive their pay before marching smartly out of the gate, around the nearest corner and back to obscurity. Some of those who lived in worked much of most days in some hidden corner, away from prying eyes, on one of several small-time rackets, a favourite being the illicit printing and dating of exact replicas of railway weekend return tickets to London which, on Fridays, in a sham booking office, were sold at a tempting price to several hundred sailors looking for a cheap way to go 'up the smoke'.

One of the coveted sinecures was that of captain of the heads or, in other words, the leader of a gang of lavatory cleaners, a species recompensed for their unattractive work by being allowed to knock off early and excused other duties. A leader of that ilk, having delegated his supervisory duties to a conscientious deputy, gained power and perks by extracting membership fees from sailors anxious to join his gang and demanding the lion's share of any 'lost' property found in his territory, a haul, sometimes, of surprising value.

One such deputy, an entirely above-board man, was Hamish Wilson, his domain comprising the latrines serving the warren of air raid shelters that had been formed beneath the parade ground of the Portsmouth naval barracks. Ordinary seaman Wilson, aged forty, had a balding pate, a smooth slightly affected accent and a rotund figure. He was on record as protesting that, as a fully trained sailor, he had applied several times for a draft to sea. An officer who befriended him in the spring of 1941 was told: 'I'm really quite nimble, sir, but I can only assume they regard me as too fat to fit into a crow's nest, or something . . .'

Asked what he did outside, it transpired that Wilson, after a successful spell as Glyndebourne's stage designer in its early days, had risen to become a leading designer both in the West End and on Broadway; and with stage lighting as a speciality, the phrase 'play lit by Hamish Wilson' in a printed programme and press review was nowadays a feather in the cap of producer and designer alike.

Soon after their first meeting, the officer sent for Wilson.

'I've been to the commodore's office and looked up your record and, if you don't mind, I'm going to apply for your discharge,' said the officer.

'Whatever you say, sir,' replied Wilson politely, but the flash of delight in Wilson's eye had not escaped the officer, who continued: 'You showed good spirit in volunteering for the Navy when we were in a real flap after Dunkirk but with the theatre in full swing once more, I suggest you'd be doing your best job for the war effort back where you belong. Chaps in the front line need good shows to go to when they're on leave. Your work will be helping morale.'

A few weeks later a plump man in civilian clothes, having surrendered his pass to the sentry, walked briskly out of the barracks gate where, after handing his kitbag and gas mask to the chauffeur, he took his seat in a waiting limousine. Hamish Wilson Esq, late ordinary seaman RN, was going home.[22]

CHAPTER NINE

Towards Victory

As the war developed the three months' initial training of most hostilities-only recruits, volunteers as well as conscripts, was spread among four large naval establishments, three of them former Butlin's holiday camps, which between them could find room for several thousand trainees. As a prelude to this experience the new entries, arriving as civilians, had spent a busy few days in one central enlistment depot being sorted out in the light of medical and dental scrutiny, psychological tests and interviews and the individual's aspirations.

A naval atmosphere and sailors' jargon were instilled from the word go, the pace was hot and the off-duty mood, in the best British tradition, sardonically philosophical. Donald Goodbrand, a volunteer entrant into the Navy in the summer of 1941, was ordered to report at HMS *Raleigh*, the initial training camp for seamen near Plymouth, where he was allocated a billet in Drake hut.

> As we rolled through the camp gates derisive chants of 'Abandon hope all ye who enter here' greeted us from three-week-old veterans, with uniform collars scrubbed and bleached to a pale blue to give the impression that their wearers were long-service matloes with oceans of experience behind them. After the first shock, our class of new entries soon settled down under the able tuition of Chief Petty Officer Tozer, a bluff Westcountryman summoned out of retirement for the duration.
>
> We were a motley crew: labourers, clerks, miners, railway workers, public servants, of all ages between 18 and 40, mostly married, mostly glad to have escaped from boring civilian jobs, English, Welsh and Scots with a tough Glasgow contingent, hard drinkers all. Dick Hughes was a merchant seaman from Anglesey, Ted Miller a train fireman from Bury, Jock Meldrum a Highland shepherd, Giddings a Wiltshire farmhand. The class leader was Capstick, a bright athletic Cumbrian. We were kitted out, mauled by the doctor and dentist, inoculated, vaccinated, received pay and identity books and discs, drilled,

lectured and royally fed. Our arms swelled from the jabs and we groaned in unison. It was the first time I had heard Scots and Welsh accents at grass-roots level. The course lasted ten weeks.

Scouse, a barrel-chester Neanderthaler from Liverpool, occupied the lower of a two-tier bed near the door of the hut, in a favourable stance to size up any incomer before anybody else, harangue the billet on his favourite subject, the myths and legends of Lime street and Scotland road, and pursue Michael Redgrave, the actor, who slept almost opposite him, with intimate questions as to the morals of his leading ladies. The rest of us regarded the film star with a mixture of wariness and awe. He left us after four days and reappeared as class-leader in a neighbouring hut. Scouse grumbled a bit, then forgot about him. He would retire to his bunk and immerse himself in the pages of *No Orchids for Miss Blandish*. Repartee flowed fast; there was great tolerance. I remember no violence.

In the mornings we rushed like berserkers to divisions, were inspected by ramrod brass, dismissed to training sessions. We felt a certain pride in becoming ordinary seamen and being part of the naval tradition and we wrote glowing letters home and sallied forth resplendent in seamen's rig to sample the local pubs. This was known as 'catching the liberty boat'. 'Deck', 'bulkhead' and 'heads' took over from floor, wall and ablutions. We drilled, fired rifles and revolvers in the butts, drilled, learned to identify enemy ships by silhouette, spliced rope, drilled, rowed in small boats, absorbed discipline, learned to salute, drilled. . . . Single men were paid 14 shillings a week. I sent home ten shillings and kept the rest, spending most in the Naafi canteen. . . .

By our last week transformation was complete. The rough camaraderie of Drake hut was about to dissolve, but not before we bought CPO Tozer a watch. 'You're not a bad lot!', he said gruffly in valediction. I believe every class that passed through his hands ended up buying him a watch. A sterling character, like most of his kind. Then we passed out on parade, collected our railway-warrants and jammed the corridors of trains going north, east and west to savour the delights of civvy street.

Leave over we returned to RN barracks, Devonport (Plymouth), slinging our hammocks in earnest for the first time. In October I was drafted to a camp at Wembury to learn high angle gunnery. But I was always keen to go to sea as a wireless operator. Before enlisting I had taught myself to receive and transmit morse at speeds up to Service standards, and at the end of December was able without too much difficulty to wangle a W/T course at HMS *Impregnable* at St Budeaux.[1]

* * *

The Royal Marines had long formed a stylish, highly-disciplined corps in its own right, with its own identity and separate quarters, and at the same time were an integral part of the Navy. Before the Second World War most of the seagoing personnel served in ships of cruiser size or above. Traditionally they manned one of the four main gun turrets besides providing guard and sentry services, officers' stewards and the ship's band, the members of the latter performing important gun control functions when their ship went into action. They had also a modest amphibious role, centred usually on a horse-drawn or manhandled field gun of a type that had been much favoured during the Boer War.

On the eve of the war in 1939, Chris Buist, from a Scottish mining family, presented himself at the main Glasgow recruiting office where he was quickly accepted into the Royal Marines. His pay was 14*s.* 0*d.* per week, of which 5*s.* 0*d.* went into a Post Office account, to help fund his fares home for leave. Out of the remaining 9*s.* 0*d.* recruits were required to buy their own cleaning materials for equipment and arms as well as uniform replacements. Under unrelenting, tough sergeant instructors, parade and ceremonial training was carried out in Stonehouse barracks, Plymouth, and the introduction to infantrymen's skills on a wet bleak Dartmoor. The recruits lived in long barrack rooms furnished with iron bedsteads fitted with the traditional army biscuit mattresses but later, at Eastney barracks at Southsea, Portsmouth, they were introduced to the hammocks used by detachments serving afloat in a warship. Here, the recruits also commenced drill on the variety of guns they would be expected to man at sea and on absorption of a doctrine soon to be laid down in their Training Manual: for example, on a bayonet charge, 'the yell is of first importance in the assault . . . and the high-pitched scream of cruel passion will shake anyone'; in action, 'every bullet must kill'; on clearing an enemy-held house, 'Kill, don't capture'; and so on.[2]

At first, after war broke out, basic training and duties afloat changed little but the amphibious role was soon given an important fillip by moves towards the formation of an inter-service Combined Operations cadre under Admiral Louis Mountbatten, the indefatigable Admiral Keyes having played a leading role at the pioneering stage. Out of this framework and in the light of raids on enemy-held territory, such as that on Dieppe in 1942, emerged that famous élite, the Royal Marine Commandos; and besides raids these were now to form a vital part of every major invasion force. These men were trained as spearheads and rearguards, able to operate and endure any coastal terrain in any climate anywhere in the world and were destined to become in war-making terms the corps' principal *raison d'être*. These seagoing 'soldiers', with their special equipment, ranging from landing craft to cliff-scaling aids, were to rank deservedly with the Guards as Britain's leading symbols of military toughness and resourcefulness.[3]

In today's shrunken and less glamorous Navy, alas, the well-known ceremonial role of the marines is but a shadow of its former self. But the sight of a white-helmeted, blue-uniformed Royal Marine guard and band on parade ashore or on a warship's flight deck, with their steady, confident gait and immaculate drill, is still one to lift the spirit and stir the heart, the more so for being a rarer experience. This exceptional gift for showmanship remains a vivid characteristic of the Navy's persona.

* * *

The Second World War provided a major step forward towards the emancipation of women. Among the many jobs in industry, transport and the forces that became open to women were those in their own fast-expanding uniformed branches of the Navy, the army and the air force; of these, the most highly regarded was the Women's Royal Naval Service, alias the Wrens. Here there was much competition among the officers for posts on staffs dealing direct with the needs and movements of operational warships, particularly where the staffs had their being in an active naval base. There was also competition among the ratings for work on or near the water, for example, as a crew member of a harbour pinnace or on shiftwork in a signal station. Such jobs offered the chance not only to work on equal terms alongside the unfair sex but to get as close as possible to the action. The women wanted to excel, but not because they had ambitions beyond the end of the war – each of them was in uniform to release a man for front-line duties and, with the end of hostilities, the jobs would be returned promptly to the men. The era of the predatory feminist had yet to come.

Meanwhile, by matching the men in drill, smartness and professionalism, and by their good-humoured demeanour, the Wrens won and held both the respect and the affection not only of their immediate colleagues but of the Navy as a whole. In off duty hours, certainly, sex would rear its pretty head but the prevailing sentiment was familial – the men generally felt protective of the women as they would of their sisters or their daughters. And the Wrens were no mere adornment. Everyone recognized that they were more than working their passage; and they were working wonders no less for morale than for efficiency.

Among those with jobs close to the water was Stephanie Batstone who, towards the end of 1942, reported at the WRNS recruiting office in Westminster:

> I had been seduced by a leaflet about a Signal School in Lancashire called HMS *Cabbala* and as soon as I saw the photographs of girls signalling with lamps and doing semaphore and hoisting flags up masts I knew that was what I was going to do.
>
> On enquiry about vacancies for visual signallers, the Wren recruiter at Westminster shook her head. 'I'm afraid that category is closed,' she said, 'and I doubt if we shall recruit any more. Can you do shorthand and typing?' 'No,' I replied. 'What a pity,' said the petty officer. 'Well, just fill in the form and where

it says "Category" put cook.' I took the form home and where it said 'Category' I put 'Visual Signaller.' A few months later, after a period for medical tests and kitting up and a wait for vacancies, I duly reported for training: at HMS *Cabbala*.

One day, on hearing laughter the training commander burst into the lecture room, 'What the devil? . . .' The instructor pulled his face straight. 'It's the International Signals Code, sir,' he said. The training commander leant against the blackboard. The instructor gave him a wary look. 'As I said,' he went on, 'the meaning of the first group of flags was "Is there room for me in your berth?"' The Wrens sat in muffled silence, their eyes on their desks. 'The next one was, "Keep close to me in the dark".' After a pause: 'Then I gave you "The buoy you are approaching is not in a proper position".' Someone gave a half suppressed snort. 'Next one, "my bottom was damaged in two places".' There was a roar of laughter. With a despairing look towards the commander, the instructor concluded, through the pandemonium: 'And the buoy to which you are attached is not to be depended on. . . .'[4]

Despite its lighthearted tone, Batstone's memoir is a serious chronicle of endurance by a group of young wartime WRNS ratings keeping twenty-hour watch on their own, in shifts of two at a time, in the Ganavan war signal station a mile outside Oban on a lonely, windswept promontory overlooking the defended waterway between Mull and the Scottish mainland. The chief duty was to challenge every passing vessel by signal lamp and, if dissatisfied with the response, to alert the local naval authority by telephone.

The conditions were spartan. In their early months the Wrens slept in a dilapidated, barely furnished, unheated house, each 'cabin' containing a single iron bed and a double bunk. With no catering on the premises 'the mice were so hungry they used to eat the soap. When we cycled off watch at 2300 in a deluge we used to strip off our clothes on the landing and hang them over the bannister to drip all night into the tiled hall below, and then drag them on again in the morning. When we came off watch at 0800 we had to go to Raasay Lodge [the main mess] for breakfast, then back [to our annexe] for towels and soap, then back to the lodge for a bath, then dress and go back to the annexe and undress and get into bed.'

The signal station at Ganavan had an outside WC and coal hole. Against the back wall stood the stove, and 'when the wind was from the east it smoked from every crack and aperture and we had to sit outside on the balcony, rain and dark notwithstanding.' The rations were of low-grade, snack bar quality. The WRNS officers were seldom seen at Ganavan, while the aloof male executive officer in charge of the base seemed content to exercise an evident taste for misogyny. No male rating would have tolerated the treatment meted out to these young women, nor would their officers have stood for it; and where uniformed men were performing similar tasks at other outposts around Oban, they were housed and fed in relative comfort and conveyed to their places of duty in motorized transport.

Conditions improved when the Ganavan Wrens acquired billets in the main mess but in retrospect, as Stephanie Batstone nostalgically records:

> Ganavan would haunt me. Never again would I be so bored, so busy, so cold, so wet, so hungry, so tired. Never did I feel so trapped in a place with no prospect at all of escape. No later relationships had the same flavour of shared adversity and of passionate pride in the job and the privilege of service with the Royal Navy. Never again would my job give me that satisfaction I had when I held the Aldis in my hand and said to a large ship 'turn to starboard' and it did. But there was always a nagging doubt. All that hardship and privation – did we really help to win the war, or were we just playing at being sailors? Once started, a war is never over in the lifetime of the people who have fought in it. In the looking glass world of war, the ones who die are the winners, and the losers are those who have to go on living without them.

Another Wren who took to the water was Margaret Seeley:

> A young girl joining the WRNS in the early 1940s found it was very similar to life at school, being presided over by schoolmistressy officers and obliged to be back in quarters by 10.30 p.m. During night-time air raids a First Officer WRNS would appear with her greatcoat thrown over her pyjamas and her tin hat perched on top of her curlers to lead her charges down the stairs, like a mother hen with her chicks. However, in the weeks leading up to D-Day, when all roads into Southampton were lined with American army vehicles, off duty Wrens would bicycle out into the country, to be greeted with whistles and cheers from the GIs who threw bars of chocolate at them, the Wrens carefully retrieving the sweets from the road or ditch where they had fallen, a bonus in those days of sweet rationing.
>
> During an important exercise of landing craft in preparation for the big day one Wren was assigned the task of recording the ETA of each landing craft as it came to the Hard to embark tanks, note its time of departure and telephone this information to headquarters. She was promised the same task on D-Day itself, so was dismayed when the time came to have to hand over to a male naval rating, the job now being considered too dangerous for a woman. Then, unless serving as Boats Crew, a Wren could rarely go out to sea. However, we weren't far off when, in June 1944, the allied troops were already embarked and the invasion fleet was berthed all the way down Southampton Water, and the weather deteriorated and D-Day was postponed 24 hours. Any of those men who stood gazing over the rails at the choppy grey water might have spotted a

naval M.L. cruising slowly down towards the Solent, with two young Wrens on board detailed off to try and raise morale by dint of waving cheerfully at the waiting ships. The D-Day secret had been so well guarded that, despite the charged atmosphere, these two girls could only guess at the historic events about to take place, and appreciate that they might be the last females the men could gaze upon before storming the beaches. How the role of women in the Navy has changed after fifty years![5]

* * *

When an officer on board a British warship joining the Mediterranean station during the last year or so of the war wanted to know what form to expect in Malta, the first name to be dropped would more often than not be that of a blue-eyed, auburn-haired Wren, known to everyone as 'Ashcan Annie'. This is her story.

At the end of 1943, after spending every waking moment of my 21 years trying to break the parental house rules, I found myself unexpectedly in battle-scarred Malta, having been taken off a troopship on my way to India. Upon reporting to the King's Harbour Master's Office, at Sheer Bastion, in Dockyard Creek, I learned that the Berthing Officer, had died at his desk: until another lieutenant-commander could be sent out, they urgently needed a spare pair of hands. So there I was, in a team led by the Admiral of the Dockyard, the Captain of the Dockyard, the K.H.M. and their Assistants, all recalled to service after retirement. They were an amusing if aged lot, some of them delighted to be back in uniform, others pining quietly for their Queen Anne houses, their Crown Derby Collections, even their dogs and wives. They were a bit bemused to have a female as part of the set-up but, happily, they soon let me write my own script; and it didn't take too long before they didn't want to change me. So, there I stayed, with enormous pride, for 2½ very busy years.

Part of the Berthing Officer's responsibility was working with the splendid fleet of tugs. Who wouldn't be chuffed that the Senior Pilot, having accepted the situation, encouraged me to accompany him. When battleships, and cruisers, or the equivalent in size, needed to enter Grand Harbour, it was necessary for the Senior Pilot to board and bring them in. This was excitement and fun for me. As we set off in his tug to meet one of them at sea, down came the Mediterranean ladder, up we'd go straight to the bridge, and we'd pilot her into her berth.

What a bird's eye view of harbour life that job gave me. K.H.M's office hummed with activity, as he was responsible for all shipping that came through Grand Harbour into H.M. Dockyard. To my delight virtually every sea going officer found a reason to call at my office, officially or unofficially, and I made many friends. I was known as Tug Boat Annie or Ashcan Annie, and of course as the King's Harbour Mistress.

So this was the ambience for my now liberated self till the end of the war. Malta though battered was a romantic reality. I could only feel warmth and excitement from the ever-changing colours of those splendid old and broken buildings and the lively dghaisas and all that lovely blue sea, and the electric atmosphere of an ever bustling population, as more and more troops and shipping came through. Of course I fell in love and what more poignant parting could we have had. I was taken out of Grand Harbour by the Senior Pilot in his tug, to escort and then follow a certain destroyer on her departure to the U.K. From our respective bridges, we could spend those last moments gazing at each other through binoculars until, at last, his ship became a mere dot on the horizon.[6]

* * *

Not all the enterprising wartime women were in uniform or ventured far from home. There were also those who, being married, remained housebound, anchored by family ties or lack of funds or ignorance of husband's movements, waiting daily for the postman to bring them news. Among those free and determined enough to follow their husbands, wherever they might be, was Barbara Sanderson:

My husband was an observer in the Fleet Air Arm. We'd met in Shanghai in 1930 when he was a midshipman on the China Station. Ten years later, at the time of Dunkirk, we decided to get married. I travelled on the night train to Edinburgh, went to the hairdressers, and was wed by special licence in the Kirk at Donibristle, no music, no flowers. After this, we went south to Ford RN air station in Sussex only to find it bombed, so on to Worthy Down near Winchester, then back to Scotland where we lodged in the policeman's house in Craill, Fife: our host, his wife and five children lived downstairs, and we shared the loo! After that I got a job in Cranleigh as a VAD at a home and machine-knitting shop for disabled soldiers from the 1914 war. I was the youngest in the house by about thirty years. One of my tasks was to look after a man with a glass eye. I had to take it out to wash it, and we got quite hysterical trying to get it back the right way up! My pay was 17/6*d* a week and full board.

In 1942, the FAA observer school was moved to Trinidad on account of the bombing and my husband was appointed there in the Spring. I was left to make my own way as best I could, *if* I could. At first, when I plagued the Ministry of Transport, neither the civil servant nor I could find Trinidad on the map! I very nearly despaired of ever leaving the country, when I received a call saying I could have a berth on a ship going to Pernambuco in Brazil, but after that I was on my own. First, I had to try and get permission to leave the country. I was calling up age and had no children – the requirements for a visa included inoculations and the promise that £25 would await me in Brazil as insurance against becoming a burden on the country. So off I went to the Bank of England, quite awe-inspiring with two gentlemen in red coats and tricornes, and carrying long staves, to escort me to the office where I got a point blank refusal to authorise the transfer of funds. Eventually, it was a friend of my sister who had a brother in a South American bank who arranged the transfer (not that it ever arrived in Pernambuco!).

I took the blacked-out night train to Liverpool, and a taxi to the docks with only a number for guidance – ever so hush-hush. The SS *Benedict* was a small ship (one of the other passengers thought it was the tug taking us out to the liner!). In peace time she would convey about a dozen tourists up the Amazon. There were ten of us, the gun crew taking up the rest of the accommodation: a commander RNR, a Cable & Wireless employee, a young professor, a member of the British Consulate, two Cornish engineers going to the Falklands (they hardly spoke, and together paced endlessly round the deck), two cipher girls bound for Rio, a young girl going to join her Dutch naval husband in Curacao, and me. The men took turns to watch for submarines, perched up in the bow, a turban of towels on their heads, as it was pretty hot. Nothing else to do, no deck games, but unlimited spirits at 5/- a bottle. One very hard-working Welsh steward for all the passengers and officers. Food was pretty awful, weevils creeping out of the cornflakes, a suet pudding when we were crossing the equator. It was an eye-opener to see what a rugged life was endured by merchant seamen, ghastly food, they only saw their families for two weeks in a year, and most had been in open boats for days after their ship was sunk. We took three weeks to cross the Atlantic, in convoy, at 8 knots, the speed of the slowest ship. We were called on deck at 5am one morning to see the lights of Pernambuco (Recife), Brazil being still neutral at the time, and we drank tea laced with whisky. Once ashore we went our separate ways and I was the only one to remain in Pernambuco, staying at the best hotel which was managed by a German! It was thronged with shipwrecked seamen waiting for a passage home. I tried to get on a flight to Trinidad, but they were fully booked by VIPs going to the States.

One night I returned from dining with some English residents to find a message saying I could get a seat in an aircraft leaving in a few hours – my escort of the evening, a Commander RNR, offered to lend me the money for my flight and hotel bill, then attempted to rape me, which I suppose he thought was a fair return! The aircraft was a tiny sea-plane on floats – it was my first flight ever. We came down on countless rivers to refuel, so sharply that I blacked out every time. You'd see the water rushing past the port hole, then a gang plank was thrown ashore. It was so hot after being frozen when we flew high. Our stopover 'lounge' was just a tin hut in the jungle, serving Coke and black coffee. That evening we landed in Belem, which is almost on the equator, and I checked into the hotel. The American who sat next to me in the sea-plane asked me out for a meal. We walked along to a rather rough kind of 'eating-house'. We pushed the swing doors and were greeted by an incredible scene, about 500 Americans, tough-looking characters in vests. I think they were Pioneer Corps building airfields. With one accord they rose to their feet, I don't suppose they'd seen many white women in months. They were a very friendly lot, and asked me if I could give them any news of their sons serving overseas! Next morning I was waiting in the hall wondering about my next move when I saw a coach about to leave for the airport. I managed to get myself and suitcase on board, and then flew by PanAm, mostly US passengers, to Trinidad.

There, we were largely cut off from the outside world by the submarine menace. For over two wonderful years, it was one long party, swimming, tennis, dancing, rum at half a crown a bottle. When I arrived, there were troubles with the so-called Robustmen, blacks who tended to threaten women who were on their own, and our house being rather isolated, my husband insisted I have a gun handy when he was on nights at the air station. At a base lent to the US Navy, they allowed us to use their beach club, where we could dance to their superb band, and they supplied the British Naval families with a weekly ration consisting of half a pound of butter, two pork chops, and a bottle of Scotch! Our elder son, Charles, was born there and he loved the blacks with their huge grins. The actors Ralph Richardson, Robert Douglas, Hedley Briggs were all in the FAA in Trinidad, and put on some excellent shows. . . . Eventually, my 10-month old son and I returned to Glasgow in a small Dutch ship, grossly overcrowded – I had to make up his bottle from supposedly boiled water brought to my cabin in an enamel can, then heat up his food in the remains of the now tepid water. We sailed in convoy, calling at New York. I was determined to go ashore, taking Charles with me, a big child, he weighed a ton. We went to Maceys to get him some winter clothes. The little Jewish shop assistants were enchanted by the fair-haired blue eyed baby. I put him on the counter and they all crowded around. We had a peaceful journey home, the only alert came off the Irish coast, but Charles and I both slept through the alarm.[7]

* * *

At a ceremonial parade in the training establishment HMS *Ganges* the last contingent to march past the visiting admiral was a platoon of about sixty smartly-drilled Wrens. Unknown to the admiral, a somewhat deaf shell-back of the old school, a microphone on the dais had inadvertently been left switched on. The Wren officer's order 'Eyes Right' to her women coinciding with a lull in the band's repertoire, the moment's hush was suddenly broken by, 'That's a rum-looking crew, like a lot of badly lashed-up hammocks, what?', through the loudspeakers right around the barracks. Ignoring the admiral's gaffe, the Wrens, their heads high, continued their march towards the men forming up at the side of the parade ground to await dismissal. Women on parade in fairly thick serge tunics are hardly at their most svelte as their high-swinging arms tend to make a swaying cushion of their bosoms, but in carrying out what was expected of them these Wrens were clearly doing their best to be a credit to their establishment. As the admiral, puce in face, retreated, those who had at first been amused by his sally soon bit their lips; and as far as could be seen in that large gathering, out of regard for their imperturbable female colleagues not a single person laughed.

* * *

Many retired admirals returned cheerfully into active service for the duration usually as the valiant commodores in charge of convoyed merchantmen; as port admirals in the firing line or as senior officers of further flung and often rudimentary bases; and as steadfast servitors in a host of behind-the-scenes offices, including that of chairman of one of the selection boards screening candidates for promotion.

As the war developed the lower decks of warships on active service became the main source of young wartime officers, the captains of such ships and, for that matter, of shore establishments, being free to submit for consideration any rating of promise whose qualifications seemed to satisfy the roughly drawn criteria. Having got back to his barracks and awaiting the next opportunity, the candidate would present himself to the appropriate admiralty selection board.

These boards, survivors of easier-going days, were pure caricature. An elderly admiral presided with gruff benevolence over a gaggle of equally obsolete officers of captain or commander rank. Facing this phalanx of gold-laced veterans sat the aspirant like a grouse on the twelfth of August hoping not to be demolished. From a vantage point behind the butts, an observer could see how the admiral having fired the opening shots, the others would respectfully take their cue and their aim from him. If the admiral went down the path of old-school ties or cricket or dropped high-ranking names, his colleagues would try to follow; and unusual courage would be needed to dispute a presidential verdict.

The star that guided such boards was the young high-flying executive officer of pre-war days, and who better to take his measure than Gieves, the 'by-appointment' outfitters? A mid-1930s edition of their beguiling *How to Become a Naval Officer* warned that the questions to be faced at an interview, having dealt with the candidate's schooling, proficiency at outdoor games and hobbies, might include such stunners as: Which do you consider to be England's best public school? As a prefect, what would you do if someone refused to be beaten? Can

45.) Commander, later Admiral Sir Charles Madden, as second-in-command of A. B. Cunningham's flagship, HMS Warspite, *during the Second World War, enjoys a moment off duty in a cabin that serves also as his office.*

46.) Royal Marines in their living quarters make the best of the cramped conditions.

47. & 48.) Groups on board a destroyer (above) and an aircraft carrier (below) are seen relaxing.

49.) However dire the circumstances, good cheer was the hallmark of life below decks – even when away from home at Christmas, the smiles in this battle-cruiser's petty officers' mess predominates.

you name some famous men educated at your school? Then, having reassured the candidate that 'all your messmates will be white men', the booklet goes on to explain how, as a member of an élite 'with the *entrée* to virtually every club in the world, and by whose behaviour Britain will gain or lose respect in the eyes of the Nations . . ., you will make many lifelong friends. . . .'

A variant from Gieves some thirty years later, *Customs and Etiquette of the Royal Navy*, although no longer concerned with skin colour and public schooling, still hankered after the gentlemanly accoutrements. On smoking and passing the port:

> On board, 'it is perfectly all right to smoke a pipe, provided your brand of tobacco does not offend others. . . . But your monkey jacket will bulge in an unsightly manner if you put pipe and pouch in your pocket, so most officers get over this by carrying their pipe and pouch in their hand when it [*sic*] really must go with them but normally leaving it . . . where it is most used – for instance their cabin. . . . Life is not quite so difficult for the cigarette smoker . . . nor is there any absolute ban on smoking a cigarette in public, although it is certainly

discouraged.' After grace at the end of a mess dinner, 'the President removes the stoppers [of the decanters] and passes the wine [port] to his left. . . . After the Loyal Toast, the President gives permission to smoke and 'invites the Bandmaster to have a glass of Port; this he has in a claret glass . . . on the left of the decanter where the President fills it and then places the glass in front of the Bandmaster [so that] the Port does not have to be passed anti-clockwise.'[8]

To twenty-year-old Frank Kermode in the summer of 1940, it seemed that,

unless the war quickly ended in national disaster [as seemed quite probable], the future consisted of indefinitely prolonged military service. In September, during the first daylight raids on the docks, I was summoned from the North to London, and, trotting naked from booth to booth, was examined by a team of perfunctory doctors and then interviewed by an amiably rough-tongued civilian who asked me if I had the power of command: was I a leader of men? This was a topic new to me, but I assured him I had this power. Taking me at my word, the brisk, over-worked interviewer sent me to Liverpool to be interviewed again, this time by a scholarly paymaster captain, his sleeves encrusted with bands of gold lace separated by bright white stripes, his breast bemedalled.

This captain seemed a rather sympathetic figure and [after collecting his thoughts] he asked me why I wasn't in uniform. 'I have no uniform, sir.' 'Well,' he said, 'that will hardly do. Very little can be done without a uniform. You must get one at once.' I sat still while he continued to ponder. Eventually he walked over to his safe, unlocked it, and took from it what looked like quite a lot of money. This he handed to me, saying, 'Go to Gieves and order yourself two uniforms, one of doeskin and one of serge. The doeskin is for number ones. Better buy a greatcoat also.' He speculated that the tailor was unlikely to be able to execute my order in less than a fortnight. 'So you'll need two weeks' leave,' he said. He unlocked the safe again and gave me more money as an advance of pay. . . . I had never had so much money all at once, and I had no intention of giving most of it to the expensive tailor nominated by the captain. Instead, I went to a meaner establishment in Paradise Street and bought a ready-made uniform. Then I went off to see my girl, and we went to the seaside, where we stayed in a small boarding house. Every night the landlady and, as we supposed, her husband, made clamorous love on an unstable bed. This struck us as the right way to behave in these difficult times.

Returning scrupulously on the due date, I sought out my pale, elegant paymaster captain. He seemed abstracted and hardly knew who I was; perhaps, after all, he had other cares, greater and more martial responsibilities. He asked me if I'd like some leave; but the money was all spent, so I honourably declined the offer, and instead asked if there was any place I could go to in order to learn my job. After some deliberation he told me to go down to the Huskisson Dock,

> find a ship called the *Sierra* and report to a Lieutenant Taylor. 'Tell him I sent you to learn the ropes.' As I was leaving the room he stopped me and examined my uniform. 'Where did you get it?' he asked. 'At Gieves, sir.' 'You did well to go there,' he said.[9]

Of all the anecdotes about idiosyncratic captains of that era, the one most enjoyed by the present author concerns a monitor's captain who, when his ship was sinking, being unable to swim,

> went aft and stood saluting the ensign. The Chief Boatswain's Mate came aft and said to the Captain: 'This isn't the time to be doing a stupid thing like that, Sir. Give me your lifebelt.' The Captain handed it over and continued saluting. The C.B.M. then inflated the life belt, wrapped it round the Captain and threw him over the side. The Captain subsequently presented the Chief with a gold watch.[10]

* * *

In 1943 it became clear to their lordships that the yield of officer candidates through the old-fashioned admiralty selection boards would not be enough to man the growing number of landing craft and escort vessels that were to service the intended invasion of northern France a year or so ahead. Joe Oram, an articulate captain of presence and authority, with an open and original mind, was called upon by the Second Sea Lord to find a way of scraping deeper into the barrel. As director of training and staff duties at the Admiralty, Oram headed a team of captains and commanders dealing with a broad sweep of innovation from design specifications for new warships to tactical doctrine. This new task came under the training part of his title, selection being regarded as inseparably linked.

While continuing to screen mature candidates sent in from ships on active service, the new idea was to earmark potential candidates at a much earlier stage, that is, during the three months of their initial new-entry training. The first question was how to identify and test the latent and hitherto overlooked officer-like qualities in this mass of untried material. The second was to devise more reliable screening methods, the prevailing wastage rate of 33% at the officer training establishment, HMS *King Alfred*, being unacceptably high. Oram later wrote:

> I was sitting pondering this problem in the United Services Club one evening when I happened to pick up *Picture Post* and noticed some photographs of an Army training establishment at Watford which subsequently became known as the War Office Selection Board. I read with growing interest that men with officer-like potential were given a special training and tests there before being

> commissioned. The problem was very similar to the one we were facing at *King Alfred* so I trotted across to the Director of Military Training and asked to go and visit the people at Watford.[11]

While it was at once clear to Oram and his advisors, notably Alec Rodger, the Admiralty's very able senior psychologist, that useful insights were to be gained from Watford, there were to be marked differences in any naval scheme. In the Navy, the selection process was now to begin at the recruitment stage. Intelligence tests and interviews to measure motivation were added to the conventional scrutinies, a minimum standard of officer potential being determined enabling all entrants above this level to be segregated and closely observed during the ensuing training. Their syllabus at this stage was then dovetailed into that of the next stage, a two-month stint afloat in a training cruiser, this syllabus in turn being dovetailed into that of HMS *King Alfred*. There were screenings at each stage, supplemented by organized reports from the training officers, the survivors of the process being ready to receive their first appointments as naval officers within only eight months of enlistment as civilians.

Another difference lay in the Navy's decision to employ industrial (vocational) psychologists, with their feet closer to the work-a-day ground, rather than psychiatrists (the army's choice), as expert advisers and as the conductors of the personality and intelligence tests. But the crux of the new system lay in the composition, procedures and criteria of the new stage-by-stage screening boards. The first such board, observed by Oram and Rodger, was held in the training establishment, HMS *Glendower*, with its captain, J. Figgins, a shrewd and salty product of one of the Navy's earlier attempts at promotion from the lower deck, in the chair.

The candidates were young seamen in their eleventh week of new-entry training. The following reconstruction is by the participating 'testing' officer, whose role soon becomes apparent:

> The first of ten candidates, wearing a numbered arm band, came in. He stood to attention, gave his name and, turning on his heel, left the room. Figgins explained: 'As you see, each lad presents himself purely to be recognized and to let him see what we look like sitting formally as a group. Having already met or performed for each of us individually, the lad knows all of us quite well, and vice versa. We'll now compare notes for the first time.'
>
> In rapid succession, the oral reports followed: from the training officer, who had observed the men over several weeks; the education officer, who had applied his traditional classroom tests; and the psychologist, in the light of his intelligence and aptitude tests and interviews. I came next, interpreting the new-fangled 'leadership' tests to which that day's candidates had been subjected in a three-hour session the previous afternoon, with Figgins and the board

commander watching from the sidelines. The commander, an experienced officer with a conventional mind, having interviewed each man privately for about ten minutes in the evening, followed me; while for the time being Figgins held his peace.

The test case for our new board proved to be candidate number seven, a rather ungainly young man with a pleasant, open face, a ready grin and natural good manners. In my group tests he had remained calm and methodical, emerging as an unflappable if unspectacular leader who, in the end, won all his peers' respect. His background was not apparently that of an officer: he was the son of a docker, an elementary schoolboy, an apprentice carpenter and he came from Hull. It was most unlikely that he would have got to, or through, an old-fashioned selection board.

The training officer, grading him D (on a scale from A to E), reported that, after a slow start, he had gained confidence and, generally, had shaped up well. But he was no high flyer: with the benefit of doubt, he had scraped through with a YES (meaning fit for promotion).

The education officer, awarding an E and a NO, explained that the man's arithmetic might cope with pilotage and chartwork but some of the calculations demanded by ocean navigation would be beyond him; and his knowledge of grammar was unremarkable.

The psychologist then weighed in with a YES, supported by A for intelligence and aptitude and C for personality. His report described 'a man whose personal qualities suggest a latent capacity for leadership with an ability that could probably make amends for a poor education.' Given encouragement, he would rise to the challenge; and to be an officer would, surely, be the making of him.

Then it was my turn. It was not in my remit to comment on intelligence and aptitude but, in other respects, my assessment was virtually an echo of the psychologist's: this was just the kind of officer material the modern Navy needed. B and YES, and for good measure, I had rated him in the first three of his group of 10.

The commander, in rather a flat voice, said he thought the candidate was uninspiring: he had graded him D and NOT YET. He would like to see him again in three months when, with more naval background, he might be more convincing.

Figgins turned to Oram. 'This is obviously our most difficult one. We have two unwritten rules. As you've seen, the most senior officers present speak last, so the others won't be influenced by rank. Then if, at the end of the day, there's not a unanimous YES, the lad goes down: one single NO sinks him for good, one NOT YET sinks him temporarily. Before we go further, would either of you gentlemen care to comment?'

Oram replied without hesitation. 'Based on the kind of evidence we've been hearing today, I would have complete confidence in your board's decisions. The last thing I'd want to do, sitting here, is to try to influence your verdict on number seven.' Rodger nodding his assent, Figgins then addressed the board. 'Each of you has now, for the first time, heard the reports of the others. In the light of these, does anyone wish to revise his earlier opinion?'

The education officer spoke. 'Yes, sir. I stand by my tests, which help to measure the present stage of a man's knowledge, but I'm impressed by the psychologist's high intelligence rating. As intelligence indicates ability to learn, I quite see that in a month or two, with tuition and experience, candidate seven could very likely pass my tests. My letter grade holds good but I'd like to change my overall verdict from NO to YES.'

'A sound decision, schoolie,' said Figgins. 'I was never any good at arithmetic myself. I learned the navigation bits as I went along and when I was stumped there always seemed to be someone around to give me a hand.' He looked at his watch. 'We've taken almost as long over number seven as all the others together. I must say, from what I saw of the lad at yesterday's tests I could well go along with the commander's NOT YET. But let's now deal with the matter with a simple vote. All those voting YES please raise a hand.'

In the silence that followed, Figgins watched every hand but one go slowly up: only the commander's stayed down. The captain looked carefully around the room, his gaze resting finally on the two visitors. But, their eyes downcast, they gave no sign. Figgins opened his mouth and was about to speak when the commander caught his eye and held it and deliberately, without any expression, raised his hand.

Figgins broke the silence. 'Well done, commander,' he said.[12]

By the early spring of 1944 the entire scheme was in full swing, with the screening boards and the new-entry training phase centred in a new establishment, HMS *Excalibur*. The wastage rate at *King Alfred* dropped to 2% and the Navy got the officers it needed for the Normandy invasion, and for the other tasks that would befall it before victory could be won.

More significantly class and the old school tie were eliminated as dominant promotion factors. These revolutionary changes, accepted so readily in the supposedly tradition-bound armed forces in the heat of war, may be regarded as the spearhead of the social revolution that, in the postwar years, was gradually to take root in the nation as a whole. And the Navy's officer selection boards of today are clearly recognizable as the offspring of those dynamic, ground-breaking parents of 1943–44.

* * *

Of all the battles and campaigns in the Second World War in which Britain had a leading role, by far the most crucial and, in economic terms, crippling for that country was the long, drawn-out and agonizing Battle of the Atlantic. As in the First World War, there were periods when it seemed that the shipping losses inflicted by the German U-boats might bring this once-greatest of maritime powers to its knees within weeks. However, for its own sake and as a springboard for the Normandy invasion, Britain was saved by the bravery and exertions of the convoys' defending seamen, mercantile as well as naval, and their supporting airmen. But it took time to create the winning technology and then the necessary weight and variety of equipment by which to gain the upper hand.

Meanwhile, a German victory could well have been on the cards at a much earlier stage had the political power and ambitious bombing strategies of the air force commanders of both countries not absorbed scarce resources. These would otherwise have gone into U-boat production in Germany and into the development of long-range U-boat hunting aircraft and close-protection escort carriers in Britain.

A glimpse of the situation in the Atlantic during the critical 1942–43 period having been given in earlier pages, it may suffice here to conclude with a summing up by Admiral Macdonald in a speech to the Royal Naval Club in 1991:

> War, they say, is generally won by the side that makes the least mistakes. So it was fortunate that we had valuable co-operation from Messrs Hitler, Goering and Grand Admiral Raeder. These three succeeded in buggering up the only individual who could have won it for them, the U-boat C.-in-C., Doenitz. Luftwaffe supremo Goering agreed with his U.K. 'oppos', such as 'bomber' Harris, on the insignificance of sea war.
>
> It is absurd that this campaign should be called a battle. It must have been, to coin a phrase, the 'mother of all battles', since in the history of man no battle has lasted as long or been fought against such odds for the benefit of so many, or indeed by so many. I cannot list all the arms, services and people, whose contribution brought us victory but, Ultra's dominating contribution apart, I offer three Oscars: One, Jolly Jack. Without the tremendous support and heart warming humour of the ships' companies that manned an incredible assortment of old and unsuitable iron in appalling conditions, we would have been utterly lost. Two, The Royal Canadian Navy, which overcame exceptional material and training deficiencies, until, by early 1943, half the escorts between New York and the U.K. were Canadians. By 1944 Canada was carrying the main burden of the mid-Atlantic war.
>
> My final Oscar goes to Admiral Sir Max Horton, C.-in-C. Western Approaches. Doenitz's memoirs claim that Churchill personally selected Horton as his, Doenitz's adversary-in-chief. All the more surprising that the victor was so minimally honoured and his name virtually forgotten. 'The evil that men do lives after them, the good is oft interred with their bones.' To these and so many others, we owe our freedom to say what we like, to refuse to pay our taxes, join

C.N.D., and vote for politicians, who in their wisdom economize on defence and turn a blind eye to the destruction of the merchant navy – something which U-boats failed to do in two world wars. Of the 138 ships chartered for the Gulf War only three were British; and without command of the sea this deployment would have been impossible.[13]

* * *

In relating the exploits of the Royal Navy from 1939 to 1945, three famous occasions now remain to be mentioned – D-day, 6 June 1944 and, in the summer of 1945, VE day and VJ day.

The invasion of Normandy, launched on D-day, and much recalled and celebrated over the years, was a sensational feat of arms and of organization on an unprecedented scale, involving the precisely scheduled movements from several ports towards numerous beach-heads of 7,000 ships and craft, some with off-shore protective roles, supported strongly by air power, most with variegated and carefully phased loads of soldiers, stores, and equipment.

Although the supreme allied commander, Dwight Eisenhower, was American and more American-cum-Canadian troops took part than British, the British had good reason to feel that the whole show, planned in London and mounted in southern England, with its antecedents four years earlier at the retreat from Dunkirk, was very much their affair; and if any service deserved pride of place, this had to be the Navy. The overall naval commander, Ramsay, was the same Briton who had led and managed the rescue from Dunkirk; he had the backing of the redoubtable A.B. Cunningham, in post as First Sea Lord; most of the vast armada of warships now heading the other way was British; and the Navy's battleground, across which the invading troops had to be conveyed, was, after all, the *English* Channel, scene over the centuries of numerous naval endeavours in defence of the homeland. If the soldiers felt in safe hands as they embarked for France, they had good reason – at great risk to its own ships and its own people, the Navy had lifted them off and landed them on many beaches since the spring and summer of 1940. As the soldiers braced themselves for the assault on Normandy and then, no doubt, for hand fighting in the northern French and Low Countries littorals, they knew the Navy would be with them.

There were only two unpredictables – the weather, and, if they discovered the timing and whereabouts of the landings, the German response. The first of these augured ill – on the eve of the great day, after agonizing sessions with his meteorologists, Eisenhower rightly postponed the operation by twenty-four hours. The seas breaking on the beaches in the prevailing north-westerly winds were considered too much for the landing craft. The fact that this huge operation could go ahead a day late said much both for the resilience of the administration and the stoicism of the participants, many of the latter being already part-way across the

Channel exposed to the elements and in acute discomfort when news of the delay reached them.

As for the second hurdle, despite all their anticipatory manoeuvres, the Germans, mercifully, were taken by surprise; that such a long-mooted and extensive enterprise suffered no breach of security was one of the miracles of the occasion.

To have been waiting on station, ready for action, before dawn on that historic day must have been a most moving experience. William O'Brien, who was there, recalls the eerie moment and what followed:

> We arrived at our position about four miles from the coast at about 3am. All quiet except for some bombing [further inland]. At 5am we anchored and waited for all the rest to turn up. A curious feeling – lying at anchor four miles off the enemy coast . . . and watching the dawn break and seeing all the cruisers gliding by to their positions and all the landing craft getting lined up. It didn't seem at all real. By six o'clock we could see the shore quite clearly. . . . Then the noise started as the cruisers opened up at the coastal batteries. . . . As we [with other destroyers] lined up [for the run in], a battery let go in our direction . . . so we let go at him and he kept quiet after that. Then we started in towards the shore – very slowly – firing at the pill-boxes on the beach and chipping chunks off the sea wall to help the soldiers get over it. . . . It all got noisier and noisier as more and more craft got within range. . . . We got to within 3,000 yards of the beach and turned broadside and stopped – letting everything we had go for the last fifteen minutes before the soldiers touched down.[14]

By the time the artificial Mulberry harbour was in place five weeks later, over a million men, a quarter of a million vehicles and a million tons of stores had been put ashore, almost entirely over the beaches. Upon completion of their eastward turning movement around the British-held pivot at Caen, the Allied armies, against strong opposition, could begin their relentless advance across France towards the Rhine. Soon Paris would be taken and, with more power to Eisenhower's elbow following the diversionary landings in the south of France, the northern flank of his armies would be into Belgium, with the great port of Antwerp to add to the string of captured Channel ports. By the spring of 1945, having crossed the Rhine, British and American troops would be battling their way into the heart of Germany where, before long, they would join forces with the Soviet armies invading from the east.

Meanwhile, there had been several setbacks, among them military reverses in the Ardennes and the failure of the British airborne assault on Arnhem. At sea the advent of the snorkel breathing tube, the acoustic torpedo and higher underwater speeds were giving the U-boat a new advantage in its anti-convoy role. But most damaging and alarming was the indiscriminate bombardment of south-east

England, and particularly of London, by the unmanned V1 'doodle-bug' missiles and the V2 bolt-from-the-blue rockets. Until their launching sites could be overrun by the Allied armies, these lethal, science-fiction weapons posed a serious enough threat to British administration for the government to consider quitting London.

But as the end of the war in Europe approached, these hurdles having been surmounted, the British fighting men and, for that matter, the British people, although weary, were in good heart. At last the troops in Germany and their supporting air and naval forces, although still meeting determined resistance, had victory in their sights, while their comrades in other theatres of war, not least the men of the Navy from the Atlantic and the Arctic, through the Mediterranean to the Indian Ocean and the Pacific, could not wait to share their home country's long-awaited and hard-won jubilation.

And so, at last, it arrived – VE day, 8 May 1945, Winston Churchill on his balcony in Whitehall, the King on his at Buckingham Palace, the cheering, singing crowds with arms linked in the bomb-scarred streets and, greatest gift of all, the lights. After almost six years of blackout, of darkened thoroughfares, of curtained or shuttered windows and, at sea, of shadowy, unlit ships and coast lines, the lights were on again.

* * *

While the people at home, although still rationed and regimented, welcomed the first batches of released prisoners of war and demobbed servicemen and, picking up the threads of family life, took steps in the July 1945 general election to oust sacrifice-demanding Churchill, their war-winning saviour, in favour of Attlee's Labour Party, the war against Japan continued unabated. British-led forces in the Indian Ocean and American-led forces in the Pacific Ocean were now on the attack against Japanese-held south-east Asia and the Japanese homeland respectively. Although an invasion of Japan was an early possibility, the common view was that it would need another two years or so of heavy, casualty-strewn combat against a fanatical enemy before victory could finally be won. For recently-joined servicemen this prospect was bad enough but for those who had already served six wartime years it was grim, the more so as the exploits, the homesickness and the aspirations of fighting men would no longer make the headlines in peacetime Britain. It was indeed hard to sail away to war at this time.[15]

Then the miracle happened – the atom bombs, heralds of the balance-of-terror age of warfare, fell out of the sky and, the Japanese having at last reaped the holocaust, their emperor decreed surrender. By now, although dominant in the South East Asia operations and king pins at the Singapore surrender formalities, poignant reminder of the debacle of February 1942, the British were clearly America's junior partner in the all-important Pacific theatre. As the fleets gathered in Tokyo Bay for the grand surrender finale, the British, although allowed a seat at the top table, were being politely sidelined. Admiral Fraser must have wondered how much of the effort, how many of the sacrifices in the common cause, had been worthwhile. What price now the global British Empire, the *pax britannica*? And as for that great instrument of 'Rule Britannia', the Royal Navy. . . ? Louis Le Bailly was there:

> The surrender and succeeding jubilation was rightly American but, as Admiral Fraser appreciated, Britain and the Commonwealth had now been at war for six long years less a day. If the forenoon had been American then the evening would be British. The last sunset ceremony having been carried out on the evening of September 2, 1939, Admiral Fraser ordered the resumption of sunset routines as from September 2, 1945. Allied and Commonwealth flags were flying from the fore and main yardarms (of the British flagship *Duke of York*) with the commander-in-chief's flag at the masthead and the white ensign at the gaff. When Admiral Fraser arrived the quartermaster reported 'Sunset, sir'. The still sounded. The Royal Marine guard presented arms and the band played, 'The day Thou gavest Lord is ended', interspersed with the sunset call as only Royal Marine buglers know how. For the first time in six bitter years the white ensign came down. Many, perhaps most, had never before savoured the magic of this moment when the busy life of a warship is hushed and the evening comes. Others of us, standing at the salute, were in tears as we remembered those who would never again see colours in the morning or hear the bugles sound sunset at dusk. As the white ensign came into the hands of our chief yeoman and the carry-on sounded, we realised that on board all the great US ships around us every activity had stopped, their sailors facing towards the British flagship and saluting us. Perhaps the special relationship between our two countries was born that evening.[16]

Perhaps. But the greatest consolation at that time was the affinity, strengthened by war, between the Royal Navy and the British people. In the thick of the fighting since 1939, this was a time of triumph, unequalled since the heady days of Trafalgar, but the more impressive as a success resting on steady and determined achievement rather than on isolated moments of dazzling splendour. The Royal Navy had never stood higher in public esteem.

Epilogue: The Ship Comes First

The setting of this book and, to an extent, the inspiration of the people described in its pages, are well summed up by Jan Morris.

> The British Empire: not long ago the very words aroused a frisson of pride in nearly every Briton; now a generation has grown up that hardly knows of the Empire's existence. Even the old phrase 'red on the map', which used to encapsulate the nation's sense of glory, has lost its patriotic as well as its cartographical meaning. Yet this discarded abstraction represents one of the most dazzling of all human achievements.
>
> At its zenith, the British Empire ruled nearly a quarter of the land mass of the world, and a quarter of its people. Its ships dominated the oceans, its engineers were at work in every climate. To the British of the imperial climax, anything was possible, nothing was beyond their strength or their ambition. And what ambition it was; a few million inhabitants of an offshore island exerting their will upon time! They founded several nations in their own image. They made their language the lingua franca of half the world. From soccer to parliamentary democracy, they left behind a legacy of Britishness that was permanently to change the face of nations. It was a colossal historical undertaking executed, for the most part, by young people, and it had all the flair and all the failings of youth. Was this really the British? Wagner once declared that the opening lines of 'Rule Britannia' expressed the whole character of the British nation. Who would say so now?[1]

The officers and men of the Royal Navy had other incentives too. The spirit of their service was nourished by several elements, high among them, tradition. And whenever that word was mentioned there would spring to mind that greatest of naval names – Horatio Nelson. Since this hero's death in the moment of victory at the Battle of Trafalgar in 1805, the example of courage and daring that he set has been a unique motivator of the British naval leadership. To emulate that example has long been considered a sure route to success. On the fringe of battle, this meant, by and large, steering towards the sound of gunfire; on sighting the enemy, to close the range and hit him hard; and to fight on whatever the odds.

But the appeal of Nelson lay also in a tenderness that was masked by his outward hard-headed resolution. His men, with whom he shared the same dangers, adored him. His habit of standing defiantly, yet calmly, in bemedalled uniform on the deck of his flagship in action, fed their own bravery. The commander-in-chief who, in the hour before battle, having signalled to his crews what England expected of them, could then pen a diary entry that, with its endearing blend of preachiness, special pleading and humility would put his stamp on what was to be, as he foresaw, a glorious if painful occasion, surely he deserved both the further plaudits of the populace and the place in history to which he clearly aspired:

> May the Great God, whom I worship, grant to my Country and for the benefit of Europe in general a great and glorious victory; and may no misconduct in anyone tarnish it; and may humanity after victory be the predominant feature of the British Fleet. For myself, individually, I commit my life to Him who made me. . . .

His prayer was, indeed, well answered.[2]

* * *

In the present century, when not at war or training for war, the Royal Navy's most picturesque and satisfying role lay in helping to protect the far-flung British raj and, to that end, in keeping the world's oceans and seaways open to peaceful commerce. It was impossible to take passage along the main imperial route, through the Suez Canal and across the Indian Ocean, without encountering at least one British warship each day and at most ports of call. At sea, whatever the nationality of the passing merchant ship, the ritual was unchanging – ensign dipped as a signal of respect to the man-of-war, white ensign dipped in acknowledgement, the warship's signalled enquiry re identity and destination duly answered. By this means the Royal Navy, in effect a maritime police force, asserted its widely recognized authority while keeping track of numerous shipping movements; and at their own destinations, the British warships brought reassurance, as well as glamour and excitement, to the locals.

When a fleet or squadron arrived, it did not need a grand setting and convenient vantage points like those of Malta to make a spectacle. The approaching array of warships with their synchronized movements, immaculate formations and simultaneous fall of anchors; their gun salutes, music, ranks of uniformed seamen, flag displays, spotless boats fanning out through the anchorage; and, later, the influx into the welcoming community of the cheerful, confident, bell-bottomed sailors – here was diplomacy at its most colourful and persuasive. National anniversary parade? Send a Royal Marine guard and band to head the procession. Threat of riot? Send the band with a platoon of sailors and march them around the trouble spots. Earthquake, act of piracy, uppish ruler or tribal chief getting out of hand, passenger liner in collision? Send the nearest British warship.

Officers and men alike, aware of their influence, took pride in their purpose, their instant readiness and their performance. Foreign navies, lacking style, were never numerous enough to make a show even had they been capable. Except, of course, the Germans before the First World War and the Americans some time after it. But their navies had little track record of diplomacy and of showmanship; their ships, when entering harbour, moved cautiously, lacked panache; and the Americans, even in the cocktail era, when it came to socializing, their officers' messes were dry, utilitarian, austerely fire-proofed and the incumbents gauche and insular as though only recently out of Utah. But then, politics, pageantry and quietly bossing people about have long been Britain's leading art forms.

* * *

As we have seen, between 1900 and 1945 the Navy survived several crises of morale of varying severity. In the decade before the First World War there were John Fisher's revolutionary reforms and dictatorial manner which drove a deep wedge in the Navy's top-level *esprit de corps*; during the war, the bungled Jutland communiqué adding to the uncertainties about the battle's outcome, and then the painful reluctance to introduce the desperately-needed anti-U boat convoys; and after the war the drastic disarmament and cost-cutting measures, culminating in the Invergordon Mutiny of 1931.

Now, as in other times of trouble, their lordships and their commanders-in-chief deployed their secret weapon – a relentless and concentrated period of training. This type of regime, under John Kelly's salty leadership, had provided the ideal cure for the Invergordon disease. Then with the emergence of new potential enemies and a gradual but encouraging move towards rearmament, the pace continued with gusto. W.W. Fisher's Mediterranean Fleet took the lead right through the 1930s; this change for the better was evident in the Navy's dazzling performance at the naval reviews at Spithead in 1935 and 1937. It says much for the leadership afloat that, following a time of shortages, including the rationing for economy reasons of fuel and ammunition, the Navy was in such remarkably good shape come the outbreak of war in 1939.

* * *

Despite the strains, reversals, losses and prolonged slog of the ensuing six-year war, the morale of Royal Navy personnel, increasingly of wartime-only composition, seldom wavered, belief in ultimate victory being universally upheld. Paradoxically, morale was never higher than at such moments of near-desperation as the evacuations from Dunkirk and later of Crete, or in the course of some of the hardest-fought convoy battles in the Atlantic, the Arctic and the Mediterranean. Perhaps the two lowest points, in both of which there was a calamitous failure of leadership at the highest level, were the loss near Singapore at the hands of the Japanese navy of the heavy ships *Prince of Wales* and *Repulse*, victims of gesture politics and a foolish disregard of air power. The second was the massacre of the Arctic convoy codenamed PQ17 following the Admiralty's over-hasty order to scatter, making it seem to some observers that the escorting destroyers had unhesitatingly run for cover, leaving the merchant ships to their fate. This was a hard-to-bear and wholly undeserved slur on that most devoted, hard-pressed and courageous band of wartime brothers, the Royal Navy destroyer captains.

* * *

In this brief review of the low points of morale one common factor becomes apparent – the fateful decisions were generally those of the Whitehall brass hats rather than of the admirals or senior commanders on active service. It is, of course, a truism that the most outstanding fleet commanders-in-chief and, in particular, the greatest fighting admirals, have tended to make a disappointing fist of high office ashore. Among the First Sea Lords in that category during the first half of the twentieth century there were two notable exceptions – David Beatty and, albeit on a shorter and less backs-to-the-wall tenure, A.B. Cunningham. For the most part an eyebrow-bristling admiral, trained to be an order-giving man of action, tended to lose his way in London's political and bureaucratic labyrinth; and the price of coming to terms with it, appeared to be a loss of feel for some of the realities of life at sea. And the corollary applied – the most constructive and effectively single-minded First Sea Lords in the present century, John Fisher, Ernle Chatfield and Dudley Pound, were not so well known as commanders-in-chief afloat.

In summary it may be said of the development of senior British naval officers at this time: too much training, not enough education; too much detail, not enough perspective; too much navel-gazing, not enough knowledge of the world; too many cards close to the chest, not enough shared decision-making. However, in terms of the quality of their fearless, hands-on leadership, their professionalism and as keepers of the spirit of Nelson they were, in their day, without equal.

* * *

In those last palmy days leading up to the outbreak of the Second World War the individual warship was, as ever, the unit of morale and custodian of the spirit of the Royal Navy. When a seaman joined a new ship he and his mates were quick to buckle to and, after working it up, strive to make it the best of its kind in the fleet. Overseas for a couple of years or in home waters for weeks at a time, it was to be their home and they wanted to be proud of it. Obviously they cared about their fleet and their squadron or flotilla but they cared most about their ship. The quality of the captain and officers and the tasks on which their ship was to be employed would vary but the quest was always the same.

The engine of their endeavours was not only a strenuously-induced competitive spirit, but also discipline, *esprit de corps* and, that manifestation of a perfectionist tradition, the habit of excellence. The close community of a ship, officers and men all in the same boat, the whole united by cause, drawn together by camaraderie and, at times, by the perils of life in a man-of-war at sea, were special factors. As John Wells has suggested:

> Whereas the Army sets great store on the military and moral value of regimental tradition the Navy relies on the ship to mould its crew into a fighting community. Whatever its size or type the ship is a miniature society embracing people with different skills, different backgrounds and different personalities, all of whom unconsciously build the ship's character. . . . The aim [is] to be the best in the squadron, the best in sport or acquire a reputation that years later springs to mind as the ship of happiest memory . . . and to [develop] that sense of togetherness that sailors feel about a home without being really conscious of it, [to the extent that] when a ship is sunk in war something deep and indefinable in the lives of those surviving is lost as well. . . . When asked how the Navy possessed the genius for evoking the best out of people and winning their affection and loyalty, a captain replied unhesitatingly: 'a system of manners'. It was, he said, a system based on long experience and the only way in which officers and men could live and work together in the crowded, confined conditions of a ship. . . . By manners he meant, quite simply, consideration for other people.[3]

But, perhaps, the strangest phenomenon of all was that, two or three years after commissioning, at the assiduously honed peak of its efficiency, its crew on its top form, the ship, with its paying-off pennant on high, went home; and its officers and men dispersed. Should so much effort and success have been thrown to the winds? Evidently. As the Navy saw it, when, by sustained effort, a peak of achievement had been scaled, the route to a new dynamism was to change the people around before staleness or fatigue could set in. This might be unsettling, but wasn't life at sea always unsettling?

50.) Home from war, the British aircraft carrier HMS Formidable *berths at Portsmouth following active service in the Far East during the closing stages of the Second World War. From a drawing by Charles E. Turner.*

Even so, as we judge the performance of the Navy, let us spare a thought for our seaman, the backbone of the system, as once again he set out from his barracks, among unfamiliar faces, to pull his weight on board yet another man-of-war. In a sense he was on familiar ground. For he knew well that whatever its character, whatever its task, whatever its human chemistry, he and his new mates would soon accept and be consoled and spurred on by one constant, reassuring goal – to make the ship, *their* ship, the best.

Throughout the period of this book, in war and peace, that is really what it was all about – *the ship comes first.*

Notes

CHAPTER ONE

1. A.J. Mills, Bennett Scott and Fred Godfrey, *Ship Ahoy*, 1909.
2. From the author's own records and collections.
3. Epes Sargent.
4. James Thomson, for a masque performed in London in 1740.
5. Bartimeus, *Naval Occasions: A Tithe of Admiralty* (William Blackwood and Sons, 1915).
6. Bartimeus, *The Navy Eternal* (Hodder & Stoughton, 1918).
7. Captain Eric Wheler Bush DSO DSC RN, *Bless Our Ship* (Allen & Unwin, 1958).
8. Lord Chatfield, Admiral of the Fleet, *The Navy and Defence* (William Heinemann, 1942).
9. Agnes Weston, *My Life among the Bluejackets* (Nisbet, 1911).
10. Sidney Knock, *'Clear Lower Deck': An Intimate Study of Men of the Royal Navy* (Philip Allan, 1932).
11. Charles Owen, *No More Heroes* (Allen & Unwin, 1975).
12. Stephen McKenna, *Reginald McKenna 1863–1943* (Eyre & Spottiswood, 1948).

CHAPTER TWO

1. These loss figures are taken from Lieutenant K.J.N.C. Rich RN, 'Why the Reluctance to Introduce Convoy as Counter U-boat Strategy' (*Naval Review*, October 1993).
2. William Jameson, *The Fleet that Jack Built* (Rupert Hart-Davis, 1962).
3. Charles R.L. Beatty, *Our Admiral, A Biography of Admiral of the Fleet Earl Beatty* (W.A. Allen, 1980).
4. Chatfield, *The Navy and Defence.*
5. Jameson, *The Fleet that Jack Built.*
6. Ibid.
7. Stanley Bonnett, *The Price of Admiralty* (Robert Hale, 1968). The tolerant attitude of ratings towards their officers' life style is confirmed by Anthony Carew, *The Lower Deck of the Royal Navy 1900–39* (Manchester University Press, 1981).
8. Lieutenant Commander W.B. Harvey, *Downstairs in the Royal Navy* (Glasgow, Brown, Son & Ferguson, 1979).
9. Knock, *'Clear Lower Deck': An Intimate Study of Men of the Royal Navy.*
10. Tom Cable RN BEM, *Crossing the Line* (Wymondham, Geo R. Reeve, 1991).
11. Lord Hankey, *The Supreme Command 1914–1918* (Allen & Unwin, 1961).
12. Stephen King-Hall, *My Naval Life 1906–1929* (Faber & Faber, 1952).
13. Beatty, *Our Admiral, A Biography of Admiral of the Fleet Earl Beatty.*
14. Owen, *No More Heroes.*
15. Madden was to have served for about a year, after which, having completed his stint as

commander-in-chief of the Mediterranean Fleet, Roger Keyes would take over. But in the interval, for reasons outlined in Chapter Four, Keyes fell out of favour and missed his chance.

16. Owen, *No More Heroes.*

CHAPTER THREE

1. Except where otherwise indicated, the author is the narrator of this chapter and, besides the author's own records and recollections, the sources include his publication *No More Heroes*. The name Goode-Ferguson is fictitious.
2. Some excerpts from the works of Bartimeus were given in Chapters One and Two.
3. Ludovic Kennedy, *On my Way to the Club* (Collins, 1989).
4. Charles Morgan, *The Gunroom* (Chatto & Windus, 1968 edn). This novel, describing the bullying regimes to which junior midshipmen were often subjected on the eve of the First World War, caused a furore when first published in 1919.
5. Three months later, HMS *Nelson* having been paid off to undergo a major refit, the Admiralty relented and offered a new appointment – to a destroyer, HMS *Westcott*, on the China station.
6. Cable, *Crossing the Line.*
7. John Douglas, *HMS Ganges* (Kineton, Roundwood Press, 1978).
8. G.G. Connell, *Jack's War* (William Kimber, 1985), to which Eric Smith was a contributor.
9. From the unpublished memoirs of Frank Bertie Coombs DSM. Imperial War Museum archives.

CHAPTER FOUR

1. The exception to this rule was, of course, the individualistic, pugnaciously led U-boat arm, virtually a 'private' navy, which alone almost brought Britain to its knees in both world wars.
2. Cecil Aspinall-Oglander, *Roger Keyes* (Hogarth Press, 1951).
3. Leslie Gardiner, *The Royal Oak Courts Martial* (William Blackwood, 1965).
4. Aspinall-Oglander, *Roger Keyes.*
5. Janet Morgan, *Edwina Mountbatten,* (Harper Collins, 1991).
6. Gardiner, *The Royal Oak Courts Martial.*
7. David Niven, *The Moon's a Balloon* (Hamish Hamilton, 1971).
8. Morgan, *Edwina Mountbatten.*
9. The incidents that follow, involving two characters, here named Charles and Barbara Blunt, were provided by the author, John Marriott, and are authentic.
10. The foregoing views about Keyes owe much to Leslie Gardiner's *The Royal Oak Courts Martial* (William Blackwood, 1965), while those that follow are mainly thanks to Cecil Apsinall-Oglander's *Roger Keyes* (The Hogarth Press, 1951).
11. During the twentieth century the most notable exception to this tendency was David Beatty. On completion of his brilliant tenure of the post of commander-in-chief, Mediterranean in 1942, A.B. Cunningham, having gained the confidence of the American top brass in Washington, served with excellent effect under General Eisenhower's supreme command as the naval commander-in-chief of the Allied expeditionary forces in the North African and Mediterranean theatres. He was First Sea Lord from October 1943 to June 1946.
12. Charles Owen, *The Maltese Islands* (Newton Abbot, David & Charles, 1969).
13. When officers were boarding a ship's boat it was the custom for the most senior among them to embark last, the best seat being left vacant for him. At the boat's destination, however, the most senior officer disembarked first. Wives trying desperately to ape their husbands rank on social occasions were, indeed, a sobering sight.
14. Cable, *Crossing the Line.*
15. From Captain John Gower DSC RN to the author.
16. Chatfield, *The Navy and Defence.*

CHAPTER FIVE

1 Among the main sources for this chapter were the records, diaries and recollections of the author whose travels in the 1930s took him to nearly all the ports of call mentioned in the chapter. In view of naval regulations about writing to the press, the author used the pen-name Alexander Headon for most of his literary activities in Hong Kong. The author's *The Grand Days of Travel* (Webb & Bower, 1979) is also relevant.

2 Paul Gillingham, *At the Peak, Hong Kong Between the Wars* (Hong Kong, Macmillan, 1983).

3 Michael St John, *A Tale of Two Rivers* (Aylesbury, Bushman, 1989).

4 Kathleen Harland, *The Royal Navy in Hong Kong since 1841* (Liskeard, Maritime Books, undated) and selected issues of the *China Mail* and the *Hong Kong Sunday Herald*, supplemented by on-the-spot research for the author in 1994–5 by Sophia Wright, a resident, and while on business trips to Hong Kong, his son Rupert.

5 Frederick Wigby, *Stoker, Royal Navy* (Blackwood, 1967).

6 See note 2.

7 A principal source for the Singapore story was James Leasor's *Singapore, The Battle that Changed the World* (Hodder and Stoughton, 1968).

8 From the author's records, diaries and recollections.

9 The Gibraltar story owes much to Sir William G.F. Jackson's *The Rock of the Gibraltarians* (Associated University Presses, 1987) and William Griffiths' *My Darling Children* (Leo Cooper, 1992).

10 For further glimpses of life in Bermuda in the inter-war years see Commander C.A. Jenkins RN's *Days of a Dogsbody* (George Harrap, 1946).

11 R.C. Riley, *The Growth of Southsea as a Naval Satellite and Victorian Resort* (A Portsmouth Paper, published by Portsmouth City Council, 1972).

12 Joy Harwood, *A Portrait of Portsea 1840–1940* (Ensign Publications, 1990).

13 Arthur Almond, *The Portsea I Knew* (Hampshire County Magazine, January 1978).

14 WEA, *Going to Work between the Wars*, Vol 3 (Local History Group, Portsmouth).

15 Admiral Sir William James KCB, *The Sky was Always Blue* (Methuen, 1951).

CHAPTER SIX

1. Le Bailly, Vice Admiral Sir Louis KBE CB OBE DL, *The Man Around the Engine* (Emsworth, Kenneth Mason, 1990).
2. Geoffrey Brooke archives.
3. Anecdote taken from Louis, Commander Geoffrey L. AFC RN, *Fabulous Admirals* (Portman, 1957).
4. Owen, *No More Heroes*.
5. Much of the nation's wealth went towards servicing the national debt, while the world economic crisis of 1929–33 was practically bringing the modernization and development of heavy industry to a standstill; this was largely in a pre-1914 condition.
6. A.J. Marder, *From the Dardanelles to Oran* (Oxford University Press, 1974).
7. Taken from Beatty, Admiral of the Fleet, Earl, What the Navy Needs (London, *Evening Standard*, 8 November 1935).
8. Geoffrey Till, *Air Power and the Royal Navy 1914–1945* (Jane's Publishing, 1979).
9. Chatfield Papers, Southampton University Library.
10. From the author's own records and recollections.
11. The journal from which these extracts are taken was kept by the author while he was a midshipman on board HMS *Barham*.
12. From the memoirs of Admiral Sir Charles Madden Bt GCB DL printed in 1988 for private circulation, with the admiral's kind permission. Madden was a gunnery officer on Fisher's staff on board the Flagship *Queen Elizabeth* from 1932.

13. Admiral Sir William James, *The Sky was Always Blue* (Methuen, 1951).
14. Patrick Tailyour, The Stokers will get up the Ashes (*Naval Review*, July 1994).
15. Geoffrey Brooke archives.
16. Frederick Wigby, *Stoker – Royal Navy* (Blackwood, 1967).
17. Anthony Hogg, *Just a Hogg's Life* (Chichester, Solo Mio Books, 1993).
18. Martin Brice, *The Royal Navy and the Sino-Japanese Incident 1937–1941* (Ian Allan, 1973).

CHAPTER SEVEN

1. Geoffrey Brooke, *Alarm Starboard* (Patrick Stephens, 1982).
2. Ibid.
3. From a letter by Petty Officer L.V. Leather, early 1942. Geoffrey Brooke archives.
4. From an unsigned letter written in Singapore on 17 December 1941, Imperial War Museum archives.
5. Brooke, *Alarm Starboard.*
6. From a letter from Sub-Lieutenant V.B. Ash, February 1942. Geoffrey Brooke archives.
7. Abbreviated account based on Geoffrey Brooke's recollections.
8. Commander William King DSO DSC RN, *The Stick and the Stars* (Hutchinson, 1958).
9. Gibson, Vice Admiral Sir Donald KCB DSC JP, *Haut Taut and Belay, The Memoirs of a Flying Sailor* (Tunbridge Wells, Spellmount, 1992).
10. King, *The Stick and the Stars.*
11. The episodes featuring HMS *Westcott* are from the author's own records and recollections.
12. François Kersaudy, *Norway 1940* (Collins, 1990).
13. Sam Lombard-Hobson, *A Sailor's War* (Orbis, 1983).
14. Extracted from Mountbatten's letter, written shortly after the event, to his sister Louise, queen of Sweden, and published in John Winton's anthology, *The War at Sea* (Hutchinson, 1967).
15. Sir Charles Madden's memoirs.

CHAPTER EIGHT

1. Roger Hill, *Destroyer Captain* (William Kimber, 1975).
2. King, *The Stick and the Stars.*
3. From Sidney Hutchison to the author. After the war, Hutchison became secretary of the Royal Academy.
4. A. and G. Franklin, in John Winton (ed.), *The War at Sea* (Hutchinson, 1967).
5. Hill, *Destroyer Captain.*
6. From Admiral Sir William O'Brien KCB DSC, 'My Bit of Navy: A Love Story' an unpublished work printed for private circulation with the admiral's kind permission.
7. D.S. Goodbrand, 'Hurrah for the Life of an H.O.: A Nautical Ambience', 1991, unpublished. Imperial War Museum, archives.
8. G.G. Connell, *Jack's War* (William Kimber, 1985).
9. C. Owen, 'The Excelsior Affair', unpublished. Written while the author was second-in-command of *Obdurate.*
10. Lieutenant-Commander P.K. Kemp, FSA FR HistS RN retd, *Victory at Sea 1939–1945* (Frederick Muller, 1957).
11. From Victor Loosemore to the author following a chance meeting at a reunion dinner in Portsmouth in November 1995.
12. From the author's own records and recollections.
13. The second-in-command of a destroyer was otherwise known as the first lieutenant, number one or Jimmy the one.
14. Goodbrand, 'Hurrah for the Life of an H.O.: A Nautical Ambience'.
15. From Bob Burns DSM to the author, January 1995.
16. Hill, *Destroyer Captain.*

17. From an address by Rear Admiral E.F. Gueritz CB OBE DSC at the funeral of Rear Admiral V.H. Selby CB DSC at Devizes, 12 July 1994.
18. Gibson, *Haut Taut and Belay, The Memoirs of a Flying Sailor.*
19. Vice Admiral Sir Roderick Macdonald, *The Figurehead* (Bishop Auckland, Pentland Press, 1993). The central character of this good-humoured and revealing biography was a wartime destroyer captain, nicknamed 'Honk', whose performance in command left a good deal to be desired.
20. Le Bailly, *The Man Around the Engine.*
21. George Melly, *Rum, Bum and Concertina* (Weidenfeld & Nicolson, 1977).
22. This story is authenticated by the present author. In London towards the end of the war, at a performance of Somerset Maugham's *The Circle* starring John Gielgud, a play 'lit by Hamish Wilson', the officer and the former ordinary seaman met once again. They were to become lifelong friends.

CHAPTER NINE

1. Connell, *Jack's War.*
2. Ibid., apart from the Training Manual excerpts.
3. With acknowledgement to *The Royal Marines: The Admiralty Account of Their Achievement, 1939–1945* (His Majesty's Stationery Office, 1944).
4. Stephanie Batstone, *Wren's Eye View* (Tunbridge Wells, Parapress, 1994).
5. Contributed specially for inclusion in this book by Margaret Seeley, now living in Surrey.
6. Contributed specially for inclusion in this book by Ann Rodney, now living in Devon.
7. Contributed specially for inclusion in this book by Barbara Sanderson, now living in Hampshire.
8. From *Customs and Etiquette of the Royal Navy*, rev edn. (Portsmouth, Gieves Limited, July 1966).
9. Frank Kermode, My Mad Captains (*London Review of Books*, 20 October 1994).
10. O'Brien, 'My Bit of Navy: A Love Story'.
11. H.K. Oram, *The Rogue's Yarn*, ed. Wendy Harris (Leo Cooper, 1993).
12. From 'The Excelsior Affair', an unpublished work by the author who, on loan from the Admiralty, was the board's testing officer.
13. Macdonald, *The Figurehead.*
14. O'Brien, 'My Bit of Navy: A Love Story'.
15. On 20 July 1945 the author, newly in command of HM destroyer *Stevenstone*, sailed from England for duty with the British Pacific Fleet. However, when Japan surrendered, his ship had only got as far as Malta.
16. Le Bailly, *The Man Around the Engine.*

EPILOGUE

1. Jan Morris, 'Now that the Sun is Setting' (*The Times*, 31 December 1994).
2. Even so, by way of warning to aspiring admirals inclined to blind devotion: early in the Second World War, the captain of a British cruiser, who shall be nameless, having sighted a German man-of-war on the horizon and set what he believed to be an intercepting course, retired to his cabin to kneel and pray for guidance. The lines to God being busy that day, it was some minutes before the captain regained the bridge, only to find that the enemy was nowhere to be seen. The Admiralty promptly relieved him of his post and did not employ him again in a seagoing command.
3. Captain John Wells, *The Royal Navy: An Illustrated Social History, 1870–1982* (Alan Sutton (in association with the Royal Naval Museum), 1991).

Bibliography

Allen, Charles, (ed.), *Plain Tales from the Raj: Images of British India in the Twentieth Century* (Andre Deutsch and British Broadcasting Corporation, 1975).
Almond, Arthur, The Portsea I Knew (*Hampshire County Magazine*, 1978).
Aspinall-Oglander, Cecil, *Roger Keyes* (The Hogarth Press, 1951).

Barnett, Corelli, *The Swordbearers: Studies in Supreme Command in the First World War* (Eyre and Spottiswoode, 1963); *Engage the Enemy More Closely* (W.W. Norton, 1991).
Bartimeus, *Naval Occasions: A Tithe of Admiralty* (William Blackwood and Sons, 1915), *The Navy Eternal* (Hodder & Stoughton, 1918).
Batstone, Stephanie, *Wren's Eye View* Tunbridge Wells, Parapress, 1994).
Beatty, Admiral of the Fleet, Earl, What the Navy Needs (*Evening Standard*, 8 Nov 1935).
Beatty, Charles RL, *Our Admiral: A Biography of Admiral of the Fleet Earl Beatty* (W.H. Allen, 1980).
Bennett, Geoffrey, *Charlie B: A Biography of Admiral Lord Beresford* (Dawnay, 1968).
Bonnett, Stanley, *Price of Admiralty* (Robert Hale, 1968).
Brice, Martin, *The Royal Navy and the Sino-Japanese Incident 1937–41* (Ian Allen, 1973).
Brooke, Geoffrey, *Alarm Starboard* (Patrick Stephens, 1982).
Brown, Malcolm and Meehan, Patricia, *Scapa Flow: The Reminiscences of Men and Women who served in Scapa Flow in the Two World Wars* (Allen Lane, 1968).
Bush, Captain Eric Wheler, DSO DSC, *Bless our Ship* (Allen and Unwin, 1958).

Cable, Tom, RN BEM, *Crossing the Line* (Wymondham, Geo R. Reeve, 1991).
Carew, Anthony, *The Lower Deck of the Royal Navy 1900–39* (Manchester University Press, 1981).
Chalmers, Rear-Admiral W.S., CBE DSC, *Max Horton and the Western Approaches* (Hodder & Stoughton, 1954), *Full Cycle: The Biography of Admiral Sir Bertram Home Ramsay* KCB KBE MVO (Hodder & Stoughton, 1959).
Chatfield, Admiral of the Fleet, Lord, *The Navy and Defence* (William Heinemann, 1942).
Churchill, Winston S., *The Second World War: Vols 1–6* (Cassell, 1948–54).
Connell, G.G., *Jack's War* (William Kimber, 1985).
Cork and Orrery, Admiral of the Fleet, the Earl, *My Naval Life 1886–1941* (Hutchinson, 1942).

Cunningham of Hyndhope, Admiral of the Fleet, Viscount, Kt GCB OM DSO, *A Sailor's Odyssey* (Hutchinson, 1951).

Douglas, John, *HMS Ganges* (Kineton, Roundwood Press, 1978).

Edwards, Lieutenant-Commander, Kenneth RN, rtd, *The Mutiny at Invergordon* (Putnam, 1937); *The Grey Diplomatists* (Rich & Cowan, 1938).

Gardiner, Leslie, *The Royal Oak Courts Martial* (William Blackwood, 1965).
German, Commander Tony, *The Sea is at our Gates, The History of the Canadian Navy* (Toronto, McClelland & Steward, 1990).
Gibson, Vice Admiral, Sir Donald, KCB DSC JP, *Haul Taut and Belay: The Memoirs of a Flying Sailor* (Tunbridge Wells, Spellmount, 1992).
Gieves Ltd, *Customs and Etiquette of the Royal Navy* (Portsmouth, Gieves Ltd, 1966).
Gillingham, Paul, *At the Peak: Hong Kong between the Wars* (Hong Kong, Macmillan, 1983).
Griffiths, William, *My Darling Children* (Leo Cooper, 1992).

Hankey, Lord, *The Supreme Command 1914–1918* (Allen & Unwin, 1961).
Harland, Kathleen, *The Royal Navy in Hong Kong since 1841* (Liskeard, Maritime Books, undated).
Harvey, Lieutenant-Commander W.B., *Downstairs in the Royal Navy* (Glasgow, Brown, Son & Ferguson, 1979).
Harwood, Joy, *A Portrait of Portsea 1840–1940* (Ensign Publications, 1990).
Hill, Captain Roger, *Destroyer Captain* (William Kimber, 1975).
Hogg, Anthony, *Just a Hogg's Life* (Chichester, Solo Mio Books, 1993).
Hough, Richard, *First Sea Lord: An Authorised Biography of Admiral Lord Fisher* (Allen & Unwin, 1969).
Hunt, Barry D., *Sailor-Scholar: Admiral Sir Herbert Richmond 1871–1946* (Ontario, Canada, Wilfrid Laurier University Press, 1982).

Jackson, Sir William G.F., *The Rock of the Gibraltarians* (Associated University Presses, 1987).
James, Admiral Sir William, GCB, *The Sky was Always Blue* (Methuen, 1951); *Admiral Sir William Fisher* (Macmillan, 1943).
Jenkins, Commander C.A., RN, *Days of a Dogsbody* (George Harrap, 1946).
Jameson, William, *The Fleet that Jack Built* (Rupert Hart-Davies, 1962).
Jellicoe, Admiral Viscount, GCB OM GCVO, *The Grand Fleet 1914–1916: Its Creation, Development and Work* (Cassell, 1919).

Kemp, Lieutenant-Commander P.K., FSA FRHistS RN, *Victory at Sea 1939–1945* (Frederick Muller, 1957).
Kennedy, Ludovic, *On My Way to the Club* (Collins, 1989).
Kenworthy, Lieutenant-Commander, the Hon. J.M., *The Real Navy* (Hutchinson, 1932).
Kermode, Frank, My Mad Captains (*London Review of Books*, 20 Oct 1994).

Kersaudy, François, *Norway 1940* (Collins, 1990).
King-Hall, Stephen, *My Naval Life 1906–1929* (Faber & Faber, 1952).
King, Commander William, DSO DSC RN, *The Stick and the Stars* (Hutchinson, 1958).
Knock, Sidney, *'Clear Lower Deck': An Intimate Study of the Men of the Royal Navy* (Philip Allen, 1932).

Leasor, James, *Singapore, the Battle that Changed the World* (Hodder & Stoughton, 1968).
Le Bailly, Vice Admiral Sir Louis, KBE CB OBE DL, *The Man Around the Engine* (Emsworth, Kenneth Mason, 1990).
Lombard-Hobson, Captain Sam, *A Sailor's War* (Orbis, 1983).
Lowis, Commander Geoffrey L., AGC RN, *Fabulous Admirals* (Putnam, 1957).

Macdonald, Vice Admiral Sir Roderick, *The Figurehead* (Auckland, Pentland Press, 1993).
Macintyre, Captain Donald, *The Thunder of the Guns* (Frederick Muller, 1959); *The Battle of the Atlantic* (Batsford, 1961); *The Battle of the Mediterranean* (Batsford, 1964); *Aircraft Carrier, the Majestic Weapon* (Macdonald, 1968).
Mallalieu, J.P.W., *Very Ordinary Seaman* (Gollancz, 1944).
Marder, Arthur J., *From the Dreadnought to Scapa Flow: The Royal Navy in the Fisher Era 1904–1919: Jutland and After* (Oxford University Press, 1966); *From The Dardanelles to Oran* (Oxford University Press, 1974).
McKenna, Stephen, *Reginald McKenna 1863–1943* (Eyre & Spottiswood, 1948).
Melly, George, *Rum, Bum and Concertina* (Weidenfeld & Nicolson, 1977).
More, Kenneth, *More or Less* (Hodder & Stoughton, 1978).
Morgan, Charles, *The Gunroom* (Chatto & Windus, 1968).
Morgan, Janet, *Edwina Mountbatten* (Harper Collins, 1991).
Morris, Jan, Now That the Sun is Setting (*The Times*, 31 Dec 1994).

Niven, David, *The Moon's a Balloon* (Hamish Hamilton, 1971).

Ollard, Richard, *Fisher and Cunningham* (Constable, 1951).
Oram, H.K., *The Rogue's Yarn*, Wendy Harris (ed.) (Leo Cooper, 1994).
Owen, Charles, *The Maltese Islands* (David & Charles, 1969); *No More Heroes: The Royal Navy in the Twentieth Century: Anatomy of a Legend* (Allen & Unwin, 1975); *The Grand Days of Travel* (Webb & Bower, 1979).

Packer, Joy, *Deep as the Sea* (Eyre Methuen, 1975).
Padfield, Peter, *War beneath the Sea: Submarine Conflict 1939–1945* (John Murray, 1995).
Pope, Dudley, *73 North: The Battle of the Barents Sea* (Weidenfeld & Nicolson, 1958).

Richmond, Admiral Sir Herbert, KCB, *Sea Power in the Modern World* (Bell, 1934).
Riley, Dr R.C., The Growth of Southsea as a Naval Satellite and Victorian Resort, *A Portsmouth Paper* (Portsmouth City Council, 1972).
Roskill, Captain S.W., DSC RN rtd, *The Navy at War 1939–1945* (Collins, 1960); *Naval Policy Between the Wars Vol 1: The Period of Anglo-American Antagonism 1919–1929* (Collins, 1968).
Ross, Alan, *Open Sea* (London Magazine Editions, 1975).

Schofield, B.B., *British Sea Power: Naval Policy in the Twentieth Century* (B.T. Batsford, 1967).
Scott, Peter, *The Battle of the Narrow Seas* (Purnell Book Services, 1974).
Simpson, Rear Admiral C.W.G., *Periscope View* (Macmillan, 1972).
Smith, Peter C., *Fighting Flotilla* (William Kimber, 1976).
Stephen, Martin, *The Fighting Admirals* (Leo Cooper, 1991).
St John, Michael, *A Tale of Two Rivers* (Aylesbury, Bushmain, 1989).

Tailyour, Patrick, The Stokers will get up the Ashes (*Naval Review*, July 1994).
Till, Geoffrey, *Air Power and the Royal Navy, 1914–1945* (Jane's Publishing, 1979).
Trotter, William Pym, *The Royal Navy in Old Photographs* (J.M. Dent, 1975).

Warner, Oliver, *Cunningham of Hyndhope, Admiral of the Fleet* (John Murray, 1967).
WEA, *Going to Work between the Wars* (Local History Group, Portsmouth, Vol 3).
Wells, Captain John, *The Royal Navy: An Illustrated Social History 1870–1982* (Alan Sutton Publishing (with Royal Naval Museum), 1994).
Weston, Agnes, *My Life among the Bluejackets* (Nisbet, 1911).
Wigby, Frederick, *Stoker – Royal Navy* (Blackwood, 1967).
Winton, John, (ed.), *The War at Sea 1939–1945* (Hutchinson, 1967).
Woodman, Richard, *The Arctic Convoys 1942–1945* (John Murray, 1994).

Yexley, Lionel, *The Inner Life of the Navy* (Sir Isaac Pitman, 1908).

Ziegler, Philip, *Mountbatten: The Official Biography* (Collins, 1985).

Index

Officers who held or later attained flag rank are described as admiral, their titles and decorations being omitted, while those below this rank are denoted naval officer. Ratings are given the ranks held at the time of the events.